T0345311

Voices and Values

Voices and Values

The Politics of Feminist Evaluation

Edited by

RATNA M. SUDARSHAN
RAJIB NANDI

zubaan

ZUBAAN
128 B Shahpur Jat, 1st floor
NEW DELHI 110 049
Email: contact@zubaanbooks.com
Website: www.zubaanbooks.com

First published by Zubaan Publishers Pvt. Ltd 2018

Copyright © individual essays with the authors 2018
This collection Zubaan Publishers Pvt. Ltd 2018

ISBN 978 81 85932 39 7

Zubaan is an independent feminist publishing house based in New Delhi with a strong academic and general list. It was set up as an imprint of India's first feminist publishing house, Kali for Women, and carries forward Kali's tradition of publishing world quality books to high editorial and production standards. *Zubaan* means tongue, voice, language, speech in Hindustani. Zubaan publishes in the areas of the humanities, social sciences, as well as in fiction, general non-fiction, and books for children and young adults under its Young Zubaan imprint.

Typeset in Adobe Jenson Pro 11/13 by Jojy Philip, New Delhi 110 015
Printed at Raj Press, R-3 Inderpuri, New Delhi 110 012

Contents

1

Introduction

RATNA M. SUDARSHAN and RAJIB NANDI

'Feminist evaluation', as the term suggests, draws upon the values and methods of feminist research. It is best understood as a set of principles and values, a lens that can be applied across different evaluation approaches in order to focus on outcomes differentiated by gender, class, location and other relevant axes of difference. Feminist evaluation seeks to go beyond mere descriptions of differentiated outcomes to articulating ways to address these, and in that sense, it is 'political'. Evaluators favouring this approach have built upon feminist research methodologies as well as upon practical experience to develop a body of knowledge on the learnings (see for example Hay, Sudarshan, Mendez 2012; Batliwala and Pittman, 2010)

The essays in this book are written by researchers, practitioners and evaluators who have been associated with a four year programme of research and capacity building on feminist evaluation, co-ordinated by the Institute of Social Studies Trust and supported by the International Development Research Centre (IDRC), Canada and the Ford Foundation, New Delhi. The project was motivated by an understanding that evaluations offer evidence-based policy advocacy, and feminist evaluations could make an effective contribution to policy formulation that is oriented to gender and social equity. Other publications from the project discuss the basics of feminist evaluation, offer a toolkit of participatory methods, and the application of gender- and equity-focused meta-analysis frameworks to evaluations of flagship programmes in India (ISST 2015 a,b; ISST 2016).

While the values and principles of feminist evaluation might be seen as 'universal' in their application, with an emphasis on individual rights, the context shapes the behaviour of people requiring interpretation and influencing the recommendations that emerge from the evaluation. Kabeer and Khan (2014) suggest that as societies begin to recognize a diversity of ways of organizing social life, there may be signs of an 'intergenerational pathway of empowerment', even if little change is evident in the lives of the current generation of women. Sudarshan and Sharma (2012) have argued that 'responsible feminism' requires that in making recommendations, evaluators need to do so with a recognition of the contextual constraints that influence the feasibility of recommended courses of action and choices. It is, therefore, extremely important to share and reflect upon experiences with evaluation in different contexts. Each particular context provides nuances that need to be captured, and which, in turn, will influence

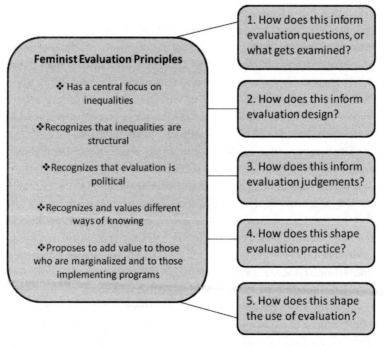

Feminist Evaluation Principles

❖ Has a central focus on inequalities

❖ Recognizes that inequalities are structural

❖ Recognizes that evaluation is political

❖ Recognizes and values different ways of knowing

❖ Proposes to add value to those who are marginalized and to those implementing programs

1. How does this inform evaluation questions, or what gets examined?

2. How does this inform evaluation design?

3. How does this inform evaluation judgements?

4. How does this shape evaluation practice?

5. How does this shape the use of evaluation?

Source: Hay (2012)

the manner in which any given evaluation method is applied or the data interpreted.

The basic tenets of feminist evaluation, drawing on work by Podems (2010) have been summarised in Hay (2012) along with questions that are useful in formulating an evaluation design that incorporates these principles (see diagram above).

The essays in this volume all subscribe to the understanding of 'feminist evaluation' that is implied above: a central focus on inequities, recognizing the structural roots of inequity, giving weight to all perspectives, adding value to those who are marginalized and those being evaluated, and taking forward the findings of evaluation into advocacy for change. In different ways, each essay advances this understanding of feminist evaluation, both conceptually and as practice.

Understanding Feminist Evaluation

A question almost invariably asked about feminist evaluation, is how it is any different from other participatory approaches that are equally concerned with exploring and addressing differentiated outcomes and which prioritize the perspective of programme participants. Of course, this question assumes that feminist evaluation necessarily needs to be differentiated from other approaches; whereas one might argue that once the principles and values it seeks to espouse can be shown to have been absorbed into other approaches, the political purpose of feminist evaluation has been achieved. There is a further question on whether, and in what ways, a 'feminist' evaluation is any different from one using gender analysis in data collection and interpretation.

This question is addressed in the essay by Ranjani Murthy. With neo-liberal ideologies gaining ground through the 1990s and 2000s, an instrumental approach to promoting gender equality has become an increasing concern among gender advocates and feminist evaluators. Murthy suggests that the term 'gender-transformative' helps to distinguish instrumental approaches from those seeking to bring about gender equality. She further argues that gender-transformative evaluations and socialist feminist evaluations are ideologically similar. Drawing on Kabeer (1994) she presents a four-fold classification of evaluation types in which 'gender' is absent or present in different ways. The first is *gender-blind evaluation* where the focus is on assessing programme efficiency and effectiveness. Such an evaluation does not assess changes in gender relations or make recommendations on gender concerns. The remaining three types do address gender, in differing ways. The second type is *gender-instrumental evaluation*, which undertakes a gender-analysis but uses the data to explore how far the programme has used the traditional roles of women and men for the success of the project. For example, targeting women in their roles as mothers for improving child health. The third type is *gender-specific evaluation* which examines how far the programme has addressed the sex or gender specific needs of women or men, but without assessing whether as a result of this, gender relations have been transformed. The fourth type is *gender-transformative evaluation* which examines how far the programme has contributed to changing power relations based on gender and other identities within institutions.

Murthy reviews the evolution of 'feminist' evaluation. This emerged out of a critique of gender evaluations rooted in a women-in-development (WID) approach. WID points to the need for promoting equality through legislation, reducing women's poverty and enhancing women's efficiency but lacks a focus on gender relations. Feminist evaluators argued for bringing gender inequalities as a central focus in the practice of evaluation, and raising critical questions on issues of social injustice that are generally absent in mainstream development and evaluation. Such an approach, that foregrounds inequities, is close to the socialist feminist strand of feminism. This latter perceives gender, class, race, caste, ethnicity, religion etc., as interlocking oppressions, requiring simultaneous struggles to transform all social relations that have a bearing on women's lives. The concept of gender transformative evaluation has a similar understanding.

Murthy then goes on to discuss different gender-transformative/socialist feminist frameworks including the Change Matrix, Making the Case, the Social Relations framework, the gender, empowerment and poverty reduction framework, Women's Empowerment Assessment tool, and their application in different contexts. She also discusses the challenges faced by gender-transformative evaluations, as these question the widely prevalent view of gender as 'smart' economics. An important point she makes in concluding is the necessity of engaging with programme formulation, as many programmes do not have gender equity as a stated goal, as well as in linking evaluation clearly to accountability through such processes as validating and disseminating findings.

Pallavi Gupta and Srinidhi Raghavan approach the question of how feminist evaluation is different, by reflecting on the experiences with evaluation that Asmita has had. Asmita is an organization that primarily works on women's human rights and gender discrimination. Over the period 1993 to 2009, six evaluations were conducted of the organization. The essay addresses three broad questions: (i) evaluation methods and the difference between gender analysis and feminist evaluation; (ii) how the institutional histories approach helps to track evolution in an organization; and (iii) how feminist evaluation helps in challenging gender bias. These are discussed in the context of the six evaluations and the methods used by the different evaluators. The authors find that the limited ability of the first evaluation to be able to understand Asmita's goals and strategies lay in the lack of a feminist perspective in the evaluators and their conventional approach to doing evaluation; thus they searched for a simple linear relation between activities and outputs through individual interviews with 'beneficiaries'. Asmita's vision and aim of creating a space for women to come together and providing a context for critical dialogue could not be captured through such a method. The failure to recognize that a movement is different from a project could make an entire evaluation a counter productive process.

The authors argue that subsequent evaluations were better able to understand the nuances of gender inequalities and power dynamics within which the organization works. Using more participatory methods, and engaging the team in reflective processes, helped to empower the organization through the process of evaluation. They argue that feminist evaluation adds perspective to the evaluation and helps in assessing whether the work of the organization has any long term benefits. Gender as an analytical category has emerged from feminist research and theory, but 'gender-sensitive' evaluation without a feminist perspective may lead one to consider women as passive respondents or mere beneficiaries rather than considering them as agents of change. In particular, the institutional histories approach is strongly recommended. It is a way of capturing institutional memory and tacit knowledge; but even more than this, the process of writing an institutional history opens up spaces for reflection and learning that can encourage institutional innovation and help in performance. The authors suggest that in a feminist evaluation the role of the evaluator shifts from merely providing technical expertise to facilitating collaborative processes where all stakeholders engage directly and feel ownership over the process. A feminist evaluation would pay attention to gender power relations and promote processes that are empowering for stakeholders. An evaluator can involve everyone in the evaluation process, even if it is not documented in the formal report. The process itself may open new paths and possibilities for interventions or recognize the importance of some ongoing interventions.

Gender-transformative Evaluations: Recognizing the 'Value Added'

A feminist or gender-transformative lens can complement, and add value, to an existing evaluation approach. Sonal Zaveri demonstrates how a feminist lens applied while implementing a Utilisation Focused Evaluation (UFE) framework, by bringing deeper understanding of gender and social equity issues, strengthened use and led to new strategies for community involvement being developed in an extension of the original programme. UFE is an approach attributed to the work of Michael Patton (2008) and the evaluation process is designed to facilitate use of the findings. The role of the evaluator is seen as being that of a 'coach, mentor and facilitator'. The project being evaluated—*Using a Mobile Application and Mapping Platform to Increase Accountability in the Delivery of Maternal Health Services for Tea Garden Workers in Assam*—used an SMS mobile and mapping platform to increase accountability in the delivery of maternal health services for tea garden workers in Assam. The evaluation approach that was being tested was Utilization Focused Evaluation, which provides a decision-making framework so that users of the evaluation actually use its findings. The author's initial role as evaluation mentor as part of an IDRC action-research project entitled Developing Evaluation and

Communication Capacity in Information Society Research, changed. As she puts it, she went beyond the non-judgemental role of a UFE mentor to become a researcher to help the implementing organizations in discovering the gaps in their theory of change. It became possible to uncover hidden assumptions in the programme theory of change and identify the additional efforts needed to achieve the objectives of the programme.

The feminist perspective led to stronger emphasis on context. It was important to understand the world of the women tea garden workers and take a closer look at issues of gender, maternal health rights and social exclusion. The initial queries could not be resolved with Skype calls, and it took field visits to uncover the 'intersectionalities' that affected women's reporting. Data was collected using guided interaction, and interpreted with sensitivity to the context. This led to changes in the programme strategies. The focus had earlier been on developing the ICT technology. This now shifted to also understanding *why* the tribal women were not reporting lapses. The underlying problem was the issue of entitlements and women's ability to claim their rights. A new action plan was developed with much more emphasis on building awareness. Zaveri argues that the feminist lens strengthened and complemented the UFE framework and this ensured that the information from the evaluation actually transformed the lives of those for whom the project was designed. The evaluation went 'beyond utilization' to improving people's lives, anchored in values of equity and human rights.

Shubh Sharma and Ratna Sudarshan suggest that a feminist lens applied to a collaborative evaluation improved the quality of the data, and contributed to developing gender-responsive programme strategies. Collaborative evaluation has been defined as 'any evaluation in which there is a significant degree of collaboration or cooperation between evaluators and stakeholders in planning and/or conducting the evaluation' (Cousins et al 1996: 210). The essay reflects on a baseline study of a development intervention that works for the economic, political and social empowerment of women in very poor and geographically dispersed settlements across several states in India. The objective of this baseline evaluation was to provide a basis for an end-line evaluation as well as to offer some pointers to the implementing team for designing area-specific interventions for the project. The essay assesses the challenges in and advantages of implementing a collaborative evaluation methodology guided by a set of feminist principles. This exercise involved a collaboration between the evaluator, implementing agency and stakeholders in data gathering, interpretation and analysis, and developing actionable strategies. The baseline study was a learning experience for both evaluator and the implementing agency; the implementing agency had deep experience of livelihood promotion but learnt how to systematically address gender issues in ongoing work. Given the geographical spread of the intervention along with the accompanying socio-cultural differences across areas, a collaborative approach to data collection using mixed methods improved the quality of the data. The evaluator got an opportunity to develop a suitable design and analysis plan that lowered the evaluator's bias, and fitted into women's day-to-day realities, rather than a pre-conceived set of indicators around gender roles and perceptions.

Rajib Nandi demonstrates how applying a feminist lens to a gender-blind project to be evaluated using conventional methodologies, can nonetheless lead to transforming the project design towards a gender-aware and responsive approach. His essay examines the evaluation of a mobile phone based free voice message service for farmers in rural India. The objective of the programme was to empower farmers and their families by disseminating timely information regarding agriculture and rural livelihoods, including health and education messages. The service provider disseminated five different pre-recorded voice messages every day in local languages. ISST conducted an evaluation of the programme in two states. The objectives of the evaluation, as per the terms of reference, were to understand the barriers between the service users and the service providers, particularly in terms of accessing and use of the service; getting feedback on the quality of the content from the users; the need and expectations of the service users from this programme; to assess the effectiveness of the programme and finally, to take the programme to more users across the social strata. The broad framework for the evaluation was predetermined. After a primary reading of the programme documents and through a series of conversations with the programme implementers it emerged that the programme was highly gender non-responsive and non-inclusive as far as women and other disadvantaged groups and small cultivators are concerned. The first challenge for the evaluators was to convince the commissioner of the evaluation (which was also the implementing agency) to make small changes in the evaluation framework, and include women and other disadvantaged groups in the evaluation process. Once this was agreed to, the evaluation was able to demonstrate that some of the programme assumptions were not valid – for example, that it is mainly men who are farmers and who use mobile phones, and the extent to which information is disseminated within and beyond households by those who hear the messages. The evaluation was able to offer specific recommendations regarding programme design, which was not part of the original TOR, and which were well received by the implementing agency.

Frameworks and Indicators for Gender-transformative Evaluations

Several of the essays demonstrate the evaluation frameworks that are recommended by a feminist approach and/or a wider set of indicators that could be used in evaluations. Renu Khanna and Enakshi Ganguly Thukral discuss the learnings from an evaluation conducted of a project to stop child marriage, being implemented by two NGOs in West Bengal and Telengana. The project showed several successes duly noted in an end of project evaluation. The evaluation, in line with the feminist tenet of being useful to the implementors, drew upon the findings of the evaluation to suggest a more appropriate multiple perspective approach to the difficult problem of child marriage. It recommended moving away from a narrow goal-focused project of stopping marriages of girls under 18 from taking place, to a more holistic approach. A sharper gender perspective would encourage working with boys and men; a contextualisation of the problem would allow strategies to be developed that are based on the community's own analysis of the problem. The role of the implementing NGOs would then be more about facilitation. The need to think around the question of child marriage, examine the wider and unintended outcomes, calls for more supporting research. In these ways, a feminist approach to an end of project evaluation, while noting what worked and what did not work, went much beyond this to shape a broader approach to the question of child marriage (to which there can be no quick resolution and which requires long term engagement), suggesting an alternative theory of change.

Venu Arora highlights the principles that ought to guide evaluations in the 'Communication for Development' (C4D) field, when the purpose of evaluation is seen to be 'to learn what we are achieving and how to improve upon it'. Theories of Development Communication have moved away from linear knowledge-transfer to participatory approaches, however programme implementation as well as evaluation practices still tend to focus on the extent to which there has been a behaviour change resulting from the project. Arora argues that a better focus would be on the extent to which there are greater probabilities of change as a result of the communication. She contrasts six evaluations of C4D conducted in the last decade and available in the public domain with two conducted by Ideosync Media Combine to show the differences that emerge when a participatory, feminist lens is applied to the evaluation. The latter set of evaluations were participatory, and research conducted during the evaluation process led to a shift in the focus of the programme towards including men, and this is turn was able to further encourage demand-driven communication.

The essay by Seema Kulkarni and Sneha Bhat examines evaluations in the irrigation sector and draws attention to the differences a feminist lens can bring. The water sector, they point out, gets divided into the domestic sphere of drinking water and sanitation where the role of women is central; and the productive sector including irrigation, which is seen as a male domain. The authors analyse and compare two sets of evaluations (i) those done by the irrigation department and (ii) those done by a pro-people, feminist group i.e. Society for Promoting Participative Ecosystem Management (SOPPECOM), a non-profit working on water and rural livelihood issues. While not directly comparable in that the scope and objectives of the two sets of evaluations are different, the essay spells out the differences in conceptual frames, data collection methods, processes of evaluation, and outcomes. The departmental evaluations view irrigation sector performance from a single point of view, that is efficiency in increasing revenue and increased area under irrigation. SOPPECOM is concerned with participation, democratisation and equity in the sector. While the department bases its analysis on secondary data, SOPPECOM used group discussions, interviews, stakeholder discussions to bring out the ground realities. The process used in the former set was non-participatory and the findings were not shared; whereas the latter used participatory and non-hierarchical processes. The outcome of the department evaluations was a presentation of the status of the programme; while in the case of SOPPECOM, the findings were shared and used for policy advocacy.

Even if 'drinking water, sanitation and hygiene' constitute the 'female' segment of the water sector, as discussed above, conventional evaluations may not recognize gender as a relevant aspect to include. Vasundhara Kaul and Neha Sanwal discuss the ways in which Water, Sanitation and Hygiene (WASH) evaluations have not adequately incorporated gender as a key indicator, and the implications this has for policy recommendations. Kaul and Sanwal's essay looks at the extent to which, and manner in which WASH evaluations have addressed gender. The authors selected, through a systematic online search, 16 evaluation reports (covering 13 distinct programmes) that were available in the public domain. Fifteen of these were published between 2005 and 2015, and one in 2000. The reports were coded using 54 indicators under three broad themes: structure of the evaluation design (8 codes); content (45 codes); funding of the evaluation (1 code). The content theme included six sub-themes focused on water, sanitation, hand-washing, impact on health, waste disposal and power relations and entitlements. The essay discusses the findings in respect of four key aspects – drinking water, sanitation, hygiene, and impact on health.

This analysis showed that gender did not constitute a focal point for any of the 16 reports. Most (fourteen out of sixteen) used mixed methods to collect data, however none attempted to get feedback from the community, even though half of the reports were for programmes under the Total Sanitation campaign which is based on community action. Most reports interpreted 'gender' as a male-female comparison but did not attempt to go beyond this. Most looked at 'access' to water and time spent, but did not go on to consider drudgery and the opportunity cost of time, thus not examining the differential impact of the programme by gender or class. Decision-making by gender was discussed in only one report. Among hygiene indicators, menstrual hygiene was mentioned in only two of the reports. None of the evaluations looked at the interplay between gender and caste or class. Overall, the evaluation reports show greater focus on access and quality and less on the drivers of behavioural change. The latter would bring up differences in power, in access to knowledge and resources, and in decision-making, and that village politics can constrain women and marginalized groups from participating in community forums. In the absence of more detailed and investigative gender and equity analysis, policy recommendations based on these evaluations focus on a supply model; while there is need for also generating demand through raising awareness and education and involving the community, specially women, in decision-making processes. In terms of the framework proposed by Murthy, these evaluations would appear to be either 'gender blind' or in some cases 'gender-specific', but would need to be differently designed to be transformative.

Feminist Evaluation as a Tool for Social Change

Through the essays in this book, we hope to show the ways in which feminist evaluation is able to offer concrete recommendations and programme strategies on how to bring about greater equity in outcomes. Some commonalities that emerge across the essays are briefly summarised.

First, the evaluations discussed here do not see the 'policy maker' or the commissioner of evaluation as the sole target of recommendations. The implementing organizations could develop new strategies or confirm the relevance of existing ones through participatory reflections during the evaluations. Thus Gupta and Raghavan show how Asmita's goals and strategies were reinforced by the evaluation processes, Zaveri shows how the project being evaluated developed a new dimension with new strategies as the evaluation uncovered hidden assumptions in the theory of change; Sharma and Sudarshan discuss the ways in which the PRADAN team began to formulate new and gender focused strategies as a result of the discussions accompanying the collaborative evaluation process; Khanna and Thukral present an alternative theory of change for understanding how to stop child marriage, and a set of indicators, as a conclusion of the evaluation; Arora shows how the communication projects shifted their focus to include men and develop demand-driven communication information and messages.

Second, these evaluations all recognize the significance of the particular context, in most cases by conducting fieldwork, capturing community insights, and using mixed methods. As Arora points out, one of the characteristics of large scale initiatives is to homogenize the community into groups such as 'young women'. It is one of the contributions of feminist evaluation to be able to explore whether there are context-specific circumstances that influence programme outcomes and call for more differentiated strategies.

Third, the essays argue for broader frameworks and additional indicators. The SOPPECOM evaluations discussed by Kulkarni and Bhat bring out the role of women's unpaid work in drawing and using water for irrigation, calling for a change in the imagery around women's roles. Importantly, they point to the need to see women's roles as dynamic, and not static, so that policy plans could visualize a different role for women in the future. The findings of the SOPPECOM evaluations bring out the need for a broadening of the goals of the water sector to move towards social justice and sustainable use, and the inclusion of new indicators such as access to water by all and voice in decision-making. Khanna and Thukral suggest that multiple perspectives need to inform interventions to stop child marriage. Both this essay and the one by Venu Arora, find that women-focused interventions could be re-shaped through the evaluation into being more inclusive of men and developing strategies that engaged both men and women.

Finally, feminist evaluation, as illustrated here, is rarely 'summative' in nature; evaluation is a part of the policy and action cycle and as long as the problem being tackled does not dissipate, dissolve or disappear, continuous engagement with the issue is necessary. Through its methods, its efforts to show how strategies could be deepened or modified, its engagement with all stakeholders and special attention to the marginalized, feminist evaluation becomes a part of the process of understanding a problem and seeking its solution.

References

Batliwala, Srilata and Alexandra Pittman. 2010. 'Capturing change in women's realities', http://brookeackerly.org/wp-content/uploads/2010/11/Batliwala-2010.pdf

Chigateri, Shraddha and Shiny Saha (eds.). 2016. A Resource Pack on Gender Transformative Evaluations, SERIES IN FEMINIST EVALUATION-3, New Delhi: Institute of Social Studies Trust.

Cousins, J.B., J.J. Donohue, G.A. Bloom. 1996. Collaborative evaluation in North America: evaluators' self-reported opinions, practices and consequences, *Evaluation Practice*, 17 (3): 207–26.

Hay, Katherine. 2012. 'Engendering Policies and Programmes through Feminist Evaluation: Opportunities and Insights', *Indian Journal of Gender Studies*, 19:2, 321–340.

Hay, Katherine, Ratna M. Sudarshan and Ethel Mendez (eds.). 2012. Special Issue on 'Evaluating Gender and Equity', *Indian Journal of Gender Studies*, Vol 19, no 2, June 2012.

Kabeer, Naila. 1994. *Reversed Realities: Gender Hierarchies in Development Thought*. London: Verso and New Delhi: Kali for Women.

Kabeer, Naila and Khan, Ayesha. 2014. 'Cultural values or universal rights? Women's narratives of compliance and contestation in urban Afghanistan'. *Feminist Economics*, 20 (3). pp. 1-24.

Murthy, Ranjani K. 2015a. Toolkit On Gender-Sensitive Participatory Evaluation Methods, SERIES IN FEMINIST EVALUATION-1, New Delhi: Institute of Social Studies Trust.

Podems, D. 2010. 'Feminist evaluation and gender approaches: There's a difference?' *Journal of Multi-Disciplinary Evaluation*, 6(14), 1–17.

Patton, Michael. 2008. *Utilization-focused evaluation*, Thousand Oaks: Sage.

Sudarshan, Ratna M. and Divya Sharma. 2012. 'Gendering Evaluations: Reflections on the Role of the Evaluator in Enabling a Participatory Process', *Indian Journal of Gender Studies*, 19(2), 303–320.

Sudarshan, Ratna, M.; Murthy, Ranjani. K.; Chigateri, Shraddha (eds.). 2015b. Engendering Meta-Evaluations: Towards Women's Empowerment, SERIES IN FEMINIST EVALUATION-2, New Delhi: Institute of Social Studies Trust.

2

Towards Gender-transformative and Feminist Evaluations

RANJANI K.MURTHY

Introduction

Evaluation has a long history. In the aftermath of World War I and II, interventions in the field of water, food rations, health and education were assessed by the war affected countries. However, it was after the formation of United Nations in 1945 that development evaluation emerged as a more systematic field of practice (Rossi et al, 2004). In South Asia, governments established an Evaluation Office after independence. The Government of India, for example, established a Programme Evaluation Organization (PEO) in 1952 within the Planning Commission for the evaluation of central government programmes (Anand, 2015). For a short period it became independent in 2013 but is now subsumed under the Niti Aayog whose functions include strategic planning, monitoring and evaluation. At a sub-regional level, in 2013 a Parliamentarian's Forum on Development Evaluation was established by the South Asian Association for Regional Cooperation (SAARC) with the objectives of ensuring that National Evaluation Policies are in place in each country, creating space for dialogue between parliamentarians and evaluators, improving the capacity of parliamentarians in development evaluation, and establishing country level performance measuring mechanisms in line with national evaluation policies

(Parliamentarians Forum on Development Evaluation in South Asia, n.d). However, not all these governmental evaluation initiatives were gender sensitive (Atmavilas, 2014)

Attention to gender issues in evaluation emerged in the 1990s. The Oxfam Gender Training Manual of 1994 included a module on evaluation of gender training modules. The Canadian International Development Agency (CIDA) evolved a Guide to Gender Sensitive Indicators in 1997[1] and the erstwhile Swedish International Development Agency (SIDA) drafted a manual on integrating gender into log frames (Shalkwyk 1998). In the early 2000s, the Organisation for Economic Cooperation and Development (OECD) evolved a guide on how gender could be integrated into the Development Assistance Committee's evaluation criteria of relevance, efficiency, sustainability and effectiveness (OECD, n.d).[2] Gender advocates pointed to the need for gender integration in terms of the reference, composition and expertise of the evaluation team, looking at who is met and who is not, the indicators, methods and ethics of the evaluation process, report writing and strengthening accountability to marginalized women in the interpretation and use of evaluation (Murthy and Kappen, 2007). Further, feminist evaluators evolved gender/feminist frameworks and tools like the Gender Roles Framework, the Moser Framework, the Gender Analysis Matrix, the Social Relations Framework in the 1990s (the first generation of frameworks) and more recently the Change Matrix, Making the Case, Women's Empowerment Index, the Substantive Equality Framework, the Socialist Feminist Theory of Change and Gender Scorecards (Batliwala and Pittman, 2010, Bowman and Sweetman, 2014). Some of these frameworks and tools focused only on programmatic aspects, while others looked at institutional and programmatic aspects. UN Women has recently established an Independent Evaluation Office whose mandate includes strengthening monitoring and evaluation capacities of government and non-government organizations from a gender lens. (UN Women, n.d)

By 2005, it was apparent that the transformative language of challenging the power relations of gender and other hierarchies was being replaced by the more neo-liberal language of 'investing in women'. More recently the World Bank and the International

Monetary Fund (IMF) argue that 'gender is smart economics' (Revenga and Shetty, 2012). While it may be smart economics, it is also true that it can overburden women. Further, the instrumental use of promoting gender equality has been a longstanding concern of gender and development advocates (Kabeer, 1994). The emphasis on quantitative methods, inadequate attention to feminist evaluation methods and the lack of attention to issues of power and accountability in evaluations have all come under question. In response some feminists have challenged the term 'gender-evaluations' and 'gender responsive evaluations' used by donors (Podems, 2010, Hay, 2012). At the same time, another section of feminists have been arguing that the baby should not be thrown out with the bath water. Using the term gender transformative evaluations clarifies that one is not referring to the use of 'gender' in evaluations in an instrumental sense. Further the term gender-tranformative evaluation is more acceptable than feminist evaluation is to governments. (Murthy, 2014)

It is in this context that this essay seeks to first explore whether the concepts of gender evaluations and feminist evaluations are really different. Taking examples from South Asia and, where necessary, outside, it distinguishes between gender-blind, gender-instrumental, gender-specific and gender transformative evaluation and argues that gender-transformative evaluations and socialist feminist evaluations are ideologically similar. The essay then explores different gender-transformative evaluation frameworks and tools, challenges to promoting gender-transformative evaluations in South Asia and suggests possible ways forward to promote gender-transformative evaluations.

ARE GENDER SENSITIVE EVALUATIONS AND FEMINIST EVALUATIONS DIFFERENT?

Drawing upon Kabeer's (1994) analysis of the different ways in which gender may be present or absent in policies, gender may be absent or present in evaluations in four different ways (Murthy, 2014).

The first type of evaluation is *gender-blind evaluation*, whose objectives do not include assessing changes in gender relations but refers to issues of assessing programme efficiency and effectiveness. The evaluation team does not normally include people who have expertise in gender and development. The evaluation methodologies may include mixed methods, but they are not gender-specific or transformative (see the next section for examples). The evaluation report does not highlight findings on changes in gender relations or make recommendations on gender-concerns. For example, the objective of the 2011 evaluation of Jawaharlal Nehru National Urban Renewal Mission (JNNURM) by Grant Thornton India was to monitor and evaluate results, impacts, and sustainability, to provide a basis for decision-making on constraints and remedial actions required and to assess the efficiency of resource use and disseminate results. The JNNURM includes components of improving drinking water and sanitation, sewage and waste management, strengthening roads and transport, beautification of urban areas, and construction of working women's hostels, marriage halls, night shelters and community toilets. Sixty six cities were covered in two phases of the evaluation. The methodology consisted of interviews of key government personnel and reviews of documents and records. While some of the findings of the evaluation are useful[3] none is gender/social relations specific. Neither are the recommendations similarly specific (Grant Thornton India, 2011). Missed opportunities to integrate gender concerns include sharing the responsibility of fetching water, safe transportation and bus stations, functional toilets, safe women's hostels etc. Further, the development paradigm which leads to eviction of slum dwellers (affecting women more than men) in the name of beautification is not questioned in the gender blind approach.

Evaluations that use the term gender could be classified into three categories: gender-instrumental evaluations, gender-specific evaluations or gender transformative evaluations (Murthy, RK, 2014, adapting from Kabeer 1994). Evaluations that use the term gender may disaggregate data by sex, may include women in the evaluation team, and refer to women and men in conclusions and recommendations, the purpose however varies.

Gender instrumental evaluations undertake a gender-analysis, but use the data to explore how far the programme has used the traditional roles of women and men for the success of project objectives (e.g. targeting women as mothers for improving child health, as adopters of family planning methods for population control). Women who are part of the evaluation team are often asked to evaluate soft aspects while financial viability, project management etc., are allocated to a male member of the team. An example of a gender instrumental evaluation is an assessment of an educational intervention with women, of infants in special care nurseries (SCN) in Kenya on breast pump use to improve the health of these infants (Friend and Chertok, 2009). The women were not able to directly breastfeed before the intervention. An evaluation (using a survey) covering 40 women with infants in the SCN was conducted which revealed that women were able to successfully utilize pumps to provide adequate milk volumes for SCN infants (Friend and Chertok, 2009). However the evaluation did not look at issues such as whether women exercised reproductive choice in having the child, whether partners fed pumped milk while the women rested or whether the contraceptive burden was shared.

Gender-specific evaluations examine how far the programme has addressed sex/gender specific needs of women or men as pertaining to it, but without assessing whether gender relations have been transformed in the process. Examples include the assessment of women's access to credit or strengthening de-addiction services for men. The evaluation team may include women members, but not necessarily with transformative views. Surveys continue to be popular in gender-specific evaluations, though may be combined with few other methods. Like in the case of gender-instrumental evaluations, women in such evaluations are asked to evaluate soft aspects like social impact, while technical viability, financial viability, project management etc., are allocated to a male facilitator. An example of a gender-specific evaluation is the impact evaluation of the USAID supported Mayer Hashi component of long-acting and permanent methods (LAPM) of contraception in 21 low performing districts of Bangladesh between 2009 and 2013. The focus was on promoting intra-uterine devices, female sterilization and, to a lesser extent, male sterilization. The LAPM interventions were aimed at increasing the demand for permanent methods and improving the skills and practices of service providers in delivering high quality services. The evaluation of 2013 used a 'before-after and intervention-comparison' evaluation framework covering six districts from the Mayer Hash programme districts and three otherwise comparable non-programme districts.

The evaluation observed that the programme districts provided greater access to behavioural change communication materials or products in facilities than non-programme districts. However, the proportion not using LAPM did not vary across programme and non-programme districts. A shortage of LAPM providers in intervention districts was felt to be one of the important reasons for poor impact (Rahman et al, 2014). The evaluation did not cover access to safe abortion services or specific hindrances to male sterilization.

Gender-transformative evaluations examine how far the programme has contributed to changing power relations within institutions based on gender and other identities (e.g. strengthening Dalit or Black women's asset base and decision making in institutions). Women in such evaluations are often team leaders or occupy a senior position in the evaluation team, and possess expertise on gender and social equity. Issues of power are placed at the centre, in community assessments, within the evaluation team, between the evaluation team and implementing agency and the implementing agency and the funding agency. Normally, a transformative conceptual framework underpins the evaluations. Mixed methods are used for such evaluations. Frameworks with examples are discussed in below.

Feminist Evaluations

Feminist evaluations emerged out of a critique of the first three ways in which gender may be present/absent in evaluations: namely gender-blind, gender-instrumental or gender-specific evaluations. The Journal *New Directions of Evaluation* brought out a special issue on 'Feminist Evaluation: Explorations and Experiences' in 2002. Contributing to this issue, Bamberger and Podems argue that international development evaluations do not adopt a specifically feminist approach but rather a Women-in-Development (WID) or, more recently, a gender approach. The authors observe that an explicitly feminist approach could strengthen the evaluation design (Bamberger and Podems, 2002).

To recall, WID approaches recognized that women play an important role in economic development (unlike the earlier welfare approach) and pointed to the need for promoting equality through legislation, reducing women's poverty or enhancing women's efficiency through tapping their economic potential (Moser, 1989). There was no focus on gender relations within the WID paradigm, or critique of the rolling back of the state which had just started.

The Gender and Development approach emphasized that gender relations are power relations, and that there was a need for both marginalized women's empowerment and challenging the mainstream development paradigm (Kabeer, 1994). Kabeer observed the need to transform institutions of family, community, market and state and interlocking social relations (gender, race, caste etc.) By the mid 2000s a different approach – Gender in Development (GID) – emerged which underlined analysis of gender roles (not relations) for efficiency of development. It is both the WID and the GID approach that have come under criticism by feminist evaluators.

Podems (2010) and Hay (2012) criticized the GID and WID approaches which underpin mainstream development and evaluations and underscored the need for feminist evaluations. Podems (2010) points to the following six tenets of feminist evaluation:

- Feminist evaluation has as its central focus the gender inequalities that lead to social injustice.
- Feminist evaluation considers discrimination or inequality based on gender as systemic and structural.
- Feminist evaluations view evaluations as a political activity; the contexts in which evaluation operates are politicized, and the personal experiences, perspectives, and characteristics evaluators bring to evaluations (and with which we interact) lead to a particular political stance.
- Feminist evaluation sees knowledge as a powerful resource that serves an explicit or implicit purpose.
- Feminist evaluators opine that knowledge should be a resource of and for the people who create, hold, and share it.
- Feminist evaluators also believe that there are multiple ways of knowing; some ways are privileged over others.

Hay (2012) adds that feminist evaluation challenges the path of mainstream development and evaluation. Mainstream evaluation has resulted in perspectives, designs, approaches, and tools which are not particularly well suited to understanding inequities. Feminist evaluation, however, foregrounds inequities. It asks whose questions are included and excluded in evaluations, uses mixed methods suited to the questions, recognizes competing definitions of success and stresses the need for taking responsible action on findings.

THE CONVERGENCE

Thus feminist evaluations, as articulated above, are close to the concept of gender transformative evaluations, and the socialist feminist strand of feminism. Socialist feminists believe that all hierarchies interlock together to subordinate women. They perceive gender, class, race, caste, ethnicity, religion etc., as interlocking and oppressing women, with the system of patriarchy, capitalism and other 'isms' underpinning them. Socialist feminists believe that simultaneous struggles to transform all social relations that have a bearing on women's lives and all 'isms' are necessary (Jagger, 1983). This strand of feminism is different from the liberal strand[4] (which sees women's secondary position as stemming from prejudices and lack of equal opportunities) or the Marxian strand[5] (which sees women's subordination as stemming from private property and capitalism) or the radical strand (which is against all manifestations and structures of patriarchy and male privilege,[6] with a few seeing men as biologically the problem).

Gender-transformative and Socialist Feminist Evaluation Frameworks

There are different gender-transformative and socialist feminist frameworks suited for different contexts.

THE CHANGE MATRIX

The Change Matrix was originally developed by Aruna Rao and David Kelleher of Gender at Work in 2002 and adapted by Srilatha Batliwala in 2008. The adapted version identifies four domains in which gendered power structures operate. These are individual, systemic, formal and informal. (See Figure 1)

FIGURE 1: The Change Matrix

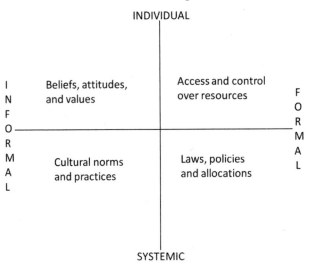

Source: Rao, Kelleher and, Batliwala (2008) The Change Matrix, http://www.inwf. org/wp-content/uploads/2014/02/10-AM-Intro-to-The-Change-Matrix-The-Case-of-the-Global-Fund-for-women-by-PeiYao-Chen-GFW.pdf Last Accessed 26th August, 2015

Access and control over resources falls in the quadrant of 'individual-formal', laws/policies and resource allocation at the 'formal-systemic' quadrant, cultural norms and practices at the 'systemic and informal' quadrant and beliefs, attitudes and values at the 'informal-individual' quadrant. When the Change Matrix is used for evaluating gender-sensitive work at the grassroots, changes in gender norms, attitudes and resources may be visible, but those in laws, policies and allocations may not be that visible. Advocacy groups, however, may have more impact on laws, policies, and state allocations, than the other quadrants. Depending on whom they fund, funding agencies may influence all four quadrants from a gender-transformative lens.[7]

The Change Matrix can also be used at the institutional level to look at, for example, job descriptions and performance evaluations (systemic-formal), to determine whether leaders are role models (systemic-informal), or if staff are motivated (individual-informal) and whether staff has a system of mentorship in place (individual-formal). (Rao, Kelleher and Batliwala, n.d)

The Change Matrix is being used by Tewa, which offers financial and technical support to small women's organizations in Nepal with the overall aim of promoting philanthropy, (gender) justice and peace. The Director of Tewa, a Board member, the monitoring and evaluation focal point and grant making team, took part in a training on gender, evaluation and learning, before choosing the Change Matrix. The work of the women's organizations it supports falls into three categories: economic and social empowerment, political empowerment, or movement building (Tewa 2015). The Change Matrix is being used to track i) which quadrant its partners work with, and ensuring that there are some partners working in each quadrant ii) what has been the impact of its partners' work on each of the quadrants. Gender-sensitive participatory methods like economic ranking (with marital and disability status) of households, a road map of change (See Box 1), confidence mapping, (reduction in) discrimination mapping, trend gender based violence mapping, and happiness index were used for ascertaining progress towards achievement of the objectives of partners. The outcomes from various partner groups are being plotted on the quadrants using an uniform scale of 1 to 5 (5 being better). Tewa plans to consolidate findings from all its partners to get an overall picture of impact of its Grant Making Unit (Tewa, 2015).

Box 1: Road map of Change from Furniture Grant

Using the Change Matrix framework it came to light that funding Nepali Rs 50,000 to a women's group for chairs and tables increased the women's self-esteem, the respect they commanded from the Village Development Council, the extent of resources they could mobilise and mediation of cases of violence. Thus a seemingly neutral intervention like furniture was in fact transformative and contributed to small changes in self-esteem, cultural norms and community resources for gender based violence (personal experience[8]).

MAKING THE CASE

The framework of Making the Case was evolved by Women's Funding Network, USA in 2004 and is used by over 100 philanthropic organizations (Nimmo, 2014). Like the Change Matrix, it can be used to explore changes in social relations of gender or other power relations. Making the Case is based on the belief that social change has to take place at the structural and cultural levels, and happens at both micro and macro levels. Social change can be slow or abrupt, and is often non-linear. Making the Case seeks to track changes of both kinds and at both levels. The framework is based on the belief that changes can be in definitions,[9] behaviour, scale of engagement, policy and (simply) maintaining past gains. Importantly, it tracks negative change, reversals, backlash and unexpected changes. After tracking changes it also analyses the contributing and hindering factors. When Women's Funding Network uses the framework, the assessments are recorded online, and a central repository of grant evaluations is made (Nimmo, 2014).

The 2007 and 2009 report of Women's Funding Report records important shifts that happened through its partnerships. For example, its partner group called NouKab in Haiti, is shifting the definition that those who protest against domestic violence are 'homewreckers', and that domestic violence is a 'private affair'. Now domestic violence is discussed in the community. Radio programmes on domestic violence, with a provision for communication, have been one of the important contributors to changes in perceptions (Women's Funding Network, 2009). Support for a capacity building programme with Latina women in Iowa on the rights of those who rent houses not only strengthened their security, but also brought about changes in policy when the women successfully engaged in advocacy with the state on responsibility for structural repairs (Clohesy and Gorp, 2007). These women worked in mobile parks, often leaving their families behind. Thus behaviour, scale of engagement and policy changed in favour of renters (ibid, 2007). Maintaining past gains is another thrust. One partner with a thrust on preventing adolescent pregnancies and fostering empowering life trajectories, points out that keeping in touch with past participants and arranging events to bring back alumni is central to ensuring that the vicious cycle between poverty, inadequate empowerment and teenage/early pregnancies is broken (Women's Funding Network, 2009).

SOCIAL RELATIONS FRAMEWORK

Evaluations using the Social Relations Framework build upon Kabeer's (1994) analysis that institutions of household, community, market and state shape gender and social relations, and that gender specific and redistributive polices are essential to challenge them. Institutions have their norms, people, structures and power, many of which disadvantage women and marginalized groups. Hillenbrand et al (2014) adapted the social relations framework to assess the impact of a 'fish on farms' livelihood based food security project on women's empowerment in Cambodia. The capacity of the implementing agency's team was strengthened on using participatory gender analysis tools, as well as baselines and end-lines. Timelines, seasonal diagrams, fish-preference ranking exercises, venn diagrams on market access, division of household responsibilities, body maps, and asset management diagrams were some of the participatory gender analysis tools used. Each day of data collection was followed by a day of analysis from a gender lens and triangulation of information from different sources. The impact assessment study revealed that household and community norms on traditional clothing were changing in such a manner that clothing helped them to work and move with ease. The norms of softness in speaking and slowness in walking have given way to assertion and speed. Silence is giving way to asserting oneself vis a vis husbands. Topics which are considered taboo like reproductive health are now being discussed by women. Gendered migration was becoming a market phenomenon, with men migrating for fishing and women for garments. It was not unusual to hear that women and men have equal status. However, the evaluation noted that decision-making, workload distribution, responsibility distribution and knowledge around care giving was unequally distributed. Alcohol misuse and gender-based violence persisted as problems. Measures to address these gaps were identified for the next phase (Hillenbardet al, 2014)

GENDER, EMPOWERMENT AND POVERTY REDUCTION

The framework of gender, empowerment and poverty reduction developed by Krishnamurthy (2004) builds on Rowland's (1997) concept of empowerment and Sen's (1981) concept of entitlements.

This framework is relevant when the objective of the programme includes women's poverty reduction and empowerment. Women's poverty is discussed at two levels: dimensions and causes. To capture the impact on gender-specific dimensions of poverty, intra-household distribution of basic needs is analysed using participatory methods, the gender-based division of labour and resources. Aspects like access to rest are taken into consideration in the definition of basic needs. Further, as women are a diverse group, issues of access to basic needs of Dalits (India), refugees (Sudan) and young people (Moldova) at the community level are explored through focus group discussions. The impact of the project on gender-specific causes of poverty is analysed through an examination of its effect on women's ownership of assets, their access to common property resources, their bargaining power in markets and vis a vis government officials. A gender-sensitive wealth ranking exercise is used to understand changes in poverty and their reasons. Deterioration (for example due to dowry or alcohol abuse) and its impact on gender-adverse coping strategies when faced with poverty is another aspect that is looked into, in addition to reduction in food consumption, trafficking of girls, unsafe migration etc. With regard to empowerment, Rowlands' (1997) framework of three levels of empowerment – power to (individual), power with (collective) and power within (deep rooted values) – is used to assess gender and diversity related impact. Body mapping and mobility mapping are some of the methods used. Changes in power to exercise control over mobility, labour, resources, body and political spaces are ascertained; power with others to influence markets, community structures and local government is explored and changes in gender and social norms are examined. Change before and after and between members and non-members is examined. When this framework was used with the team of Gorakhpur Environmental Action Group for a participatory evaluation of their sustainable agriculture and women's empowerment interventions, it emerged that women's poverty as well as that of their households had indeed reduced in terms of access to basic needs and the ability to claim entitlements, although differences in workload persisted. The expansion of women's mobility, their participation in the Gram Sabha, their participation in farmers' organizations and their earnings were visible; but dramatic changes in asset ownership by women were not visible. Violence against women had declined. Gender and caste norms were slowly changing. Improvements among members was more than among non-members of similar status, and over time (Krishnamurthy, 2004).

WOMEN'S EMPOWERMENT ASSESSMENT TOOL

In 2011, as part of a broader effort to understand organizational effectiveness, a team within Oxfam GB began implementing impact evaluations on a small sample of projects largely focused on women's empowerment. The resulting 'Women's Empowerment Effectiveness Reviews' employed a quasi-experimental evaluation design,[10] and were undertaken in more than a dozen sites over three years, including in parts of Asia. Assessing the impact of projects of Oxfam GB with a women's empowerment focus (which often begins with livelihood as a starting point) posed a difficult task, given that baselines were rarely available. Two sets of issues were posed in the first year of impact evaluation: first, women's involvement in several aspects of household decision-making, such as decisions regarding the purchase of new assets, or choices related to children's education or family planning, and second, their participation in community-level leadership and decision-making. Also, other questions that were raised pertained to self-confidence and women's ownership of assets. The reviews of the first year found that women participants in the projects were more likely to have the opportunity and feel able to influence affairs in their community than non-participants. In contrast, there was no clear difference in intra household decision-making (Bishop and Bowman, 2014).

In years 2 and 3 the indicators were broadened, drawing upon Oxford Poverty and Human Development Initiative and IFPRI's Women's Empowerment in Agriculture Index. Four dimensions were explored, namely (i) Household decision-making (productive and other spheres), (ii) Control over resources (access to credit and strategic assets), (iii) Public engagement (group involvement, community influence) and (iv) Self-perception (efficacy, attitude to sharing household duties, attitude to women's rights, and attitude to the position of women). The findings were similar to the first year. In addition, contradictory findings were found, like higher levels of self-confidence along with traditional views on the role of men and women in households. Based on lessons learnt from the three year review, an additional dimension – support from social networks – has been added. The final menu of women's empowerment dimensions and characteristics evolved is given in Table 1 with characteristics being chosen according to the context of the project (Bishop and Bowman, 2014).

Some of the lessons drawn from the assessment were the importance of avoiding composite indices (which do not disaggregate and give a nuanced picture), the need for a menu of indicators from which project and evaluation teams can choose, valuing the right steps and not just outcomes, and the need for evaluation to move from promoting accountability to promoting accountability and empowerment (Bishop and Bowman, 2014).

TABLE 1: Suite of Economic Empowerment Characteristics

Dimensions	Characteristics
Ability to make decisions and influence	• Involvement in household investment decisions • Involvement in livelihood management decisions • Involvement in income-spending decisions • Involvement in general decisions • Degree of influence in community decision-making
Self-perception	• Opinions on women's property rights • Opinions on women's political rights • Opinions on women's educational equality • Opinions on women's economic and political roles • Opinions on early marriage • Self-confidence • Psycho-social well-being
Personal freedom	• Literacy • Autonomy in work • Time to pursue personal goals • Support from family in pursuing personal goals • Attitude to violence against women • Experience of violence

Dimensions	Characteristics
Access to and control over resources	• Ownership of land and property • Ownership of other productive assets • Independent income • Extent of role in managing/keeping family's cash • Savings • Access to credit
Support from social networks	• Degree of social connectivity • Participation in community groups • Level of support provided by groups to pursue own initiatives

Bowman, K & C Sweetman (2014) 'Introduction to Gender, Monitoring, Evaluation and Learning,' *Gender & Development*, 22:2, 201–212.

Challenges to Institutionalizing
Gender-transformative/Socialist-Feminist Evaluations

Of late, some of the aid agencies have begun to look at 'gender as smart economics'. Citing the World Bank, the IMF notes that greater gender equality can enhance economic productivity, improve development outcomes for the next generation, and make institutions and policies more representative (Revanga, and Shetty, 2012). While it is good that gender equality is seen as smart economics, unless care-work work is shared, and gender norms in the workplace change, women have ownership of assets and women's safety can be assured in all spaces and women exercise strategic political power, it is difficult to empower women. Evaluations in this ideology are rarely gender transformative. There is also a danger that this ideology may extend to evaluations, in other words that you should churn in gender for smart evaluations!

Another hurdle is that in their designs, programmes seek to address gender-specific issues (e.g. access to credit) but are weary of the transformative ones as they go against the cultural norms (e.g. women's land rights). Assessing the transformative potential of the programme design may or may not be part of evaluation, especially if the evaluation is summative in nature. The feminist evaluator is then asked 'Why are you assessing empowerment when it is not part of the objectives?' Further, with few exceptions, programmes for women's empowerment are targeted only at women and do not seek to work with men on masculinities. The limited work with men is on the sexual and reproductive health of women and men and prevention of violence against women. The discourse of 'happy families' underpins some of the work on masculinities (Care Sri Lanka, 2012) which restricts life choices for women.

There is a tendency for some of the simplistic gender frameworks that underpin evaluation – which compare men and women and but do not examine the interlocking with other social relations – to not examine exclusions. Sabharwal (2015) observes that Dalit women in India had lesser access to Janani Suraksha Yojana (a maternity benefit scheme) when compared to the caste Hindus in seven states covered through her study.[11] In some cases Anganwadi workers refuse to hold the infant of a Dalit to weigh or give immunization. Such observations are not reflected in the government reviews of the same scheme. It is not just a shortage of frameworks which grapple with complexity which is a problem, but also evaluators who are sensitive and competent. There is also a need for gender and social transformative indicators (Jandhyala, 2012). Such indicators may be evolved in consultation with marginalized women.

Yet another challenge in feminist evaluation is the need to carefully assess not just the transformative potential of ends achieved, but the means as well. Khanna (2014) in her evaluation of the Sabala-Tarang (adolescent girl empowerment) programme in India observes that some of the reasons used by Sakhis and Sahelis (peer leaders amongst adolescent girls) to persuade people against child marriage were that 'during delivery it would be easy' and that the 'health of mothers and babies would be better.' They did not focus on health as an intrinsic right for the girl. The paths and ends have to be feminist, and if possible rooted in the history of social reformers and feminists in the area.

Baselines and endlines are important for evaluations, and should be combined with qualitative methods. However, not all programmes have baselines (UNICEF, UNFPA, PHD, 2012). Further, when available not all are sex and socially disaggregated or have the required information related to outcome or impact indicators. A study of evaluations of irrigation sector programmes in Maharashtra, India from a feminist lens found that most baseline and endline surveys of the irrigation department of the government focused on irrigation system performance, canal use efficiency (ratio of water released to actual supply), maintenance costs etc. Data on equity in the distribution of water, distribution between productive vs reproductive needs in women's participation in water-use/irrigation decision-making was not available (Kulkarnai, 2013).

The political economy of dominant evaluations is another challenge to gender-transformative evaluations. In large evaluations gender-experts are positioned as members of the team, and not as team leaders. The TORS given for the evaluation may not look at gender/social relations as a cross cutting issue; and restrict such assessment to women focused programmes or soft sectors like health and education (Murthy, 2012). Further, the time available for evaluations is normally short (10-20 days) while the demands of assessing gender-transformative changes, analysing them, and taking the findings back to community women is longer. The linking of evaluations to future funding (often the case) leads to the emergence of a hierarchy between the evaluation team (including gender experts) and the implementing agency, wherein the true impact and lessons may not emerge. This is also true of community interactions, wherein women/girls and men/boys know how to respond, and questions have to be posed carefully (Khanna, 2014). Evaluations often do not budget for the validation of findings and recommendations with (different groups of) women and men in the community and follow up visits to facilitate implementation of recommendations (Murthy, 2012, Khanna, 2014).

Finally, there is a lot to be done on building capacities on gender-transformative/socialist feminist evaluations and increasing the number of evaluators. Training courses on evaluations normally do not reflect the above perspective, and courses on gender do not comprehensively cover gender-transformative evaluations. The USAID and MEASURE Evaluation Learning Center offers several certificate courses on M and E (USAID and Measure Evaluation n.d). A look at the course outlines of seven courses suggests that none address gender concerns. However, USAID offers a special module on Gender in Evaluation, rooted in analysis of gender norms and power relations, but not on any of the frameworks discussed earlier (USAID, n.d). That is, gender and evaluation is ghettoized. A review of a Gender Course in the Netherlands reveals that it discusses core concepts, including sex, gender, sexuality, and intersectionality; gender biases in research, the historical and political context of gender dynamics, and gender and education, work and careers, as well as politics. There is no reference to monitoring and evaluation (Radbound University, n.d). Short courses on quantitative evaluation methods are also the need of the hour, as feminist evaluators are familiar with qualitative methods, but need hard skills to quantify findings, and prove validity (Hay, Sudarshan, and Mendez, 2012)

The Way Forward

Our discussion has drawn attention to the fact that development evaluations need to move from being gender-blind, gender-instrumental and gender-specific to being gender-transformative. Gender-transformative and socialist feminist evaluations are similar in their theoretical underpinnings, principles and frameworks. Yet there are several constraints to furthering such evaluations which pertain to efficiency paradigms, programme design, evaluation frameworks, methodologies, methods, indicators, and evaluation processes which are at best gender-specific. The limited capacity in gender-transformative evaluation is another issue.

Given that many programmes do not have the promotion of gender equity as a stated objective, it is important, first of all, to engender programme objectives and design through engagement with programme formulation. Care needs to be taken that women's involvement is not promoted in an instrumental sense. Baselines that capture strategic gender/social issues and monitoring systems are crucial. Such data and information needs to be quantitative and qualitative.

Equally it is crucial to engage with mainstream evaluations and challenge them as much as possible. Nandi (2015), for example, took up the evaluation of a voice messaging service to farmers on agriculture in Rajasthan and Punjab, India. While the official purpose was to get feedback from (male) users on issues such as quality, timeliness, usefulness, future needs etc., the evaluator's recommendations included responding to women as primary users, employing them as marketing agents, and adding other information as well, such as land rights for women, violence against women, etc. Thus, fielding more gender experts as mission leaders is imperative.

Another strategy that is required is building theory from our own practice. Several of the women activists in South Asia have evolved their own ways of doing evaluations. Underpinning these evaluation initiatives is the Social Relations or Empowerment Framework. They have, however, used different methods and indicators and rooted them in issues of diversity. These methods and indicators need to be documented, and extended to evaluating emerging issues like climate change adaptation.

Building gender-transformative evaluation capacity from within the sub-region is also important. Modules on gender-transformative evaluations may be included in general courses on monitoring and evaluation, in addition to being a cross cutting issue. This equally applies to courses and degrees on Gender and Development. In addition special training on gender-transformative evaluations could be promoted.

Finally, evaluation and accountability are related. This requires that findings and recommendations from evaluations are taken back to marginalized women and men as well as women's rights groups in a form accessible to them and once these are validated, they are widely disseminated. At the same time it is important to engage with policy makers (including parliamentarians) from the sub region on promoting and learning from gender-transformative evaluations.

Notes

1.   BRIDGE evolved its own pack of gender indicators in 2007 (Moser, 2007).
2.   Around 2002 as implied by the list of reference used (OECD, n.d).
3.   Example, the evaluation team noted exclusion of small cities, lack of translation of city development plans into, lack of environmental and social impact assessment of some projects, restriction of consultations

to government departments and lack of adequate funds for some reforms etc (Grant Thornton India, 2011),

4. See Betty Friedan. 1963. *The Feminine Mystique*. New York/London. W.W, Norton and Company.

5. See Engels, F. 1942. 'The Origin of the Family, Private Property and the State', *in Marx/Engels Selected Works*, Volume Three (Translated by Alice West, Hottingen: Zurich.

6. See Daly, M. 1973. *Beyond God the Father: Toward a Philosophy of Women's Liberation*. Boston: Beacon Press.

7. The Global Fund for Women uses the Change Matrix for tracking the outcomes of its support (Global Fund For Women, 2012).

8. Personal experience while demonstrating participatory gender transformative evaluation methods in different districts of Nepal between 1st and 5th of February, 2015.

9. For example as in concept of women's work.

10. Participant-non participant comparison.

11. Madhya Pradesh, Chattisgarh, Jharkhand, Bihar, Uttar Pradesh, West Bengal and Orissa.

References

Anand, P.K. 2015. Presentation on PEO Evaluations in workshop on 'Evaluations for Development with Equity and Equality' organized by ISST and UNDP on 15–17 April, New Delhi: India Habitat Centre.

Atmavilas, Y. 2014. Draft: State Evaluation and Accountability Mechanisms: Where do Gender and Equity Criteria Figure, Engendering Policy Through Evaluation Project, New Delhi: Institute of Social Studies Trust.

Bamberger, M. and Podems, D. 2002. 'Feminist Evaluation in the International Development Context: New Directions for Evaluation' 96. Wiley Periodicals Inc.

Batliwala, S. and A. Pittman. 2010. 'Capturing Change in Women's Realities: A Critical Overview of Current Monitoring & Evaluation Frameworks and Approaches' Toronto, Mexico City, Cape Town: Association for Women's Rights in Development, http://brookeackerly.org/wp-content/uploads/2010/11/Batliwala-2010.pdf; Last accessed 26 August 2015.

Batliwala, S. 2011. 'Strengthening Monitoring and Evaluation for Women's Rights: Insights from 12 Donors' Toronto, Mexico City, Cape Town: Association for Women's Rights in Development, https://static1.

squarespace.com/static/536c4ee8e4b0b60bc6ca7c74/t/54381234e4b
0cc14e48e6919/1412960820285/Awɪᴅ+-+Strengthening+ME+for
+Women%27s+Rights.pdf. Last accessed 26 August 2015

Bishop, D. and K Bowman. 2014. 'Still learning: a critical reflection on
three years of measuring women's empowerment in Oxfam', *Gender &
Development*, 22:2, 253-269.http://www.tandfonline.com/doi/pdf/10.
1080/13552074.2014.920993. Last accessed 26 August, 2015.

Bowman, K. and C. Sweetman. 2014. 'Introduction to Gender, Monitoring,
Evaluation and Learning', *Gender & Development*, 22:2, 201-212http://
www.tandfonline.com/doi/pdf/10.1080/13552074.2014.934525.
Last accessed 26 August, 2015.

Care Sri Lanka. 2012. 'Mid-term Evaluation of Engaging Men Project',
Care International; http://www.engagingmen.net/content/mid-term-
evaluation-engaging-men-project-care-international-sri-lanka. Last
accessed 26 August, 2015.

Clohesy S. and S.V. Gorp. 2007. 'The Powerful Intersection of Margins &
Mainstream: Mapping the Social Change Work of Women's Funds', San
Francisco: Women's Funding Network; http://www.clohesyconsulting.
com/PDFfiles/wfn_full_report.pdf. Last accessed 26 August, 2015.

Daly, M. 1973. *Beyond God the Father: Toward a Philosophy of Women's
Liberation* Boston: Beacon Press.

Engels, F. 1942. 'The Origin of the Family, Private Property and the State',
in *Marx/Engels Selected Works*, Volume Three, Hottingen-Zurich
(Translated Alick West).

Friend, D. and I.R.A. Chertok. 2009. 'Evaluation of an educational
intervention to promote breast pump use among women with infants in
a special care nursery in Kenya: Populations at risk across the lifespan:
Program evaluations'. *Public Health Nursing* 26(4): 339-345.

Friedan, B. 1963. *The Feminine Mystique*, New York and London: W.W.
Norton and Company.

Global Fund For Women. 2012. 'The Global Fund For Women Impact
Report: Gender Inequality in Asia and the Pacific', San Francisco:
Global Fund for Women, USA https://www.globalfundforwomen.
org/storage/documents/impact/Global_Fund_for_Women_Impact_
Report_Breaking_Through.pdf. Last accessed 26 August, 2015.

Grant Thonrton. 2011. 'Appraisal of Jawaharlal Nehru National Urban
Renewal Mission (JNNURM) Final Report – Volume I', http://jnnurm.
nic.in/wp-content/uploads/2012/06/Appraisal-of-JnNURM-Final-
Report-Volume-I-.pdf. Last Accessed 26 August, 2015.

Hay, K. 2012. 'FIE/MME Week: Katherine Hay on How to do Feminist

Evaluation' http://aea365.org/blog/fiemme-week-katherine-hay-on-how-to-do-feminist-evaluation/#sthash.xivlihUb.dpuf. Last accessed 26 August, 2015.

Hay, K., R. Sudarshan and E. Mendez. 2012. 'Why a Special Issue on Evaluating Gender and Equity?' *Indian Journal of Gender Studies*, June 19: 179–186.

Hillenbrand, E., P. Lakzadeh, Ly Sokhoin, Z. Talukder, T. Green & J. McLean. 2014. 'Using the Social Relations Approach to capture complexity in women's empowerment: using gender analysis in the Fish on Farms project in Cambodia', *Gender & Development*, 22:2, 351–368, http://www.tandfonline.com/doi/pdf/10.1080/13552074.2014.9209 92. Last accessed 26 August, 2015.

Jaggar, A. 1983. *Feminist Politics and Human Nature*, Maryland: Rowman & Littlefield.

Jandhyala, K. 2012. 'Ruminations on Evaluation in the Mahila Samakhya Programme', *Indian Journal of Gender Studies* 19 (2): 211–231.

Kabeer, N. 1994. *Reversed Realities: Gender Hierarchies in Development Thought*, London: Verso and New Delhi: Kali for Women.

Khanna, R. 2014. 'Evaluation of SABLA – TARANG: a User Focused Evaluation?' New Delhi: Institute of Social Studies Studies Trust.

Krishnamurthy, R. 2004. 'Gender and Poverty Impact of Social Mobilization, Sustainable Agriculture and Micro Credit Interventions: Lessons from Gorakhpur Environment Action Group, Gorakhpur, UP' http://www.geagindia.org/pdf/Ranjani's%20Impact%20Assessment%20Report-FINAL.pdf. Last accessed 26 August, 2015.

Kulkarni, S. 2013. 'Reflections', Presentation in Workshop on 'Engendering Policy Through Evaluations', organized by Institute of Social Studies Trust, Pune, February 8.

Moser, A. 2007. 'Gender and Indicators: Overview Report', BRIDGE, Sussex: Institute of Development Studies, http://www.bridge.ids.ac.uk/sites/bridge.ids.ac.uk/files/reports/IndicatorsORfinal.pdf. Last accessed 26 August, 2015.

Moser, C. 1989. 'Gender Planning in the Third World: Meeting Practical and Strategic Gender Needs', *World Development*, Vol. 17, No. 2, pp. 1799–1825.

Murthy, R.K. and M. Kappen. 2007. *Institutionalising Gender within Organisations and Programmes: A Training Manual*, Bangalore: Visthar.

Murthy, R.K. 2012. 'Decade of Evaluation of Micro-finance and Livelihood Projects from a Genderand Equity Lens', *Indian Journal of Gender Studies* 19 (2) 279–301.

Murthy, R.K. 2014. 'Are Gender-Sensitive Evaluations And Feminist Evaluations Different?' *Gender and Evaluation* http://gendereval.ning. com/profiles/blogs/are-gender-sensitive-evaluations-and-feminist-evaluations?xg_source=activity. Last accessed June 25, 2015.

Nandi, R. 2013. 'Towards engendering a voice messaging programme for rural communities in India through evaluation with a feminist lens', Paper presented at a workshop on 'Engendering Policy through Evaluation', Pune, February 8.

Nimmo, C. 2014. 'Making the Case: A Tool to Measure Social Change', http://www.inwf.org/wp-content/uploads/2014/02/1-PM-to-4-PM-Interactive-In-Depth-Training-on-the-Making-the-Case-INWF-+-IHRFG-LME-Institute-Cynthia-Schmae-Nimmo-WFN.pdf. Last accessed 26 August, 2015.

OECD, n.d, Sheet 12, 'Gender and Evaluation' http://www.oecd.org/social/gender-development/44896217.pdf. Last accessed 26 August, 2015.

Parliamentarians Forum on Development Evaluation in South Asia, n.d, http://www.mymande.org/evalyear/parliamentarians_forum. Last accessed 26 August 2015.

Podems, D. 2010. 'Feminist Evaluation and Gender Approaches: There's a Difference?' *Journal of Multi Disciplinary Evaluation*, Volume 6, Number 14, August, 2010; http://journals.sfu.ca/jmde/index.php/jmde_1/article/view/199/291. Last accessed 26 August, 2015.

Radbound University Nijmegan, 2015. 'Gender: A Core Concept in Society and Science,' http://www.ru.nl/radboudsummerschool/courses/social-sciences/@969991/gender-core-concept/. Last accessed 26 August, 2015.

Rahman, M., S.L. Curtis, M.M. Haider. 2014. 'Impact Evaluation of the Mayer Hashi Program of Long-Acting and Permanent Methods of Contraception in Bangladesh, Measure Evaluation/USAID', Chapel Hill: USAID www.cpc.unc.edu/measure/publications/tr-14-102/at.../document. Last accessed 26 August, 2015.

Rao, Kelleher, Batliwala, S. 2008. 'The Change Matrix', http://www.inwf.org/wp-content/uploads/2014/02/10-AM-Intro-to-The-Change-Matrix-The-Case-of-the-Global-Fund-for-women-by-PeiYao-Chen-GFW.pdf. Last accessed 26 August, 2015.

Revanga, A. and S. Shetty. 2012. 'Empowering Women is Smart Economics', *Finance & Development* March 2012, http://www.imf.org/external/pubs/ft/fandd/2012/03/revenga.htm. Last accessed 26 August, 2015.

Rossi, P., M. W. Lipsey and H.E Freeman. 2004. 'An Overview of Program Evaluation', in Rossi, Lipsey and Freeman, *Evaluation: A Systematic Approach* (Seventh Edition), Thousand Oaks: Sage Publications.

Rowlands, Jo. 1997. *Questioning Empowerment: Working with Women in Honduras*, Oxford: Oxfam GB.

Sabharwal, N. 2014. 'Study of Janani Suraksha Yojana.' New Delhi: Institute of Social Studies Trust.

Sen, A. 1981. *Poverty and Famines: An Essay on Entitlement and Deprivation* Oxford: Clarendon Press.

Shalkwyk, J. 1998. 'Mainstreaming Gender Equality into the Use of Logical Framework Approach (LFA)', Stockholm: Swedish International Development Corporation Agency. file:///E:/gender%20and%20feminist/mainstreaming-gender-equality-into-in-the-use-of-the-logical-framework-approach-lfa_2717.pdf. Last accessed 24 June, 2015.

Tewa. 2015. 'Learning and Evaluation Training: 1st February 2015–5th February 2015,' Kathmandu: TEWA.

United Nations. 2012. Evaluation policy of the United Nations Entity for Gender Equality and the Empowerment of Women, UNW/2012/12, Second regular session of 2012 28-30 November.

UNFPA, UNICEF, PHD. 2012. 'Evaluation report 2012 Nepal: Evaluation of Conflict-Related Sexual Violence Project', http://www.unicef.org/evaldatabase/index_69979.html. Last accessed 24 June, 2015.

UN Women. n.d. Evaluation, http://www.unwomen.org/en/about-us/evaluation. Last accessed 26 August, 2015.

USAID and Measure Evaluation n.d. Measure Evaluation – M and E Learning Center: Certificate Courses, USAID and Measure Evaluation, https://training.measureevaluation.org/certificate-courses. Last Accessed 26 August, 2015.

USAID, n.d. Module 13, Gender in Evaluation, http://usaidlearninglab.org/sites/default/files/resource/files/mod13_genderinevaluation.pdf. Last accessed 24, June, 2015.

Women's Funding Network. 2009. Making the Case Report to Women's Fund of Miami-Dade County, For Grants Awarded in 2007–2009, San Francisco: Women's Funding Network.

3

Feminist Approaches to Evaluation

Institutional Histories, Participatory Evaluation and Gender Analysis

PALLAVI GUPTA and SRINIDHI RAGHAVAN

Introduction

The primary purpose of an evaluation is to assess whether an organization is proceeding in the right direction. Secondly, an evaluation assesses the extent to which the organization has been able to achieve its objectives. While doing this, it seeks to explore the congruence and incongruence that could have arisen between the organization's stated objectives and contemporary social reality. Social political conditions are constantly changing and often organizational strategies need to be altered. Sometimes even the objectives need to be altered, however slightly. The evaluation is a significant mediator in helping the funding agency to understand changing priorities and to judge whether their requirements/objectives are being met. When evaluators have a clear political perspective, in this case a feminist perspective, it immediately raises the value of the evaluation from a mechanical exercise of measuring outputs to assessing the needs of stakeholders and bridging gaps in theory and practice.

The evaluation consists of discussions with staff, and consultation at various levels. The meeting with the expert team or the governing body assists in assessing whether the organization is moving in the right direction. What fits into the existing objective and framework of the organization and what does not? Feminist evaluation adds perspective to the evaluation and helps in assessing whether the work of the organization has any long term benefits. This essay will draw from six evaluations of Asmita, a women's organization based in Hyderabad, that have been undertaken from 1993 to 2009 and flag significant aspects in each. The essay will also attempt to address three broad set of questions:

1. What are the specific methods employed? When have feminist evaluations been conducted? How is gender analysis different from feminist evaluation?
2. How important is it to document institutional histories? How does the institutional histories approach help to track the evolution of an organization?
3. How does feminist evaluation help in challenging gender bias? What are the key learnings from Asmita's evaluation? How does one analyse the most significant changes within organizations working on gender issues?

The first section of the essay explores the six evaluations Asmita has undergone in the last two decades; the second looks at the institutional histories approach and its application in India by other civil society groups. The last section focuses on gender strategy and explores the various strands that emerge in the process, whether in the form of gender analysis or a gender responsive framework and the efficacy of gender trainings. A brainstorming with evaluators was conducted to understand their learning and experience. This can be found as an appendix.

Section I
Our First Evaluation

Asmita Resource Centre for Women was founded in 1991 and has been working on women's human rights, gender discrimination and human rights. The organization aims to create a space for women to come together; provide a context for critical dialogue and reflection; facilitate feminist analysis and action on critical issues and provide resources to women in need. The first evaluation in 1993 was carried out when 'the donor agency (HIVOS) felt the need to gauge the long term capacity of Asmita and its scope to develop into a strong women's organzsation with potential to influence government policy'.[1]

From Asmita's point of view the evaluation was felt to be necessary to determine the organizational capability of the members, to gauge the effectiveness of the programme and its activities and to modify the structure and programmes, if necessary, to help it grow into a strong and unique organization dedicated to bringing about socio-political empowerment of women in Andhra.[2]

METHODOLOGY

A participant-oriented approach to evaluate Asmita was adopted as the organization was barely a year old. It was also a formative evaluation that would provide the Asmita team and HIVOS objective feedback on the effectiveness of the structure and activities, the feasibility of the programme as well as its acceptability to the various stakeholders. The Terms of Reference were clearly laid out and the evaluators tried to address the various aspects in the evaluation report.

Information about the organization being evaluated and prior discussion of plans is important for a successful evaluation. The evaluators assumed that, like most organizations, Asmita would have beneficiaries that they could meet and question. 'On reaching Asmita and discussing our plans with them, we realized that some of the above would not be possible due to time constraints (eg: visits to various places), and prior engagements of the participants (eg: journalists).' The evaluators had also planned to meet women who had approached Asmita for legal aid.

An analysis of the evaluation report showed that while the evaluators tried to address the various aspects like Asmita's vision and philosophy, translation of their vision into activities and networking, their lack of a feminist lens negatively impacted the assessment.

In terms of Asmita's vision and philosophy, the evaluators felt that Asmita's vision to work towards a socio-economic transformation by trying to bridge gender inequalities and helping women to be equal partners in a just society and the feminist philosophy that was inherent in this vision, had been clearly internalized by the staff and founder members of Asmita. Their clarity of purpose had strengthened their motivation and determination to work towards their goal. Since many of them had been associated with leftist groups, their ideology was a healthy combination of Feminism and Marxism. In fact the members felt that Asmita could provide a space for young people to join the women's movement and even provide leadership to women's struggles in the local context.

Institutional Histories

Drawing from Asmita's vision and philosophy, since 1991, it is clear that the organization has been able to provide space to young women to join the women's movement and leadership in the local context. Some examples are G. Sucharita who coordinates programmes at CWS; Jameela Nishat who runs Shaheen Welfare and Resource Centre for Women in old city of Hyderabad; Sumitra who heads Ankuram centre for children in Hyderabad. All these women have received hand holding and support from the founder members of Asmita.

Apart from those who worked in Asmita, a large number of women working in organizations across the state had participated in Asmita's capacity building workshops and used Asmita's publications. This created a cadre of second line leadership throughout the state thus fulfilling Asmita's objective of building a cadre of women leaders in the state.

DANGERS OF A MISPLACED PERSPECTIVE

In the section on legal aid and help to individual women, the evaluators reflect 'Asmita has not advertised their availability for such cases and individuals have approached them only through word of mouth. Most of the cases have come to them at the last stages of the conflict where legal action is the only recourse available. This has a danger in Asmita being perceived as approachable only in divorce cases.'

Asmita provided a space for women to approach the organization when in need of help. There was no need to advertise as a steady stream of cases kept coming in, referred by members and contacts in the state. There was also a deliberate decision not to take up dowry death cases as the motive was often vengeance, ending in financial settlement rather than justice. Advertising would have brought a flood of dowry death cases where it was too late to help the victim who had been let down by her own family. The evaluators could not grasp this logic.

Feminists are trying to break away from stereotypical assumptions about family, marriage and divorce in assessing work on legal aid and help to individual women. To assess the work of a feminist organization requires knowledge and skills on women's human rights beyond traditional monitoring and evaluation. The excerpt mentioned below clearly highlights the danger of a technical know-how with lack of a perspective:

> We see two dangers in this process – first – as many cases come to Asmita at the last stage; a divorce is the only option. It will do Asmita a lot of harm if it cultivates an image of an organisation advocating divorce. This may be unnecessarily and wrongly linked to the presence of divorced and single women in Asmita. Such an image would have an adverse effect on the entire organisation. The second danger, which is very real, is that the young staff team who are continuously exposed to sad and frightening situations of these women are being negatively influenced with all sorts of fears of marriage, of men, etc. This needs to be looked into seriously.

Rather than understanding the realities of women's lives, the unequal nature of roles and responsibilities for women within most marriages and maintaining that violence is a non-negotiable within relationships, the evaluators focus on the dangers of employing single and divorced women and warn the organization of the dangers of a negative public image while fighting for the rights of women who are facing violence or are in unhappy relationships.

Initially, Asmita was reluctant to respond to the evaluation report as it felt that the evaluators lacked the comprehension and competence to evaluate a feminist organization. The carefully worded response was seen as a requirement from the funders. Consider the following excerpt from Asmita's response to the report:

> We did have a problem arranging meetings with the women who came for help. This is not to do with the team or its attitude but to do with the process of evaluation itself. The relationship between the women in crisis and the counselling group is specific and intimate. For these women to discuss their problems or the nature of the help received with strangers was traumatic. They complained of

feeling interrogated. It also caused some problems for us as some of the women seemed to think we ought to start giving them financial help to settle their debts. This has to do with the situation of the victim and the nature of the problem. Ideally we would like the evaluators to question the staff and perhaps meet the women in a group meeting where the issue is discussed and women may come up with experiences. But the fact is that once the problem is settled the women have no time or inclination to come back.

We are also aware that as our work is more in the nature of campaigns and interactions than directly of an institutional/ beneficiary kind, the conventional interview may be impractical or even counter-productive. We cannot for instance produce journalists or writers for an evaluation meeting without losing whatever stature we earn through our interactions which is vital for our continued effectiveness.

On the issue of divorce and the dangers of their work Asmita did try to convey to the evaluators the lack of perspective.

The only problem we had with the evaluation report was one of perspective. The team seemed to feel that patching up a broken marriage was a positive result. We as a feminist group believe that helping the woman to find a solution of her choice is important. We neither advocate nor advise divorce or patching up.

We are also deeply disturbed by the comment that the presence of single women in the group and our work might have a negative effect regarding marriage on the minds of young women working with us. We see marriage as an option, a personal choice that women, like men, may or may not want. We strongly contest the assumption that marriage is the norm for women. And we feel that if the young women with us begin to be released from the pressure to marry that drives millions of women to desperation and death we have achieved something truly worthwhile.

Learning to Walk: Asmita's Second Evaluation

The second evaluation was conducted in 1997 and was aimed at:

a)   Providing the organization to be evaluated with the opportunity to reflect on its activities and organizational functioning, and with inputs for formulating a sound plan for follow-up programmes;

b)   Providing HIVOS with inputs for taking decisions concerning ways of continuing its support to the organization.

Asmita had been supported by HIVOS since its inception. HIVOS's approach being organizational rather than project-based, the evaluation takes account of all of Asmita's activities with particular attention being paid to the inter-linkage between the various components. These components include the structure of the organization, the division of labour, decision-making, efficiency, communication patterns, systems of checks and balances, planning capacity, accountability, leadership, staff qualifications, openness to the target group etc. Besides the internal organization of Asmita, the evaluation also included a look at its 'social embedding' to assess what linkage it has with other groups and movements, to what extent networking plays a role in its strategy, how far the organization has progressed in its effort to empower its target group through organization building, awareness-raising, and improvements in the positions of women and the environment.

The fact that the evaluators had a clear feminist perspective, considerable experience in women's issues and were determined to help the organization by identifying possible gaps and suggesting means of rectifying them was positive. It was a funder's evaluation but the whole effort was to strengthen and support the organization's efforts. Significantly the evaluators made a great effort not only to look at programmes carried out but to track the changes and the evolving responses to the needs of the community.

> As of now the emphasis is on curative work – each case being handled on its merit. Sooner or later the centre will have to take up the question of how it hopes to link its curative with preventive measures so that the fundamental causes of dowry and family harassment are also addressed.

Overall Impact of Programme

The nature of work undertaken by Asmita (issues in relation to human rights and gender justice in all spheres in general) and the mode through which Asmita operationalizes its programmes (campaigns, jatras, legal aid, media intervention etc.) necessarily bring it into contact with, (sometimes against), other groups, local communities, government bodies, policy makers at the local, national and international levels. The theme of a particular programme and the mode employed to implement it decides whether Asmita does it alone and/or whether it teams up with other bodies. As already mentioned, the jatras, training and workshop programmes are conducted in collaboration with NGOs who are directly working with grassroots women in rural areas. Through these programmes Asmita's outreach in terms of number of people (men and women) is quite large.

ON GENDER

It is not necessary to labour the point that Asmita's primary goal is to work towards bringing about a socio-economic transformation by trying to bridge gender inequalities and help women be equal partners in the creation of a just society. Hence, every programme that Asmita has taken up and/or organized is informed by a gender perspective.

Feminist Movement and Reflexivity

An evaluator with a feminist perspective was able to appreciate the fact that an organization working on women's human's rights cannot always take up issues which are merely funder driven.

Sabala states '*In a nutshell one can say that Asmita is an organization different from other NGOs. It is sensitive to the need of the hour. Every day there is some issue or the other. Asmita is so vibrant and live. Never lets an opportunity go by. Constantly on the move. So much is happening at every level.*'

The articulation of the need to address the problem of girl children between the ages of 9-14 years (as set out in Asmita's future plans) is a local extension of the nature of work that Asmita has been doing among basti women. Through such work among the urban poor, through their trainings, workshops, jatras and research output, Asmita has been highlighting the structural nature of women's subordination.

As already mentioned, Asmita has succeeded quite reasonably in consciousness-raising as far as gender issues are concerned; how far these impacts have resulted in changes in the sexual division of labour within the households of the participants and/or how far it has enabled women (thus empowered) to participate in decision making in their communities, needs a different kind of impact analysis, which Asmita has not attempted so far.

Asmita has not so far consciously targeted men in its gender sensitization programmes particularly at the jatras and in the bastis. However, some organizations like the police academy, road transport corporations etc., have invited Asmita to provide a gender input into their training programmes. The bulk of the participants in these programmes have been largely male. Once again there is no way of finding out what impact such gender inputs have on male participants.

Seven years of Asmita

Apart from funder recognized/sponsored evaluations, Asmita has also commissioned evaluations to track its growth. The third evaluation of Asmita was conducted in 1998. The evaluator had experience in conducting extensive trainings on health issues in rural India since the 1970s. One of her well-known works was based on a health project facilitated by Asmita. The evaluation report highlighted the origin, structure, culture, system, skills, style of management, programmes, problems encountered, strengths, lessons learnt and shifts.

METHODOLOGY

Group discussions, individual interviews and life cycle mapping of the organization were part of the participatory methodology. Groups were divided programme wise to discuss aims and objectives, processes involved, constraints, impact and future plans.

One of Asmita's core activities includes campaigns on a range of issues. During the evaluation Sabala highlighted its impact. 'Over the past years Asmita has become a centre of information dissemination on local, national, regional and international issues. Campaigns and media advocacy is a preventive measure in which they attempt to create awareness on gender issues. Their campaign work gets linked to trainings.'

BUILDING PARTNERSHIPS FOR DEVELOPMENT AND CHANGE

The evaluator valued the work undertaken by Asmita in building partnerships and solidarity for change. The work on women's human rights required collaboration and alliances of several groups who have a similar vision.

Asmita has been the nodal agency for a UNESCAP NGO project, has been a state level facilitator for the National Alliance of Women (NAWO) and plays an important role in the activity of the Indian Association of Women's Studies (IAWS). Asmita has popularised and disseminated information on the Platform for Action (PFA) and translated material in Malyalam, Telugu and Tamil. Asmita has developed a kit of booklets, posters and scrolls highlighting different elements of PFA. Thirty thousand kits have been circulated in these three languages. Booklets and posters have also been brought out on violence, the environment, the status of the girl child and the PFA.

Through partnerships with different groups, Asmita has been able to build a special focus on gender issues. Apart from the ones mentioned above, Asmita was also part of Indian National Social Action Forum, Telugu Writers Network and Asia South Pacific Bureau for Adult Education.

Exploring the need for hierarchy with a feminist organization

While it was said that there would be no hierarchies, a slow development of hierarchies did emerge of those who run the organization and those who work for the organization. When there is no commitment a certain kind of hierarchy becomes evident. Hierarchies were there and they were confused. Things that were assumed to be basic values in the women's movement came in for questioning. The top down structure too came in for questioning. These were not comfortable questions.

The first evaluation questioned the lack of structure. However, in the second evaluation it was seen that the lack of strict hierarchies within the organization allowed for staff lower down the 'hierarchy' to democratically take part in programme planning.

Intersectional Approaches and Understanding Different Voices

An evaluator with field based experience and an understanding of women's rights could relate to the activities of Asmita. Working on violence against women alone cannot address the concerns on women's human rights and social justice. Women are not a homogenous group and therefore their varied concerns need to be taken into account. Asmita's work reflects these concerns and challenges.

> Asmita has campaigned on issues of violence against women, communal harmony, women's political participation, food security, CEDAW/PFA. They have involved Muslim women in their outreach activities. The rapport and interventions with Dalit groups has been effective.

Due Diligence and State Accountability

The kind of societal transformation that a feminist organization envisages involves a multifaceted approach. Apart from campaigns, the evaluator was sensitive to the current environment and identified the work the organization had undertaken to hold the media house liable for sexist representations. 'As part of their media intervention, they have carried out a campaign against a sexist cartoon. They have also been writing articles, giving interviews – Press and TV and holding press conference on all important issues. They have kept an ongoing dialogue with the press to make it more gender sensitive.'

The evaluator identified various milestones and drew from the institutional histories approach to understand the nature of progress made and the lessons learnt in running a feminist organization. She also looked at the way the institution has evolved over time and what their experiences have been.

Asmita at Fifteen

Review of publications and field level engagement

In 2007, as part of our reflection and review process of fifteen years of work we invited two renowned members from Andhra Pradesh to evaluate our publications and engagement with five field level organizations. The evaluators—an educator and political activist, and a Dalit feminist writer—travelled to five NGOs in Andhra Pradesh to review Asmita's impact.

One of the evaluators highlighted the need for groups like Asmita to bring out publications. His report says:

Asmita's publications on a variety of topics deepen knowledge on gender politics. The work undertaken by Asmita is worth emulating. A group involved in the struggles of an oppressed community for emancipation must theorise its own experiences. The hegemonic classes use the available institutions for guidance whereas the subaltern groups evolve an alternative world view through its own intellectuals to guide its practice. Many groups representing the subaltern classes must learn from Asmita's experience. In the absence of a theorisation of its experience many organizations collapsed as they faced new situations and encountered opposition from new quarters. The publications are not only useful to guide feminist practice but also helpful to the civil rights activists and dalit activists to understand the nature of the criminal justice system. Andhra Pradesh also is witnessing a number of identity movements. These movements can use the publications to understand the dynamics of power relations in Andhra Pradesh. They also offer a clue to evolve a basis for coalitions.

Undertaking monitoring and evaluation in a development organization that seeks to 'challenge unequal power, reduce economic and political inequality and support a changed global order which takes into account the interests of the poorest in our societies is a massive challenge'. (Bowman and Sweetman 2014) Women's rights groups, feminists and evaluators have been asking for new frameworks and approaches that engage with partner organizations without merely 'mining for facts'. This evaluation was an attempt to join the dots between the organization's work and the context within which it was working.

The second evaluator's review process was undertaken by visiting NGOs. The evaluator interacted with the organization head and staff. The report notes:

Asmita helped us to develop advocacy skills and question government officials, landowners and those holding powerful positions about the relevance and impact of their work. Working with Asmita gave us clarity and focus about our course of work and where we were heading. We were able to define our work better. Contact with Asmita also reinforced and restored our belief and confidence in our work.

The evaluator focussed on the approach and ideology used that translated into questioning the economic empowerment schemes of the government. The evaluation emphasized the importance of Asmita's rights based approach which focussed on the denial of basic needs and rights, and the importance of political participation and the right to a life with dignity. The trainings encouraged network organizations to use this approach in their work and integrate the importance of political participation and the right to a life with dignity.

The evaluator's feminist perspective helped to highlight the difference in the 'denial of basic needs and rights which has a greater impact on lives'. These comments reaffirm the organization's work, direction and contribute to its growth.

CHANGE IN PERCEPTION: QUALITATIVE ANALYSIS

Qualitative analysis of Asmita's work would help monitor both short term and long term change that is being brought in the community. The process of a feminist learning evaluation must attempt to capture complexity and nuance. For instance, women's organizations engaged in building capacity through training and other means, including research and knowledge building, challenging dominant perspectives and discourses, shifting public attitudes through campaigns and consciousness-raising with women, all find it quite challenging to show the impact of their work. Consequently, they are compelled to measure their *processes, outreach, and outputs* (number of training programmes held, number of participants, publications, attendance at rallies and meetings), rather than the *results* of the process. (Batliwala and Pittman 2010) In her evaluation the evaluator drew an important connection between the trainings and the change in attitudes after.

> After the gender trainings, the attitudes of men towards their wives have changed a lot. The perceptions of women about their rights have also changed. Before the training, both men and women thought wife-beating was normal. Men have begun treating the women in their families with greater respect. Women have begun to question their husbands. The number of girls going to school has increased.

A FEMINIST LEARNING SYSTEM

In a feminist evaluation, the role of the evaluator shifts from merely providing technical expertise to facilitating collaborative processes where all stakeholders engage directly and feel a sense of ownership.

The process itself must be enabling and a learning one. The feminist learning system aspires to be an interconnected, non-linear system that responds to the need for programmatic monitoring and evaluation that is simple and flexible, and that reflects our partners' realities and is centred on learning whilst maintaining the ability to meet back-donor accountability requirements. (Miller and Haylock: 297)

In June 2009, a three member team consisting of a social activist, an academic and a chartered accountant carried out an evaluation to assess organizational structures, human resources and financial management.

> Using a participatory methodology like SWOT (Strengths, Weaknesses, Opportunities and Threats) analysis, informal interviews, focus group discussions, programme mapping, interaction with outreach organizations and constituencies, this review attempted to provide an analysis of the programmes in relation to the organzation's stated vision, mission and overall goals and suggest ways and means of strengthening the organizational structures and resources to further enable the organization to achieve its goals.

The evaluators engaged with the staff, the core management team, the board of directors on the work undertaken in the organization, the staff's assessment of the organization and relevant factors in this. Through the discussions, the evaluators provided Asmita their suggestions. They observed:

> Asmita is one of its kind in the state. It has made significant contribution to inform all processes of the state and non state actors and policy makers of a gender and human rights perspective. (…) In keeping with the vision of providing an inclusive space, Asmita provides not just a physical space where women from various walks of life, children of the urban poor and other marginalized groups and NGO leaders come together but also an ideological space to address issues that affect women and marginalized.

The analysis of the staff's assessment of the organization showed their engagement in the work, the perspective of those who carry out the work within the organization and the democratic work atmosphere. A feminist evaluation process allows for 'monitoring and evaluation systems which systematically bring different voices and perspectives into sense-making and valuing of processes'. (Bowman and Sweetman 2014: 208)

Asmita Institutional Histories

The strength of this evaluation was that it engaged with not just reports and staff but all minutes of the staff meetings and day-to-day planning of activities. For instance, the report talks about the internal planning, monitoring and evaluation systems:

> Monitoring of the programme takes place at various levels. Sometimes programme monitoring begins with the facilitator being asked to share her presentation within the organization for a possible feedback from the staff and from the coordinators. This also allows for the learning process of the staff that could fine tune their presentations and sharpen the perspective. The coordinators monitor the work through constant updates from the project staff and from the target groups. Monitoring also takes place through the process of registrations during each programme and during the group discussions. In addition, the process is systematically documented.

Asmita Institutional Histories

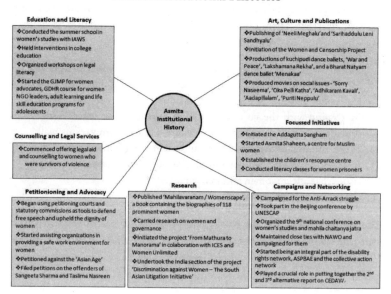

Education and Literacy
- Conducted the summer school in women's studies with IAWS
- Held interventions in college education
- Organized workshops on legal literacy
- Started the GJMP for women advocates, GDHR course for women NGO leaders, adult learning and life skill education programs for adolescents

Art, Culture and Publications
- Publishing of 'Neeli Meghalu' and 'Sarihaddulu Leni Sandhyalu'
- Initiation of the Women and Censorship Project
- Productions of kuchipudi dance ballets, 'War and Peace', 'Lakshamana Rekha', and a Bharat Natyam dance ballet 'Menakaa'
- Produced movies on social issues - 'Sorry Naseema', 'Oka Pelli Katha', 'Adhikaram Kavali', 'Aadapillalam', 'Puriti Neppulu'

Counselling and Legal Services
- Commenced offering legal aid and counselling to women who were survivors of violence

Focussed Initiatives
- Initiated the Addagutta Sangham
- Started Asmita Shaheen, a centre for Muslim women
- Established the children's resopurce centre
- Conducted literacy classes for women prisoners

Asmita Institutional History

Petitionioning and Advocacy
- Began using petitioning courts and statutory commissions as tools to defend free speech and upheld the dignity of women
- Started assisting organizations in providing a safe work environment for women
- Petitioned against the 'Asian Age'
- Filed petitions on the offenders of Sangeeta Sharma and Taslima Nasreen

Research
- Published 'Mahilavaranam / Womenscape', a book containing the biographies of 118 prominent women
- Carried research on women and governance
- Initiated the project 'From Mathura to Manorama' in colaboration with ICES and Women Unlimited
- Undertook the India section of the project 'Discrimination against Women – The South Asian Litigation Initiative'

Campaigns and Networking
- Campaigned for the Anti-Arrack struggle
- Took part in the Beijing conference by UNESCAP
- Organized the 9th national conference on women's studies and mahila chaitanya jatra
- Maintained close ties with NAWO and campaigned for them
- Started being an integral part of the disability rights network, ASPBAE and the collective action network
- Played a crucial role in putting together the 2nd and 3rd alternative report on CEDAW.

2015	**Asmita today**
2014	
2013	
2012	
2011	
2010	
2009	**Evaluation: organizational structure**
2008	**Asmita an institutional history**
2007	**Asmita at fifteen** / **Review of publications**
2006	
2005	
2004	
2003	
2002	
2001	
2000	
1999	
1998	**Evaluation: 7 years of Asmita**
1997	**Second Evaluation - HIVOS**
1996	
1995	
1994	
1993	**First Evaluation - HIVOS**
1992	
1991	**Inception of Asmita**

An evaluation process must allow for reflection on the programmatic activity at various levels and not merely on the outputs. The report addresses the fact that the translation of relevant texts into Telugu: 'is not merely of a language translation or adopting of a simple style but of translating international agendas on women's rights and of feminist perspectives and ideologies of human rights to the regional and local context.' Additionally, it looks at sustained engagement on the issues in the region by tracking all the research and documentation done over the years. 'The best example is Asmita's sustained interest and engagement with the research project on censorship and women's writing for more than a decade, which has resulted in several publications of books. Another important aspect, the activism content, to this particular research project has been the spawning of several networks of women writers and the founding of Women's World India, which now actively carries out the publications of women's works.'

For instance, when these evaluator's comments and reflections on the legal aid and counselling is compared to the first evaluation experience of Asmita, one can see the importance of the evaluator's perspective:

> Providing a non-judgemental and supportive environment is an important aspect of counselling which has enabled women to share their fears and inhibitions and reluctances in engaging with the issue of violence. The process of providing legal aid had been a long drawn out one with the organization having to visit the court and the police station other than continuously monitoring the cases.

An evaluation undertaken with participatory processes while taking into account the vision of the organization can help in reaffirming the objectives and provide direction to the organization being evaluated.

Over the years, we can see the influence of the perspective of the evaluator in providing the necessary guidance to the organization.

Section II
Institutional Histories

The Institutional Histories approach enables us to effectively map our path and assess what has worked and not worked in the life of an organization. Institutional histories have been used by scholars from new institutional economics (a branch of economics that emphasizes the embedded nature of economic activity in social and legal institutions) and sociology. Researchers applied this approach to document an institutional history of watershed research at ICRISAT and other agricultural research.

The process of preparing institutional histories, and the dialogue that can be fostered around them, can contribute to learning and capacity building. (C. Shambu Prasad: 2006)

Institutional histories are narratives of ways of working that stem from the rules, conventions and routines governing behaviour, sometimes referred to as habits and practices. The purpose of writing institutional histories is to introduce institutional factors into the legitimate narrative of success and failure in research organizations, by routinely drawing institutional lessons and promoting new working practices. The need for institutional innovation in research organizations is urgent – especially to cope with changing development agendas, which often demand partnerships with non-research organizations in the innovation system. These are the emerging realities to which development practitioners must adapt. (C. Shambu Prasad: 2006)

WRITING ORGANIZATIONAL HISTORIES: OUR EXPERIENCE

When questions about the institutional histories were brought up, participants at the consultation felt that evolution of the organization and dynamics, change in politics (if any), had not been mapped in the annual reports which dealt mainly with the organization's activities. The connection of the activities to the larger politics had been left out. This was attributed to the capacities of the organization and the kind of time one needs to invest in the exercise.

It was felt that since many of the organizations have a history of over two decades and there is high staff turnover, there are very few who understand the entire, expansive history. They might be equipped to write the report but might not be clued in and know what the changes are; they might not know or understand the rationale and dynamics that went into the idea.

Some participants felt that photo documentation, case studies, videos and publications on lessons learnt were among the ways in which the history of the organization and its work were being documented.

An institutional history can be used to: document institutional innovations in programmes and projects; diagnose the system of innovation of which the particular project or programme is a part; highlight barriers to and mechanisms that assist change.

In 2008 Asmita Resource Centre for Women came up with an institutional history report for the seventeen years of work (1991–2008) undertaken by the organization. Learning is central to the institutional histories approach. According to the authors (C. Shambu Prasad: 2006) an institutional history can be written up in a polished document that captures institutional memory and tacit knowledge; but more importantly, the process of preparing the history opens up spaces for reflection and learning that can help redirect projects towards better performance. Asmita's institutional history compiled and edited by Dr Kalpana Kannabiran is a learning document that highlights the institutions's concerns and broad areas of work. Asmita's institutional history traces the birth of the organization:

> Most of us who came together in 1991 were women who had been active in autonomous women's groups in different parts of the country since the late 1970s and had participated in major debates on questions of equality, the state and violence against women through the 1980s. We brought this understanding with us into the group that we were setting up with the clear objective of spreading the consciousness of women's rights with enthusiasm, diligence and cheer.

The document justifies the reasons behind the birth and growth of the programmes and the classifications therein. 'Education as a fundamental human right is our guiding principle; peace and respect for diversity are the cornerstones of our education programmes.'

In addition to sketching the various programmes and activities undertaken by the organization

Seven broad areas of work:
1. *Arts, Culture, Publishing*
2. *Education and Literacy*
3. *Focussed initiatives*
4. *Counselling and Legal Aid*
5. *Campaigns and Networking*
6. *Petitioning and Advocacy*
7. *Research*

over the 17 years, the institutional history report focuses on the vision behind each programme and the challenges faced in achieving these. The document maps the highs of the organization through innovative documentation like photographs, press clips, articles written by the staff, poetry of the founder members.

INSTITUTIONAL HISTORIES: A REFLECTIVE PROCESS
ARROW'S REPORT

In a similar effort, ARROW produced an institutional history report of 20 years, a learning document not just for the organization but also for other women's rights groups. The authors state in the preface that the document was prepared after a lot of consultation and took up the voluntary time of many of its members. Institutional histories are in part based on recollections and may be biased. However, the final draft of the history must be arrived at and agreed upon in a reflective, participatory manner.

> Too often, activist groups are occupied with programmatic matters, especially advocacy work that requires immediate attention, that they put organizational development matters on the back burner. From our early years, we have decided to give equal priority to programme and organisational development, believing that a strong and fair organisation is the backbone of a strong and effective programme. We are pleased to say that at 20 years of age, ARROW has been assessed by our donors and external evaluators as strong in both aspects. Through the ARK process though, we realise that we need to put more time and effort now into organisational development as the demands of the programme and raising funds has been ARROW's priority in the last five years. (ARROW Resource Kit 2014)

The ARROW Resource Kit (ARK) discusses: 'the history; how we built a strong organization; partnerships; building our future.' The core values of the organization and its strong commitment to women's rights are one of the driving forces for the focus on systems. The organization even defends its stance on putting in place a hierarchal system despite being a feminist organization: 'ARROW deliberately chose a hierarchical structure of organization, even though we were founded by feminists, because we believed that we could better ensure accountability and efficiency towards responsibilities and programme implementation if our decision-making processes were unambiguous, transparent and functional.'

Section III
Gender Analysis

This section looks at gender analysis and tries to ascertain whether there is a link between gender strategy and feminist evaluation. If not, how are the two different?

According to evaluator Donna Podems, evaluators always tend to confuse feminist evaluation and gender approaches. This lack of clarity may be a result of the limited examples of feminist evaluation in academic journals, books, and published papers, compared with the many examples of gender approaches to evaluation.

A gender analysis begins with diagnostic activities to identify the causes of gender inequality focusing on the differential socioeconomic and political status of men and women with regard to the division of labour, access to resources and benefits, and decision-making power. The analysis then proceeds to the identification of the causes of gender gaps, using an analytical framework that examines legal and policy frameworks, stakeholder and institutional analyses, and stereotypes associated with decision-making. Finally, plans for interventions are developed to address the causes and gaps. (Mertens, 2004)

Principles of Gender-sensitive Evaluation

In a discussion on Gender-Responsive Research and Evaluation Mertens (2004) highlights the six basic principles underlying a gender sensitive evaluation from Sielbeck-Bowen, Brisolara, Seigart, Tischler, & Whitmore (2002). These are as follows:

1. The central focus is on gender inequities that lead to social injustice. Every evaluation should be conducted with an eye toward reversing gender inequities.
2. Discrimination or inequality based on gender is systemic and structural. Inequity based on gender is embedded in the major institutions and other shapers of societal norms such as schools,

religion, media, pop culture, government, and corporations. This affects who has power and access.

3. Evaluation is a political activity: the contexts in which evaluation operates are politicised, and the personal experiences, perspectives, and characteristics evaluators bring to evaluations (and with which we interact) lead to a particular political stance. Acknowledging the political nature of evaluation raises questions concerning the definition of objectivity within traditional norms of science.

4. Knowledge is a powerful resource that serves an explicit or implicit purpose. Knowledge should be a resource of and for the people who create, hold, and share it. Consequently, the evaluation or research process can lead to significant negative or positive effects on the people involved in the evaluation/research.

5. Knowledge and values are culturally, socially, and temporally contingent. Knowledge is also filtered through the knower. The evaluator must recognize and explore the unique conditions and characteristics of the issue under study. The characteristics of the knower will influence the creation of knowledge; critical self-reflection is necessary.

6. There are multiple ways of knowing; some ways are privileged over others. Transformative knowledge is sought that emanates from an experiential base.

In her essay she also addresses the tensions and challenges that the term 'feminist and gender sensitive evaluation' throws up:

Considerable discussion ensued around the use of the term feminist versus gender-responsive. Many of the participants indicated that they were more comfortable with the term gender-responsive evaluation rather than feminist because feminism is subject to many different interpretations amongst third world women's rights advocates. The term feminist is often associated with white women to the neglect of concerns of women of colour, or with women who are lesbians. To counteract this more exclusionary interpretation of the term, the UNIFEM staff recommended the term gender-responsive. (Mertens, 2004)

The literature review also flags the various Gender Analysis Frameworks that are present and are employed to achieve different aspects of gender equality.

Gender Analysis Frameworks

A. Harvard Analytical Framework
B. DPU[4] Frameworks
    a) Moser (triple roles) Framework
    b) Levy (web of institutionalisation) Framework
C. Gender Analysis Matrix (GAM)
D. Equality and Empowerment Framework (Longwe)
E. Capacities and Vulnerabilities Framework (CVA)
F. People Oriented Framework (POP)
G. Social Relations Framework (SRF)

Source 1: Gender Analysis: UNDP Learning and Information pack

EVALUATIONS OF GENDER STRATEGIES BY ASMITA

A review of some of the activities undertaken by Asmita staff from 1994-2007 on gender strategy is useful in order to understand the evolution of the term and the different ways in which it has been employed by various funding and other groups. In 1994, the India desk of Overseas Development Association (ODA)[3] took steps to define a strategy for gender, aimed particularly at promoting the social, economic, legal and political status of women. The objective of the consultancy was to contribute to India's gender strategy by identifying the best practices amongst the array of gender approaches available and being used by ODA projects.

One of the areas considered important was the mapping of resources and organizations that were doing dedicated work in the area of gender. A list of organizations was attached to the report. One of those listed as a useful resource by the participants in the consultation was Asmita, Hyderabad.

However, the strategies used to study the existing problems were neither expansive nor qualitative. They merely looked at the gender related expenditures for the projects; the number of projects that had undertaken gender planning training for the staff; the ratio of male to female project staff; the number of projects that employed an individual with a specific WID or gender brief.

Though it was apparent that women were suffering from inequality, it became clear that 'development experts and policy makers soon realised that men and women at different levels had to be *taught* to see the differential impact of development measures on men and women. That men did not automatically and naturally include women. This resulted in the emergence of a whole new field called gender sensitisation or gender training.' (Kannabiran 1996)

In 1997, a gender strategy was written for Department for International Development, India (DFID, India)[4] which highlights a few key points involved in the development of a gender perspective. These include:

> Working towards attitudinal change; full commitment to gender issues at all levels; greater allocation of resources to training and capacity building; increased technical support on gender for different ministries and departments; improved research skills and data management systems; innovation in organizational structure towards more flexible, open and responsive organizations; enhanced accountability through promotion of the right to information of primary stakeholders.

The draft strategy also went on to suggest how the priorities for DFID India's support for gender equality "must maintain a critical balance between gender-sensitive sectoral focus and cross-sectoral interventions."

Evaluating an International Partnership

Vasanth Kannabiran and another evaluator were invited in 2007 to evaluate the partnership of DVV International and the Asia Pacific Bureau of Adult Education (ASPBAE). Their evaluation focuses on the larger, existing environment of adult learning and the challenges faced before proceeding to evaluating the partnership. The final section of the evaluation focuses on the recommendations on the strategic learning partnership of ASPBAE and DVV International.

The evaluation "is in the spirit of strategic learning that the partners look to this evaluation as a tool for self-reflection on their contribution to strengthening the capacities of civil society organisations (csos) in their adult education work aimed at improving the conditions and advancing the interests of disadvantaged people."

Apart from the review of documents and literature, key informant interviews, group discussions and informal interactions, as well as field visits were conducted to the partner csos. The richness of the report lies in the infusion of multiple methodologies. The annexures also contain quotes from the partner civil society organizations which show the strength these organizations gain from this fruitful international partnership. Additionally, the quotes focus on the importance of the voices of the partners in the process of evaluation. According to Priyanka Dale of pria, "The Festival of Learning was a first hand exposure to a global movement. All the workshops at the festival built a perspective and I advanced professionally and personally in the process. There was a constant upgradation of learning.'

Sharing the Fish Head

The essay 'Sharing the Fish Head'[5] looks at the work of gender trainers in South Asia to design a conceptual understanding of gender training as practised by women's groups in the region and to document how gender training is being institutionalized within organizations in this region. In Kannabiran's words:

> The very emergence of gender as an analytical category was to emphasise the relational aspect of man and woman relations keeping in view the subordination of women. It was intended to avoid the problems that came up with using patriarchy without reference to its historically changing dynamic nature. Today gender training cuts away from the politics of subordination and is reduced to a set of bland exercises that leave participants feelings they have grasped everything but which in fact have not even scratched the surface. (…) Training should be an extension of activism. Instead of extending the frontiers of activism, we find that there is dichotomy between gender training and the women's movement. (Kannabiran 1996)

The gradual movement towards the dilution of politics was highlighted in the essay. Questions were raised on whether tools could replace content; do trainings retain their connections to the women's movement? Though raised in the context of gender training, these questions can be extrapolated to the evaluation process. Also, the strength of gender training lies in the ability of the trainer to infuse the training with a degree of activism. 'Gender sensitisation efforts in trying to impact and change a series of gender regimes have therefore to address a whole range of complex factors that come into play. No training can stop with access and control of resources but has to go far beyond to grasp the ramifications that range from the local to the international.' (Kannabiran 1996)

In her guide to gender 'Engendering Adult Learning', Vasanth Kannabiran[6] explores the theoretical outline for the social relations of gender and the key concepts and tools for gender analysis. This was part of ASPBAE initiative to mainstream gender. While discussing the different approaches, she talks about WID, WAD and GAD which have 'emerged with different strategies based on varying underlying assumptions about the participation of women in the development process.' The guide is a sample of the work in the area which helps deepen and enlarge our understanding of issues in gender and development. It provides a long list of tools across frameworks like the Harvard analytical framework, the social relations framework, the women's empowerment framework etc. It also argues the strengths and weaknesses of these frameworks to enable a critical understanding of the tools. The paper provides a list of questions to be asked about a project's contribution towards women's development. The questions are broken up into problem identification, project strategy, project objectives, project management, project implementation and project outcome.

In Conclusion

Gender sensitive evaluations follow the same principles of feminist evaluation given that a focus on gender emerges from feminist research and theory. (Haylock 2014) The authors state that two factors are important: first how much attention is paid to gender power relations and second, how far it promotes the use of evaluation processes that are themselves empowering for stakeholders.

In international development organizations, gender sensitive evaluation often involves integrating gender analysis into the programme design, and then collecting sex-disaggregated data as part of the monitoring process, exploring gender-differentiated programme outcomes for women and men in evaluation. (Haylock 2014) Therefore gender analysis is integral to any gender sensitive evaluation. A gender sensitive evaluation is driven by feminist principles and values, at the core of this is the effort to bring about social change. As Humphries says, the aim of feminist evaluation is not only to understand the world but also to change it. (Humphries 1999)

The six evaluation reports that we have reviewed in this essay have also flagged the critical role of an evaluator in feminist evaluation. In such evaluations, the role of the evaluator shifts from primarily providing technical expertise to facilitating collaborative processes that are empowering and contribute to a sense of ownership for stakeholders. (Haylock 2014)

Each organization has its own set of strengths and weakness therefore one size does not fit all. Any evaluation thus has to take into account the context, historical background and the experiences within which the organization and its work are located.

1. Make M&E a key ingredient in our learning and accountability
2. Develop M&E capacity
3. One size does not fit all
4. Track reversals or "holding the line"
5. Balance quantitative and qualitative assessment
6. Prioritize approaches that assess our contribution to change, not those that demand attribution
7. Less is more
8. Flexibility and adaptability
9. M&E systems must be appropriate to organizational architecture
10. Negotiate M&E systems with donors
11. Tailor indicators and results to time frames
12. Create baselines
13. M&E that works for us will work for others

Apart from the collaborative processes, the manner in which evaluation is facilitated, the opportunity to participate and connect to one another and the programme becomes important. Srilatha Batliwala, provides thirteen key insights into how women's rights organizations and movements can strengthen capacity to track and assess the contribution of our organizations and interventions (Batliwala 2010). She states that monitoring and evaluation is most useful and relevant when it is approached as a learning process, rather than a reporting or fundraising requirement. Solid, comprehensive and rigorous assessment of our effectiveness is a critical expression of our accountability to our constituency, and to our longer-term mission of building a gender just world.

Notes

1. Asmita Evaluation Report. 1993. p. 1.
2. Ibid.
3. Sarah Ladbury. 1994. 'Evolving a Gender Strtegy'. ODA.
4. Vashanth Kannabiran, Vimala Ramakrishna, Ramya Subrahmanian. 1997. 'Draft Gener Strategy—Working Group'.
5. Vasanth Kannabiran. 1996. 'South Pacific Bureau of Adult Education and FAO-NGO South Asian Programmes. New Delhi.
6. Vasanth Kannabiran. 1998. 'Engendering Adult Learning—A Guide to Gender.' ASPBAE

References

African Development Bank, Operations Evaluation Department (OPEV). 2011. 'Mainstreaming Gender Equality: A Road to Results or a Road to Nowhere?' An Evaluation Synthesis, working paper.

———. 2011. 'Mainstreaming Gender Equality: Emerging Evaluation Lessons', *Evaluation Insights*, 3. November.

Arrow Resource Kit. 2014. Asian Pacific Resource and Research Centre for Women (ARROW) Link : http://www.arrow.org.my/download/ARK-final.pdf. Last accessed 15 April 2015.

ASPBAE and DVV International. 2007. 'Strengthening A Strategic Learning Partnership', Report of Evaluation of ASPBAE-DVV International Cooperation.

Batliwala, Srilatha and Alexandra Pitman. 2010. 'Capturing Change in Women's Realities: A Critical Overview of Current Monitoring and Evaluation Frameworks and Approaches,' AWID.

Batliwala, Srilatha. 2010. 'Strengthening Monitoring and Evaluation for Women's Rights: Twelve Insights for Donors', AWID.

Bowman Kimberly and Sweetman Caroline. 2014. 'Introduction to Gender, Monitoring, Evaluation and Learning', *Gender and Development*, Vol. 22, No. 2, 201–212.

C. Shambu Prasad, Andrew Hall and Laxmi Thummuru. 2006. 'Engaging scientists through institutional histories.' ILAC *Brief 14*: 1–4.

Department for International Development, India. 1997. *Draft Gender Strategy*, DFID India.

Eguren, Inigo R. 2011. 'Theory of Change: A thinking and action approach to navigate in the complexity of social change processes', UNDP/ Hivos.

Engaging scientists through institutional histories, Better Evaluation *http:// betterevaluation.org/resources/tool/institutional_history*. Last accessed 16 April 2015.

Hay, Katherine, Sudarshan, Ratna M. and Mendez. 2012. 'Special Issue: Evaluating Gender and Equity', *Indian Journal of Gender Studies*.

Kannabiran, Kalpana. 2008. 'Asmita: An Institutional History', Hyderabad: Asmita Resource Centre for Women.

Kannabiran, Vasanth. 1998. 'Engendering adult learning – A Guide to Gender', Asian-South Pacific Bureau Of Adult Education.

———. 1996. 'Sharing the Fish Head', *A Study Sponsored by Asian-South Pacific Bureau Of Adult Education* FAO-NGO *South Asian Programmes*, New Delhi.

Ladbury Sarah. 1994.'Evolving a Gender Strategy For ODA in India' *Sponsored by the Overseas Development Administration*.

Mertens, Donna M. 2004. 'Transformative Research and Evaluation and Dimensions Of', *Sixth International Conference on Logic and Methodology*. Amsterdam: Sage Publications, pp. 17–20.

Miller Carol and Haylock Laura. 2014.'Capturing changes in women's lives: The experiences of Oxfam Canada in applying feminist evaluation principles to monitoring and evaluation practice' *Gender and Development*, Vol. 22, No. 2, 291–310.

Podems, Donna R. 2010. 'Feminist Evaluation and Gender Approaches: There's a Difference?' *Journal of Multidisciplinary Evaluation* Vol. 6 (14), August.

Annexure

REFLECTING FOR CHANGE: BRAINSTORMING SESSION WITH EVALUATORS AND PEOPLE FROM ORGANIZATIONS THAT HAVE BEEN EVALUATED

A round table discussion with ten feminist evaluators and people from organizations that were evaluated, have been pulled together in this part of the essay. Experience has proved that the term 'feminist' evokes a certain apprehension and distaste based on the stereotypical notions of what feminism represents.

Feminism with its emphasis on women's rights and marginalization presented a threat to funders and funding agencies which have not lost their patriarchal character. Gender, on the contrary, was accepted as a more inclusive term since men were part of the analysis. That it was a feminist formulation did not matter.

For funding agencies, donors and local NGO heads (largely male) it seemed a much more palatable category of analysis.

One of our efforts during this collective exercise was to explore the importance of feminist monitoring and evaluation in the assessment of an organization. In undertaking feminist evaluation it is important to take into consideration the nature of the organization being evaluated. There is a significant difference between a movement and a project; the failure to recognize that and factor it into the evaluation can be counter-productive. The institutionalization of women's groups grew out of a desire to put back some of the movement learnings and growth into grassroots communities. Institutionalization meant an increased need for people, material resources, and infrastructure to name a few. Rules, regulations, discipline, measuring of output all became mandatory with the need for output and progress reports to funders. This meant that the ideals of a collective would not work unless the organization was set up and run by the collective.

A major concern was the need to analyse the strengths and weaknesses of collectives versus hierarchical organizations. One truth that was self evident but that feminists took time to grasp was that a collective works well when all the members are evenly matched in terms of commitment and ideology, even if the level of their skills varies.

The reality is that a small group of committed people try to carry a whole team along, dealing with issues on the ground and issues internally. Yet there is a lot of progress and gradual change as the vision of the organization is internalized and a commitment is born.

Bringing in the Gender Angle and the Feminist Perspective

Several small groups have emerged in the last three decades to cater to the needs of people in the area. They have mobilized around land, water, wages, violence and labour. They have struggled for material and intellectual resources to carry on this work. Unfortunately the state has co-opted these groups and diverted them into becoming delivery agents for government programmes and microcredit finance. Political parties also use them to garner votes and retain control. Their potential is sapped and they are unable to function independently. Through the last decade the World Bank definition of funding and empowerment and the consortium of funders have choked off small groups with innovative ideas and created mega organizations. These large organizations can produce reports that can fit into tables and columns while marginalizing processes. There is pressure to tell a positive, simple story that demonstrates programme impact and is preferably backed up by numbers. Telling the story of changes in women's lives is, however, complex and messy. (Batliwala and Pittman 2010; Wallace *et al.* 2013)

However, one positive trend is that now women's organizations are called upon for support and have gained greater visibility. This has been the result of feminist interventions and recommendations at International and United Nations fora. From a hierarchy of causes where for instance land, wages, environment and poverty stood high on the list, feminist interventions have forced the issue of gender on to the table and now women's rights to wages, land, and security have moved up. Even where health was once focussed on infant mortality, malnutrition, epidemics and population control, the focus has shifted to reproductive health and reproductive rights, placing women's bodies and wellbeing centre stage. As a result a gender approach which includes women is seen as a necessity by csos.

An evaluation needs to take into consideration all these factors. While sifting out the ritualistic responses and gender rhetoric and perceiving the genuine efforts and possibility for change, a feminist evaluation, if sensitive and nonjudgmental, can help steer an organization on the right track.

Project Evaluations vs. Evaluating Organizations

There are programme evaluations, project evaluations, organization evaluations, institution evaluations etc. When one is evaluating an organization, the whole process of building the organization, interaction with the people and the organization's values need to be taken into consideration. In evaluating projects or programmes, processes are important but more important are the project objectives, goals and activities. The evaluator looks at access and control, voice and agency, and other, similar concepts. A tool can be a valuable aid to understanding something but can never become a substitute for understanding.

Often one has to see if technology is appropriate because it can also become an obstacle. In NREGA one can see that women are forced to use tools designed for men. Gender budgeting is another problematic area. Organizations are not ill intentioned but just not exposed to feminist values and feminist perspectives on issues. The feminist evaluation process can expose these gaps. Everyone in Kerala glorifies Kutumbasri and the self help group model is used to systematically organize women. But a feminist point of view reveals that such a model does not address violence against women. Women are not looked at as agents, but as passive respondents/beneficiaries, as mere actors in poverty eradication. Even consultants who evaluate this programme from a gender perspective often do not address this – instead a feminist intervention is required to do so. There are other things like sexuality, control of body, reproductive health that need to be looked at. Economic empowerment alone is not enough.

Hence it can be said that gender-sensitive evaluation and feminist evaluations follow the same processes. Carol Miller and Laura Haylock argue in their essay that the difference depends on two factors: one that it takes into account existing power relations and two that the evaluation processes are empowering for stakeholders. (Miller and Haylock 2014) Many of the evaluators gathered at the brainstorming session reiterated that direct emphasis must be placed on the ways in which the programme challenges gender-power relations.

For instance, 40 per cent of elected women are from Kutumbasri. This is seen as a superb indicator. But deeper analysis raises the question of whether they are able to articulate critical issues in a male dominated environment. Additionally, they are restricted till the Panchayat level. Why is this? Thus, sustained engagement with the programme and with the women who contest might bring their challenges and, by extension, the issues in the programme, to the fore.

One of the evaluators present at the meeting was of the view that gender evaluation only looks at gender roles whereas feminist evaluation looks at the impact of activity in the context of the power relations between men, women and social institutions. The impact at the personal level, the community level and the family level is also measured. Having said that, one must acknowledge that gender evaluation is useful in framing gender relations. Gender analysis has a certain framework which requires people to have studied the literature and comprehended the structure. Feminist evaluation, however, looks at the long term impact. Often, evaluators may function through a feminist lens but not term the evaluation feminist. A woman might have land in her name but is she the real owner?

A well-funded sericulture programme saw six women commit suicide when the programme ended. The two-year training was meant to make them entrepreneurs but they were not taught entrepreneurial skills. Then, the training was extended for another year. The perception was that the government would eventually make the programme permanent. When the funds dried up, many women in the programme had already married and some committed suicide for lack of a livelihood. This kind of long term decision making/impact is better understood within a feminist evaluation.

BALANCING LEARNING AND ACCOUNTABILITY

The purpose of each evaluation is different. Most are meant to ascertain future funding for the group, based on the findings of the evaluators. Members are often coached in how to conduct evaluations; male and female evaluators speak a different language in the process. How information is collected and authenticated is a challenge for evaluators. Gender as an analytical tool doesn't provide a hold on everyday life and therefore a feminist evaluation is not easy.

The context of the evaluation is, therefore, important. This is so because contexts are changing so fast. Currently there is an environment of being smart in the reporting of your project, like a smart city, which is result oriented with smart objectives. There is accountability to the donors who, in turn, need to report to their donors. And accountability to the stakeholders or groups we work with. But we really need to make a case on why we need feminist groups to make a change.

Any evaluation is expected to demonstrate that everything has been positive. Yet the learning process through the evaluation is more important. Rich experiments in the field need to be documented. But unfortunately, to the organization this feels like a scrutiny. It is essential in a feminist evaluation to remember the larger power relations at play (with donors) while evaluating organizations and their partners, reiterating whose voices matter most in evaluation and whose stories count. (Miller and Haylock 2014)

EVALUATION AS A POLITICAL ACTIVITY

One of the consultant evaluators stated that evaluation is a political activity and involves power. How the organization experiences the evaluation is important. The evaluator can display power or be participatory. The process is more important than the final report as one can see in Asmita's old evaluations as well. Within the process itself, if there is need for changes in the organization and its activities or processes, this can be conveyed. Everything need not be documented in the formal report. There can be a set of recommendations for the organization which are not part of the formal report.

One example that came up was the evaluation of the Sumangali scheme where adolescent girls are taken as contractual labourers in cotton mills. Three adolescent girls reported similar problems in menstruation and conception after having worked in the mills. But a doctor's report to support the claim was very difficult to provide. This foregrounds the qualitative aspect of the evaluation. The evaluators wanted evidence of the health impact and problems which the adolescent girl's stories provided. This is the difference between qualitative and quantitative proof. Feminist evaluations often use experiences to illustrate a finding. Other evaluators demand hard core data. Some adolescent girls work for 16 hours rather than 8 hours. Many of them cannot sit down after standing for 12 odd hours. The evaluators need to make an effort to understand these aspects. Even safety or sexual assault was not taken into account while evaluating the project. It was dismissed as something common that happens in all workspaces. Despite the fact that these issues were flagged by the feminist organization, the report hasn't taken them into consideration. This underlines the difference between evaluators with experience and perspective and those who merely fill in a few boxes. There are many registered organizations for monitoring and evaluations that have no perspective. They bid for their projects and conduct them. This often results in evaluations that are insensitive and commercial. It is imperative to articulate the difference in conducting evaluations *on* organizations, projects and women and men rather than *with* them – one of which has inherent connotations of power.

THE ROLE OF THE EVALUATOR

Looking at the evaluators themselves, their experience, knowledge and attitude are important. An evaluator who has theoretical knowledge but no field-level experience faces a number of problems. A committed feminist evaluator will be ideal for a gender project/group. Feminist evaluators can bring out power relations more sharply than others. There is no single tool/framework that is perfect. We need to use several tools to complete the picture. Story-telling and life stories are one of the most powerful ways of speaking about change. The ultimate aim of an evaluation for the organization that is being evaluated and for the evaluator/donor (and for society as a whole) should be to produce a learning document. This will open new paths and the possibility of saying that important interventions need to be continued even if they are no longer fashionable.

The evaluation/learning process should be participatory and should help organizations in identifying where they have moved ahead and what is yet to be done. Local factors that might have been inhibiting rather than enabling need to be understood by the evaluator. The resources for the evaluation must be used for maximum advantage to the organization. The growing need to ask for quantifiable data or number crunching is disturbing and difficult. Often, this kills the nuances, the narratives, the lived realities of the people. Working towards change is slow. Funders need to take into consideration the whole context. The evaluator needs to be firm about this and to support the organization being evaluated. Evaluations must aim to strengthen work rather than obstruct it.

Some evaluators find no meaning in project evaluation and only conduct organizational evaluations. The specific cultural context is crucial. The evaluator needs theoretical knowledge but also the requisite experience and attitude. It is difficult for an external person to understand the cultural context. The evaluator must have the humility to accept that the cultural context is new.

While interacting with the field level staff, the context is important. Many decisions taken by the organization are dictated by the context. A good evaluator must be able to foresee that. The vision of the organization and the vision of the evaluator need to be attuned. There are a lot of values attached to an evaluation such as respecting diversity, respecting the cultural context and specificity. If the evaluator is not able to do all of this, the evaluation becomes a hierarchical power exercise. Many of the evaluated organizations shared experiences of how a bad evaluation exercise nearly destroyed the organization.

Despite the fact that monitoring and evaluation exercises are immensely important for growth, they have been reduced to being seen as a mechanical activity rather than a political one. Hence, it is best for evaluators to remain open to learning and evolving new ways of assessing the impact of development on men and women, and on women's rights and gender equality. (Bowman and Sweetman 2014)

4

Using a Feminist Lens for Utilization Focused Evaluations

Lessons Learned

SONAL ZAVERI

Introduction

In this essay, I explore how Utilization Focused Evaluation (UFE) provided the framework within which, as a feminist evaluator, I encouraged a deeper understanding of gender and social equity issues, as a result of which the interpretations of the evaluation findings allowed a more nuanced and equitable way forward. This knowledge building addressed issues of disempowerment, hierarchy and vulnerability within an evaluation context. From the UFE point of view, I share the overall methodology, how data was collected and analysed, who the evaluation users were and what the evaluation was used for. From the feminist point of view, I share how important it was to understand the context in order to interpret the findings. I use a practical example to illustrate these intersections and synergies. This essay also represents my personal values as an evaluator because I believe that capacity building in evaluation is not just about methods and tools but about understanding the larger context in which interventions occur. It is about encouraging those who are evaluating or being evaluated to reflect, contribute and debate about the evaluation process so that they not only *own* the process, but also *use* in the evaluation to make a difference in people's lives.

UFE is an approach that has been attributed to the work of Michael Patton (2008). Patton's central premise is that the entire evaluation process must be designed to facilitate use of the findings. For this reason, his evaluation approach is structured to move from general ideas of what to evaluate to the *real* and the specific. 'Use', according to Patton, means, 'how real people in the real world apply evaluation findings and experience the evaluation process' (Patton, 2008, p. 37). The UFE approach does not advocate either a qualitative or quantitative model and encourages methodological flexibility. The evaluation focuses on producing useful programme information directly to the individual primary users. UFE is a broad decision-making framework that gives structure to the evaluation process (Ramirez and Brodhead, 2013) and is driven by the intended users and their specific information needs. The role of the evaluator is that of a coach, mentor and facilitator. 'The evaluator facilitates judgment and decision-making by intended users rather than acting as a distant independent judge' (Patton, op.cit.: p. 38). In this sense, UFE is neutral in its approach towards gender and evaluation methodology in general. The decision to layer the UFE approach with a gender or feminist lens depends upon the evaluation needs of the intended users as well as the perspective of the evaluator.

A feminist lens has specifically emerged as an approach to evaluation because it critically looks at gender and other sources of inequality (Hay 2012). According to Batliwala (2008), a feminist ideology advocates for the transformation of *all* social relations of power that oppress, exploit or marginalize any set of people, women and men, on the basis of their gender, age, sexual orientation, ability, race, religion, nationality, location, ability, class, caste or ethnicity. Gender represents the socially constructed differences between men and women and not the biological differences that distinguish them. Gender always discusses not just gender roles but power relations between men and women. So, gender is not exclusive to women but because the social constructs for women are skewed, women face gender inequities and a lower status. The feminist point of view argues that all hierarchies such as patriarchy, caste, ethnicity, class and so on, oppress women. A feminist evaluator must therefore be aware of these inequities and in the use of UFE, mainstream these concerns.

Although UFE does not necessarily have to incorporate gender analysis, there is added value in using a feminist lens because it helps, as in the case example regarding marginalized women's use of mobile technology to access their rights to health, to assess how the programme affected these women in different ways. The mobile application to report health violations was created because poor and marginalized women's access to timely and quality health care is usually compromised. The feminist UFE mentor takes on an additional role: probing for key evaluation questions (KEQs) that call for engendered evidence, as many gender issues are not easily visible and can be overlooked.

This essay is organized in the following sections: a) the context of the project, b) focus of the evaluation and justification of the hybrid approach, c) findings, various interpretations and their suggested use, and d) reflections on the synergy between a feminist lens and the UFE.

The Context

BEGINNINGS

Nazdeek India[1] is a human rights organization that, along with its partners Pajhra[2] in Assam and ICAAD in New York,[3] won a grant from ISIF Asia[4] for its project named – *Using a Mobile Application and Mapping Platform to Increase Accountability in the Delivery of Maternal Health Services for Tea Garden Workers in Assam.*[5] In 2014-15, ISIF offered to three grantees – out of the twelve ISIF Asia grant recipients – an opportunity for mentoring in evaluation and research communication. Mentoring was provided as part of an IDRC action-research project entitled Developing Evaluation and Communication Capacity in Information Society Research (DECI-2).[6]

This essay summarizes my work as a DECI-2 evaluation mentor under DECI-2 from September 2014 to June 2015 with one of the three possible grantees, Nazdeek. Nazdeek was selected because it fulfilled several organizational 'readiness criteria', such as a buy-in and commitment from senior management to receive mentoring, assignment of a staff person who was willing to learn and experiment, and who expressed willingness to spend the time and money to implement the evaluation and communication plans so that they would be more strategic and focused.

The Project

Tea garden workers (mostly women) in Assam have insufficient access to health facilities and essential services. Although women are entitled to free of cost maternal health services to be provided by both the government and tea plantations, they are often neglected or discriminated against because of their ethnicity and socio-economic status. Existing facilities are severely underequipped and understaffed, and many villages are located in underserved and remote areas. As a result, tea garden workers, many of them from the indigenous (Adivasi) community, suffer high rates of maternal and infant mortality with minimal access to legal and advocacy resources to address violations. In fact, Assam has the highest maternal mortality rate in India.

Nazdeek, a legal empowerment organization, received funds to pilot a nine-month project that tracks, maps, and analyses gaps in health and nutrition services delivery. This work takes place through a mobile and web-based platform that collects and maps reports sent by SMS on cases of denial of timely and quality access to maternal and infant health services in one district with a high Adivasi population. Nazdeek collaborated with ICAAD, a human rights organization, to develop the technology and with Pajhra, a local activist organization, to implement the application. Pajhra, Nazdeek's grassroots partner for this project, has worked for many years in three districts of Assam including the community around Tezpur, Sonitpur District, (located in the state of Assam, India) promoting the rights of indigenous labourers working in the tea garden areas as well as the villages near the estates.

The Nazdeek project recognized that the rights of marginalized women were being violated because of their gender and ethnicity and socio-economic status. The aim of the SMS Mapping platform was to build an evidence base for litigation and advocacy. It was evident that the tea garden workers did not have the *means* to report health rights violations and thereby prevent or combat maternal deaths. Nazdeek's field experience indicated that about one in 20 women (including non-Adivasi women) owned a phone, and one in five women had access to one (through family members). Women were also unfamiliar with sending information through SMS technology. The intention of the project was therefore to marry community mobilization and technology to collect evidence that could be used to hold both public and private entities accountable for the timeliness and quality of health services for women tea garden workers and their children.

In the project, forty women volunteers were given mobile phones to report health rights violations. The phones have a list of codes for both the type of violation and the location of health facilities in the coverage area. Women are able to text the appropriate code of the violations, which are received at the Pajhra office and within two days are verified by a staff member through a call-back. Sometimes the Pajhra team also does site verification. The violations are populated on a map, which informs the location and type of violation. The aim is to increase the documentation of gaps in the health system, by using the online platform to map the data and visually identify areas of concern and patterns of abuse. This mapping and tracking enables health rights advocates like Nazdeek and Pajhra to use the evidence to demand accountability from the government and tea plantations for the delivery of health services to women and their children.

Focus of the Evaluation and Justification of the Hybrid Approach

THE UFE APPROACH

As an evaluation mentor for UFE, my task was to guide Nazdeek and Pajhra through the evaluation process. Patton has articulated the UFE approach in a series of steps. His book *Utilization Focused Evaluation* (2008) describes 12 steps which were later expanded to 17 steps in his latest *Essentials of Utilization-focused Evaluation* (2012). I chose to use the 12 steps (and kept the additional five steps as options) to provide guidance to the grantee's evaluator-facilitator regarding how to structure UFE.

UFE builds the evaluation capacity of the user of the evaluation. The user is usually defined as a person or persons who has/have the influence and commitment to take the findings of the evaluation forward (in contrast to an audience that will only read the evaluation

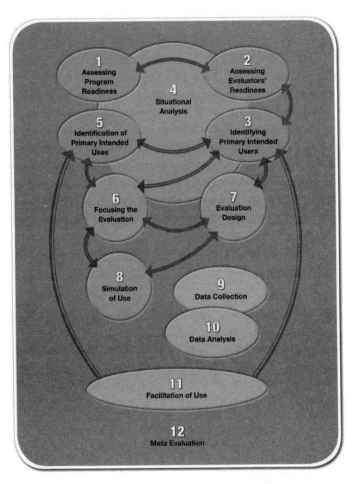

report). Other DECI-2 partners preferred the term evaluation "owners" to underline the control they have over the evaluation design. The user contributes to the focus of the evaluation since he or she has a use in mind. UFE is like a work in progress with both the evaluator-facilitator and the user iteratively working through the UFE steps. Experience has indicated that an external evaluator who is aware of the UFE process and understands the context can meaningfully mentor the organization doing the UFE.

The above diagram explains the 12 UFE steps and indicates that UFE is not a linear process (Ramirez and Brodhead, 2013). Although

Patton described the 12 steps in a linear fashion, in practice some steps have typical interactions between sequential steps; plus there are also strategic interactions across steps that are not sequential. In fact there is considerable back and forth in the steps. UFE is 'messy' and 'political' and reflects the real world in which projects take place. The situational analysis, attention to the context and involvement of different stakeholders in discussion regarding who the user will be, the use and the questions of interest makes the UFE process 'political'.

The first five steps include: a review of the readiness of the project for UFE and include assessing the organization's and evaluator's readiness, identifying the users and the uses of the evaluation and doing a situational analysis. In this case, the organizational readiness had already been ascertained during the selection of Nazdeek for UFE mentoring. UFE demands that the use for the evaluation findings be defined at the design stage and not thought of at the end of the evaluation. To ensure use, UFE emphasizes that a small group of 'users' be identified who will take ownership of the UFE process. Though the steps of identifying the user(s) and use(s) appear simple, in practice a number of iterations are required before finalizing.

Nazdeek and Pajhra went through several iterations to decide on the users, uses and Key Evaluation Questions (KEQs).

Initial users and uses	Final users and uses
1) Local activists including Nazdeek, Pajhra – USE: to collect data to advocate and litigate with government.	Project Coordinator, Pajhra
2) Community members and local leaders – USE: to create awareness for access to maternal health services	USE: a) To learn about implementation to improve the programme, b) to better inform Pajhra and Nazdeek to source the next round of funding.
3) Local government and courts – USE: for policy level choices to improve health services	

Nazdeek had challenges in deciding who the user(s) should be, what to evaluate and how to use the evaluation. According to the UFE approach, all three are linked because the users make decisions about what to evaluate depending on what use they have identified. The first approximation is shown on the left column of the table. Skype calls to unravel this proved to be inconclusive and it was difficult for me to understand the causes behind these bottlenecks.

During a site visit to Pajhra, I visited the tea gardens, met the volunteer women and observed what happens in a health facility. The situational analysis (Step 4 in the UFE approach) enabled a project audit to take place. This immersion allowed me to learn what exactly Pajhra's strategy was, as well as the role of Nazdeek, the plight of the women working in the tea gardens and the political undercurrents regarding documenting health rights violations. Face-to-face meeting with the volunteers revealed that they were able to map the health rights violations but that the tea garden owners and government were unaware of it. It became clear to me that it was highly unlikely that the local government and courts could be evaluation users – as had been suggested – when they were not even aware of the tracking and mapping of health rights violations!

During the discussion with Pajhra and the women volunteers, I understood that the women volunteers were afraid to report health rights violations as some of them were employed by the government (as frontline health workers, nursery teachers, etc). It was unlikely that community members and local leaders could be evaluation users since the extent of violation reporting was in the initial phase. In fact, the defining feature of the project was greater community involvement in reporting human rights violations, and was in itself being questioned since the community (tea garden workers and women volunteers) were yet to take charge. Furthermore, it was also unlikely that persons from Nazdeek and Pajhra could be users. They were already in a combative role, using a litigation strategy to advocate for change. Also, Assam at that time was facing various agitations related to overall Adivasi issues. For these reasons, it was decided that the Project Coordinator of Pajhra would be the evaluation user and by focusing on the challenges and possible solutions in implementation (that the Project Coordinator was responsible for), Nazdeek and Pajhra could write a Phase Two proposal to extend their work and approach potential funders. For the next tranche of funding, Nazdeek wanted to emphasize how technology empowers the community, in this case marginalized women working in the tea gardens. This goal meant a closer look at implementation and what Pajhra was achieving. It was important to consider how Nazdeek and Pajhra communicated (or not) with various stakeholders and how to weave this information into the evaluation. This step meant listening carefully regarding *what* Nazdeek and Pajhra wanted to communicate *to whom* and *how*. So, the UFE added a dimension of reflection regarding the purposes of evaluation, and communication practices. The UFE framework does not have an inherent link to communication but the DECI-2 research project does integrate both UFE and Research Communication (ResCom) into a hybrid approach to support actionable decision-making. These reflections and analyses contributed later to a revised realistic theory of change.

A preliminary analysis of the monitoring data indicated that some women volunteers were not texting infringements because they faced problems in selecting the right code and did not seem to be motivated. Many women had never reported while others were very active (texting started in May 2014). Without good community level data, Nazdeek would not be able to gather solid evidence on the gaps in healthcare delivery which was essential for advocacy with the government. In fact the success of the mobile technology for which Nazdeek had received funds from ISIF depended on the active participation of the women volunteers. As a result of these discussions and analysis, the focus of the evaluation turned to better understanding the barriers and challenges the women volunteers faced, their motivation to work and the nature of the health violations reporting.

Although the grant was to test a mobile and web-based application, the contextual analysis and the focus of the evaluation suggested the need for a feminist lens to the UFE approach. It was important to understand the world of the women tea garden workers and take a closer look at issues of gender, maternal health rights and social exclusion.

The Feminist Lens

The women tea garden workers belong to the Adivasi[7] community. They are the descendants of tribal people who were brought by the

British colonial planters as indentured labourers from other parts of India into Assam from the 1860-90s onwards for the purpose of labour in the tea gardens industry. (Sutradhar 2015) The tea industry is labour intensive and has a high proportion of females in the workforce. Tea estates are located in the interior and deepen women's sense of isolation and disempowerment. The women tea garden workers for – whose health rights Pajhra and Nazdeek are defending – belong to one of the most backward communities in Assam due to decades of continuous exploitation. In spite of over a century of living in Assam, the Adivasi community has been marginalized from mainstream groups. Poor standards of living, low access to education and minimal health facilities compounded the problems women tea garden workers face. All of the women volunteers who are supposed to document health rights violations in the ISIF funded project, belong to the Adivasi community or live in and near the tea gardens.

This contextual understanding was important in Nazdeek/Pajhra's project analysis that emerged during discussions of who the user would be, what the uses would be, and what to focus the key evaluation questions on. In principle, the theory of change for the project was sound – that once the local community women (including Adivasi women) were trained to use mobile technology and the violation codes, they would be able to report health rights violations which could be tracked and mapped, which in turn would result in advocating and litigating with the government and other bodies responsible for maternal and child health services. Once the government responded, the impact would lead to improved access and quality of maternal and child health services for the women tea garden workers. Yet, clearly the pathway to change was more complex than it seemed since the reporting of incidents regarding health violations were lower than expected. Although there was a strong mobile platform available to report health violations and it was common knowledge that there were health violations, volunteers were not reporting them in the numbers required. In other words the assumptions behind the theory of change had not been addressed.

Nazdeek/Pajhra's strategy of community involvement was also sound – the most affected were selected to participate and intensive training to use the SMS platform was given to them. As a feminist evaluator, I felt that we could understand what was happening if we dug deeper and unpacked the assumptions in the theory of change regarding how social exclusion could be affecting women's active involvement in addressing their health concerns.

It is well documented that women's health rights are violated because their caste and class further exacerbate their lower status. (Khanna, 2012) The women tea garden workers belonged to the most marginalized tribal or Adivasi communities and were excluded because of their gender, caste, location and occupation. (Sutradhar, 2015) Amartya Sen draws attention to various meanings and dimensions of the concept of social exclusion (Sen, 2000). A distinction is drawn between the situation where some people are being kept out (or at least left out), and where some people are being included (maybe even forcibly included) – at greatly unfavourable terms. These two situations are described as 'unfavourable exclusion' and 'unfavourable inclusion'. 'Unfavourable inclusion' with unequal treatment may have the same adverse effects as 'unfavourable exclusion'. Sen's concept of unfair inclusion is similar to the concept of discrimination. Women tea garden workers were not only excluded from claiming their health rights but when included, they did not receive the same treatment as others because of their caste and class. The concept of social exclusion is essentially a group concept. This concept helps us to understand the meanings and manifestations of caste and untouchability-based exclusion in India. Research indicates that in comparison to higher caste mothers, mothers from the lower caste group lack necessary information regarding maternal health services, under-utilize available services and their benefits, and face caste-based discrimination (unfair inclusion) when utilizing the services (Sabharwal, 2014).

The feminist lens (which encompasses all forms of power relations and discrimination) demanded that we take a closer look at who the women volunteers were and what the barriers and challenges were that they faced.

FOCUS OF THE EVALUATION

The UFE recommends that once the Users have identified a set of Uses, they also formulate two or three key questions to anchor the evaluation. From a feminist point of view, we needed to come up with KEQ that would address barriers faced by these women.

Pajhra had enrolled women working in and around the tea gardens but did not have demographic information regarding their caste, class, occupation and education. We needed to first understand the 'intersectionalities' that may affect women's reporting. Feminist evaluation recommends understanding how gender intersects with social cleavages (such as gender, race, class, sexuality, caste, religion) that define and shape the experience and exercise of power in different contexts (Hay, 2012). It was a leap of faith for women, mostly marginalized, to be willing to be volunteers to document health rights violations and we needed to understand what their motivation was to join the project. We then needed to understand what processes they followed to obtain information, understand their challenges and barriers, and ask them about how to make the programme better.

The Use identified by the User, the Project Coordinator (who was male), was: a) to learn about implementation to improve the programme, b) to better inform Pajhra and Nazdeek to source the next round of funding. Based on our understanding of the context and using a feminist lens, two questions were finalized:

UFE Key Evaluation Questions	Implications from a feminist lens
What are the factors that affect the participation of women who use the mobile phones to report violation of health rights?	Do marginalized women tea garden workers know and act on their health rights? What are their barriers in communicating with women who have experienced these health violations and reporting about it? Which women have the greatest difficulty reporting and why?
How do the women whose rights have been violated, frontline health workers (known as ASHAS and Anganwadi Workers), health facility staff and community leaders perceive the changes from the project? What more can be done?	Has the tracking of violations led to change in awareness about maternal health rights? Do communities recognize women's role? Are women's voices heard and acted upon by decision makers (in the health services)? What suggestions do women have to improve the project results?

The KEQS, as well as the 'feminist lens' were the foundation for the choice of the data collection instruments. To develop the data collection tools, it was important to have a series of focus group discussions (FGD) with the women to understand the issues that were of concern to them. The user also felt that it would be easier to approach funders with some quantitative data, and it was decided that a mix of quantitative and qualitative data would be useful for proposal preparation. It is important to note that the use of quantitative methods with communities empowers because quantitative data and indicators are perceived to be the territory of the 'elite academics and researchers'. Understanding quantitative indicators and being able to use them appropriately is potentially transformative (Khanna, 2012). However, most of the women volunteers had limited writing skills and open-ended questions would be difficult to record and analyse. Closed questions would not provide a clear understanding of the issues. Nazdeek put together a list of open-ended questions for a focus group discussion in one implementation area, which was then refined to develop a draft version of the questionnaire. This questionnaire was piloted with five or six participants and amendments made for the final version. The questions had multiple-choice answers and they were read out to each woman, and she could choose the answer closest to her perceptions. They also had a translated written copy of the questionnaire where they could read and write their choices.

The feminist evaluation paradigm ensured that we listened to women's voices (through the FGDs) to prepare the questionnaire. The administration of the questionnaire also took cognizance of women's hesitation to work with paper and pencil and used a guided interaction approach.

Selected Findings and Their Interpretation

EVALUATION FINDINGS

The profile of women volunteers was disaggregated by location (village/tea garden), age group, literacy level, religion, and occupation.

Almost an equal number of volunteers lived in the villages and the tea gardens but the women residing in the tea gardens were the low-performance reporters. High-performance reporters were students and teachers, and some government workers; the low reporters were housewives and a few government employed nursery teachers. Some had never reported. Many mentioned that they were not sure of the code to be texted, others did not text because they were scared of the repercussions – most of the people who chose the latter answer were housewives from tea gardens, perhaps because they were afraid of repercussions from garden managers in general since the work was their family's only source of livelihood About a third of respondents said they faced pressure from their own family members who discouraged them from texting. This has negatively impacted the participation, since people who chose this answer were either medium or low reporters (Nazdeek, 2015).

Low reporters in the tea gardens had more informal communication about rights violations with women who accessed health services. High reporters resided in the villages and they were able to get information from the government frontline workers such as the field health workers and nursery teachers (the most literate in the communities) as well (Nazdeek, 2015).

The initial decision with this evidence was: a) to reduce the number of women volunteers, especially the large number of low to medium reporters; b) to develop a selection criteria – younger age group (because they performed better), more educated (although literacy did not impact reporting) and from the villages (not the tea gardens); c) to meet monthly to provide more assistance with the coding and for the managers to meet the families of the volunteers so that they would support the volunteers for texting; and d) for project coordinators to assist the high reporters in finding out more information for accurate reporting of violations. These decisions constitute an immediate utilization of the findings, which in turn is how the success of a UFE evaluator is gauged.

Pajhra had assumed prior to the evaluation that the volunteers selected were either not competent or not motivated or had a conflict of interest (since some were employed by the government as teachers and field health workers) and it was perhaps necessary to recruit new personnel.

The first interpretation of the findings was that it was the tea garden worker women who were the least responsive; they had difficulty interacting with health workers/government staff to obtain information from them; yet they did interact with other women just as the high reporters did.

As a feminist evaluator, I initiated discussions with the User and the rest of the team. Just as we had understood the context of the women tea garden workers from a rights and feminist lens and formulated the questions to understand the lived realities of their work and challenges, we needed to put on our feminist 'spectacles' to interpret the findings.

A FEMINIST INTERPRETATION

A feminist lens demanded that the contextual analysis question the hierarchies that keep marginalized women in a subordinate position (Ehrenreich, 1976) and understand how this impacted their use of technology and reporting of health violations.

According to this approach, patterns in participation of volunteers reflect existing social structures/hierarchies within the community. While project participants, being Adivasi women, already belong to a marginalized group, volunteers qualifying as 'low reporters' are even more marginalized. Low reporters mostly live in tea garden areas, are housewives or are home-employed, have little understanding of mobile technology and, more importantly, have lower social status, which hinders relation/communications with ASHAS and frontline workers. Conversely, high reporters have higher self-esteem and social standing, crucial to obtaining information from ASHAS and Anganwadi Workers (AGWs). While 'social status' is difficult to define, it plays a very clear role in the ability of volunteers to report.

Indeed, the findings suggest that frontline health workers (ASHAS and AGWs) are a key source of information for volunteers, and the difference between high and low reporters often lies in their ability to obtain information from health workers. The discussion also focused on the attitude of ASHAS (government field health workers) towards patients and some of the volunteers, who have reported feeling disregarded by ASHAS and therefore unable to obtain information. Challenges in approaching ASHAS result in too much time being spent on sourcing information, and therefore low reporting (Nazdeek, 2015).

ASHAS command respect and have influence in the tea gardens and tend to blame the pregnant (Adivasi) women for being in poor health or not taking their medicines. Among Adivasi women, there is a culture of silence, and a tacit acceptance of the violation of their rights – such as when entitlements are not received. Pajhra reported for example that government Anganwadi workers (who provide food, health and educational services to children at village level) did not receive nutrition for the under fives in their care for six months but did not report this in the tea gardens and villages because they feared they would have to face repercussions from their supervisors. In villages, volunteers are more educated and can access ASHAS who will provide accurate information on health care lapses. But the context is very different in the tea gardens where there are cultural barriers for tea garden workers to access the ASHAS and their health records.

Furthermore, the findings showed that documentation and reporting also require interaction with community members and families of patients. Low rights awareness results in women (patients) and relatives having little information to share with volunteers. The data indicated that as a result of the project, women were beginning to perceive the health violations as representative of human rights violations. All their life they had seen such violations and had accepted them as routine or their fate. What emerged was exactly what Pajhra as a human rights organization had been fighting for years – the need to empower tribal men and women who for generations had seen exploitation, and educate them about their entitlements. Pajhra had spent all its energies on developing the ICT technology rather than on understanding *why* the tribal women were not reporting lapses. A third of the community members including families of participants were not supportive of the women volunteers' work because the idea of claiming entitlements was 'new' and questioned the 'hierarchy' of the societies they lived in. My feminist lens led me to become a 'researcher' at this stage (along with my mentoring role) to help Nazdeek and Pajhra discover a gap (the unexpressed set of assumptions) in their theory of change. In fact, disaggregating reporters by age, religion, literacy level, occupation and location showed how their access to technology can reproduce inequalities existing within the community. (Feruglio, F. 2015)

Nazdeek's objective was to 'increase accountability in the delivery of reproductive health services and therefore strengthen enforcement of laws, policies and programs' (ISIF Asia Grant with Nazdeek, p. 2). To do so, the pilot 'married community mobilization and technology' to ensure individual incident reporting that would provide factual evidence to track incidents of human rights violations. The overall objective was that once community capacity was built for good data gathering using technology, the information could be used for litigation to prevent maternal and infant mortality. The assumption was a) an easy mobile (such as SMS) platform was needed to improve data gathering b) women whose health and human rights had been violated would use their training to report these incidents to the project's field volunteers c) the community volunteers would track incidents and be involved in the litigation and d) government would positively react to the litigation and make improvements.

The use of the UFE framework and the feminist lens enabled Nazdeek and Pajhra to closely review these assumptions underlying their Theory of Change. The project audit reviewed a) the difficulty of the SMS platform for reporting because many women were using the cellphone (their very own) for the first time in their lives b) women had been so disenfranchised that they did not understand that they had entitlements related to their health c) community volunteers were afraid to report lapses since they were either dependent on the government for their income or due to their historical low status, had never questioned those in power and d) since the government had no idea that incident tracking was taking place by the community in their health services they were likely to feel threatened and less likely to respond positively to advocacy.

The UFE framework and the feminist lens encouraged reviewing the assumptions underpinning the Theory of Change and suggested a more actionable pathway to achieve the overall objective. For example, Nazdeek and Pajhra considered the option of developing a communication strategy that would enable collaboration and provide government with data so that they could take action to improve health services. Another option under review was to further strengthen the women volunteers and disenfranchised women about their rights and entitlements, invest in leadership building and motivational strategies so that they were more likely to report lapses in health services. In time, Nazdeek and Pajhra reviewed the roles of the women volunteers and considered retraining high performers as paralegals.

From a feminist lens, the data raised questions about the interrelationships of the volunteers with the community, health care workers and the historical structural inequalities that subtly impacted the responses for an ICT application that was otherwise technologically sound. The underlying problem for Pajhra was the issue of entitlements and how confident women are to claim their rights. Unless this issue was resolved, the ICT application was unlikely to report the real numbers of health rights violations. Technology is put to effective use according to underlying human intentions and the degree to which technology makes an impact depends on existing human capacities (Gurstein, 2003; Toyama, 2015).

The volunteers needed more empowerment sessions than those initially carried out – to know and to exercise their rights as tribals and women; and to be more confident in reporting lapses in health care. Having minimal education, the women also needed more interactive ways to better understand and report codes that represented specific violations. Finally, the women needed to understand their collective strength as advocates and to share and learn from each other. Women needed to see change happening. Perhaps the reporting was important from a legal perspective but community action and dialogue with the government was the priority at the community level. The evidence helped Pajhra to decide on the followings: a) to retain the existing volunteers; b) to further strengthen legal empowerment and rights based training sessions along with lessons on how to key in different health violations on a mobile phone; c) to focus and strengthen the community component through trainings/meetings on cultural identity and self esteem; d) to translate the training materials into the tribal language Sadri; and e) to work with block level (administrative division) government officials to collaboratively bring change (this was a huge step as Nazdeek and Pajhra were already engaged in two legal suits against the government in the Assam High Court).

Even before the UFE process was complete, as a supplement to the reporting of health violation lapses, the team initiated follow-up meetings with the relevant government authorities, creating a dialogue with them around the need to redress health rights violations. The UFE and the communication component of the mentoring had suggested the need to engage the local government early on based on the audience analysis for communication which was carried out in parallel with the stakeholder analysis for UFE. Without engaging government, the campaign for better and timely health rights for tea garden workers and their children would backfire. The strategic communication plan strengthened the use of the UFE and in turn advocacy for health rights of marginalized women and children.

Pajhra developed the Action Plan below. It is worth noting that there is only one section on mobile technology use, while the rest of the items are related to empowerment and efficacy strengthening. This constitutes evidence of a shift in the theory of change of this project.

What – Action Plan

Discussion/Training on Adivasi (tribal) cultural identity and permanency (residence) question of Adivasis in Assam.

Training on leadership and communication

Training on the use of mobile technology

Awareness meeting with community leaders, members of community organizations

Phone conference with block leaders (managers)

Smaller meetings with participants (women volunteers)

Reflections on Valuing a Hybrid Approach

The UFE provided the basic framework within which a feminist lens was introduced and through this hybrid, the use of findings from a gender transformative (feminist) lens was placed centrestage. One of the challenges in equity and gender transformative evaluations is the *use* of findings as they usually inform whether there has been change in power structures or not. The use of UFE in this case strengthened advocacy and the use of the equity and gender related findings. A broad analysis of the UFE process and feminist thought (Sielback-Bowen et al, 2002; Podems, 2010) indicates the synergy between the two.

1. Evaluations are Political

A UFE evaluator understands the importance of doing a situational analysis to understand that use is dependent upon who the user is and on asking the questions that matter the most for the use of the evaluation. While deciding who the users could be, a stakeholder analysis takes place with discussions regarding who has power, who decides and who does not. Feminist evaluations view evaluation as a political activity; the contexts in which evaluation operates are politicized. UFE recognizes that the evaluator brings his or her own perspective to the evaluation and challenges the evaluator not to judge but to be open to learning. As a feminist evaluator, I went beyond the non-judgmental role of a UFE mentor and by introducing feminist values, brought value to what the project was trying to achieve and carefully balanced both UFE and feminist evaluation. Feminist evaluations value the personal experiences, perspectives, and characteristics evaluators bring to evaluations (and with which feminist evaluators interact) and accept that it may lead to a particular political stance. Understanding the context of the Adivasi culture, the exploitation of women, the marginalization of tea garden workers and the struggle to claim their rights was critical in understanding the relationships of activist organizations (Pajhra), human rights advocates (Nazdeek) and service providers (government and private).

2. Knowledge is a Powerful Resource

Recognizing that knowledge is a powerful resource, UFE ensures that the user is involved right from the design stage so that the evaluation, its data, findings and use are 'owned'. This stress on ownership and use ensures that not only are users involved in the process of evaluation, but that they come forward to take action on the information from the evaluation. The intense debate on how to interpret the information in order to put it to use, resulted in a very different action plan. Feminist evaluators recognize that knowledge has an implicit and explicit purpose and that it is important to determine who owns it, who uses it and who benefits from the information. Feminist evaluators opine that knowledge should be a resource 'of and for' the people who create, hold, and share it. Feminist evaluators also believe that there are multiple ways of knowing; some ways are privileged over others. UFE has no restriction on what tools should be used but stress that they must be related to the use. So, in this case the need for quantitative or qualitative data did not emerge from the KEQs, but rather from an evaluation *use* that combined learning with fund-raising. In discussions with Nazdeek and Pajhra, it was suggested that donors would prefer some data that was quantitative and the UFE should provide scope to collect such data. Further, the voices of the women were heard through FGDs and the questionnaire was designed based on their responses.

3. Understanding the Process of Change

The identification of Users, Uses and KEQ triggered a 'project audit' and an informal unravelling of the theory of change – what resources was the organization investing in the project, what were the underlying assumptions for selection of the activities, what change was expected initially and more long-term and how the change would impact the target population. The organization was introducing an ICT technology that had cultural and political overtones and it was important to understand the context in which the technology was trying to introduce change and to assess if the change was likely to be sustainable. This analysis also challenged the organization to be clear about what their communication purposes were, who the audience was for communication and what changes they expected. This integrated evaluation and communication approach enabled a debate on the project structure, the underlying assumptions and outcomes expected.

A feminist lens looks at change from the perspective of gender inequities that lead to social injustice and exclusion. Feminist evaluation considers discrimination or inequality based on gender as systemic and structural and digs deep into the assumptions that underpin a project's theory of change. This lens was important during evaluation design and interpretation of information from the evaluation. Which key evaluation questions to focus on in the UFE can be guided by a feminist approach to evaluation. As mentioned above, this also means that the UFE evaluator moves beyond a purely facilitative role, and participates in a collaborative inquiry.

4. *Knowing and Telling the Story*

The Step 12 of the UFE is a meta-evaluation that encourages reflexivity so that evaluators can be thoughtful. Feminist evaluators encourage this reflection to understand the nuances that impact inequities. They also value multiple ways of knowing, communicating and listening to the 'target' population. UFE encourages taking the evaluation forward and in this case would encourage sharing the evaluation with the participants of the evaluation, the women volunteers.

To conclude, this example of a hybrid approach to evaluation highlighted the need in mainstream evaluations like the UFE to capture potential effects of gender-targeted programmes and to understand the causes of gender inequality. Social psychologists have stressed the latent nature of discrimination – that gender inequality is deeply ingrained in the attitudinal and psychological make-up of individuals. Not addressing these issues led to compromised uptake of a mobile platform that was meant to redress marginalized women's own health rights violations.

In many ways, the UFE and the feminist lens strengthen and complement each other to ensure that the information from the evaluation transforms the lives of those for whom the projects are designed. By strengthening the evaluative capacity of the organization, by encouraging its reflexivity, by stressing ownership and use and designing evaluations that are most relevant to the organization's work, we ensure that evaluations go 'beyond utilization' to improve people's lives, anchored in values of equity and human rights

Notes

1. www.nazdeek.org
2. www.pajhra.org
3. http://www.icaad.ngo/
4. The Information Society Innovation Fund Asia (ISIF Asia) is a grants and awards programme aimed at stimulating creative solutions to ICT development needs in the Asia Pacific region. ISIF offers grants and awards on a competitive basis to groups interested in ICT action-research. The ISIF programme is hosted by APNIC in Brisbane, Australia.

5. http://nazdeek.org/assam-using-mobile-technology-to-address-maternal-mortality/
6. The predecessor DECI-1 project focused only on evaluation mentoring in Asia whereas DECI-2 included mentoring on communication as well. Since 2012 DECI-2 has supported research networks and grantees under IDRC's Networked Economies programme.
7. Adivasi is an umbrella term for a heterogeneous set of ethnic and tribal groups considered the aboriginal population of South Asia.

References:

Batliwala, Srilatha. 2008. 'Changing Their World: Concepts and Practices of Women's Movements' Association for Women's Rights in Development.

Ehrenreich, B. 1976. 'What Is Socialist Feminism?' (Reproduced From Win Magazine) https://www.uic.edu/orgs/cwluherstory/CWLUArchive/socialfem.html; accessed 5 October 2015.

Feruglio, F. 2015. 'The role of Technology for Legal Empowerment in India' in *Gender, Sexuality and Social Justice: What's Law Got to Do with It?* Sussex: Institute of Development Studies.

Gurstein, Michael. 2003. 'Effective Use: A Community Informatics Strategy beyond the Digital Divide', *First Monday*, Volume 8, Number 12, 1 December. http://firstmonday.org/ojs/index.php/fm/article/view/1107. Accessed 7 October 2015.

Hay, K. 2012. 'Engendering Policies and Programmes through Feminist Evaluation', *Indian Journal of Gender Studies*, 19(2), 321–340

Khanna, R. 2012. 'A feminist, gender and rights perspective for evaluation of women's health programmes', *Indian Journal of Gender Studies*, 19(2), 259–278.

Nazdeek. 2015. 'Findings Of The Utilization-Focused Evaluation (Ufe) "End Mm Now" Project', See www.nazdeek.org

Patton, M.Q. 2008. Utilization-focused Evaluation. Thousand Oaks: Sage.

Podems, D. 2010. 'Feminist evaluation and gender approaches: There's a difference?' *Journal of Multidisciplinary Evaluation*, 6 (14), 1–17

Ramirez, R. and Brodhead, D.P. 2013. *Utilization focused evaluation: A primer for evaluators*, Penang: Southbound.

Sabharwal, N., et al. 'Caste Discrimination as a factor in poor access to public health service system. A case study of Janani Suraksha Yojana Scheme', *Journal of Social Inclusion Studies*, Vol. 1, No. 1, 2014, 148–168.

Sen, A. 2000. 'Social Exclusion: Concept, Application, And Scrutiny', Asian Development Bank.

Sielbeck-Bowen, K. Brisolara, S. Seigart, D. Tischler, and E. Whitmore. 2002. 'Exploring feminist evaluation: The ground from which we rise,' *New Directions for Evaluation*, 96, 3–8.

Sutradhar, Ruman. 2013. 'What Caused Marginalization: A Study of the Tea Plantation Women of Cachar', *International Journal of Science and Research* (IJSR), Volume 4 Issue 5, 2771–2774, http://www.ijsr.net/archive/v4i5/SUB154798.pdf; accessed 2 October, 2015.

Toyama, Kentaro. 2015. 'Geek Heresy: Rescuing Social Change from the Cult of Technology', *Public Affairs*, New York.

5

A Feminist Approach to
Collaborative Evaluation

*Innovation for Relevance and
Constructivist Learning*

SHUBH SHARMA and RATNA M. SUDARSHAN

This essay discusses our learnings from and experiences of a collaborative evaluation with a feminist lens of a development intervention with women in very poor and geographically dispersed settlements across several states in India. We were commissioned to carry out the project baseline, which had the dual objective of providing the basis for an endline evaluation at the close of the project period, as well as offering some insights to the implementing team for designing their area-specific interventions for the project. The method used, of collaborative evaluation, evolved in the course of designing the baseline study. We discuss the project and the design as it evolved, and assesses the challenges in and advantages of implementing a collaborative evaluation methodology.

The first section briefly discusses the perspective with which the baseline was designed, that is using a feminist and participatory lens. The second section describes the programme to be evaluated. The third section discusses the formulation and implementation of the baseline using a collaborative evaluation methodology. The last section concludes by summarizing the key learnings from this exercise.

At the Outset: Perspectives

We begin by highlighting the present discourse on conceptualizing and measuring women's empowerment, as well as by deconstructing the collaborative and feminist approaches to evaluation before we describe the programme and the baseline, and its objectives and methodology.

Empowerment (Kabeer 1999) is defined as the process by which those who have been denied the ability to make strategic choices acquire such ability. Kabeer (1999) finds that there is an implicit assumption underlying many attempts to measure women's empowerment that we can somehow predict the nature and direction that change is going to take. She cautions that this, without some knowledge of ways of 'being and doing' which are realizable and valued by women in that context, runs into the danger of prescribing the process of empowerment and thereby violating its essence, which is to enhance women's capacity for self-determination.

Batliwala and Pitman (2010) further elucidate that the challenges of measuring change in the context of gender relations, and the social relations within which they are embedded, are somewhat more complex. This is because while changes in the social power relations of North-South, race, class, caste, ethnicity, sexuality, ability etc., are also difficult to achieve, patriarchal norms are embedded and normalized within each of these power structures. Therefore, challenging and transforming them is a doubly daunting task. Since gender power is integral to both public and private institutions and relationships, shifting it in one domain does not guarantee that it has been uprooted in another.

Feminist evaluation is rooted in an understanding of these realities. It (Sielbeck Bowen et al 2002, Podems 2010:4, Hay 2012) is an approach to evaluation that places emphasis on reflexivity, participatory and inclusive methods, and an ethical sense in evaluation design, data collection and use, and can be characterized by the following broad principles:

- Feminist evaluation has a central focus on inequities – this informs evaluation questions;

- It recognizes that discrimination or inequality based on gender is systemic and structural – this will inform evaluation design;
- Evaluation is a political activity; the contexts in which evaluation operates are politicized; and the personal experiences, perspectives, and characteristics evaluators bring to evaluations lead to a particular political stance, this will impact judgements;
- Knowledge is a powerful resource that serves an explicit or implicit purpose. Knowledge should be a resource of and for the people who create, hold and share it. Consequently, the evaluation or research process can lead to significant negative or positive effects on the people involved in the evaluation/research;
- Knowledge and values are culturally, socially, and temporally contingent. There are multiple ways of knowing – some privileged over others. Recognize and value different ways of knowing.

These principles were a guide to the way in which the baseline study was to be designed and conducted. In particular, this is an approach that points towards the need to recognize the structural basis of gender and social group inequities; to ensure that multiple perspectives are captured; and that the process of evaluation becomes useful to the programme implementers. These were, for us, powerful guidelines for this study.

Equally, we were committed to a participatory process for the evaluation. This was partly because given the nature of the programme, we believed this to be the best approach to fulfil feminist principles of evaluation. There was also a pragmatic consideration, that given the geographic spread of the intervention and accompanying socio cultural differences, it would be difficult to collect data without a strong participation of the implementing partner (thus ensuring that language, communication, culture, access did not become barriers). The method that evolved is best described as a 'collaborative evaluation', in which collaboration between the evaluator and the implementing agency was essential to successful data gathering, and also informed design and judgement.

Collaborative evaluation is rooted in a movement that emerged over the latter half of the nineteenth century toward participant-led approaches to evaluation (Brisolara 1998). The term collaborative evaluation is often used interchangeably with participatory and/ or empowerment evaluation. The Topical Interest Group (TIG) in the American Evaluation Association is called Collaborative/ Participatory/Empowerment Evaluation (Sullivan and Agostino 2002:373). Cousins et al (1996:210) define collaborative evaluation as 'any evaluation in which there is a significant degree of collaboration or cooperation between evaluators and stakeholders in planning and/ or conducting the evaluation'. Participants in a collaborative evaluation decide the evaluation questions, the evaluation design, the data collection strategies, the data analysis techniques, an interpretation of the findings, and a strategy for dissemination of the results, consensually and collaboratively (Brisson 2007:25).

Stakeholders are technically participants in an evaluation, when they provide information for it, but are not necessarily collaborators in its design (Sullivan and Agostino 2002: 373). To us, as for Sullivan and Agostino (2002: 373), collaborative evaluation rather than the term participatory evaluation, implies the desired level of involvement. The approach considers programme staff and other stakeholders to be part of the evaluation team, to the extent they are able (Sullivan and Agostino 2002: 374) and to the extent feasible. This does not imply that the evaluator is relieved of the expert role of leading the evaluation and producing evaluation findings. A significant positive outcome of collaborative evaluation is that it empowers participants to enhance their understanding of evaluation and gain new skills. However, Fetterman (1996) argues that it is not an intended outcome.

Utilization of evaluation findings continues to be a central problem in the field (Patton 2008, Hay 2010: 223). Some assert that the evaluator should be the person responsible for promoting evaluation use (Cousins et al. 1996). Many believe that involving stakeholders in the evaluation process will improve evaluation utilization (Fetterman 1996; Patton 2008; Sullivan and Agostino 2002: 374). Logic would suggest that if programme personnel are collaboratively involved in the evaluation, their understanding and thus the use of the findings would increase (Sullivan and Agostino 2002: 374).

Scriven (1996) critiqued collaborative evaluation and the potential co-option of the evaluator, as familiarity with programmes and programme staff increases. Conversely, programme staff in collaborative evaluation can be considered extensions of the evaluation team. Strengthening evaluation skills among team members is a desirable practice, from both a micro perspective of effective management (Sullivan and Agostino 2002: 374) as well as the macro perspective of evaluation field building.

It needs to be noted that the collaboration in this example primarily refers to the manner in which the implementing agency partnered with the evaluators in the process, and that while other stakeholders were approached in a manner that allowed expression of views and sharing of experience, they were not part of the design formulation or of analysis and judgment matters. We believe that this has significance in a country context where, given the size of the population and the geographic spread, many or even most programmes are implemented as a set of projects, and when time and resource constraints do not allow a wholly participatory process to be followed (as in the case of appreciative enquiry ((Cooperrider and Srivastva 1987:152)), for example), collaborative enquiry offers a promising approach to evaluation. In our experience this approach helped to reduce the distance between external evaluators and the community, even though it fell short of being a fully participatory process.

A Women's Empowerment Intervention

The baseline study was conducted for a women's empowerment programme. The goal of this programme is that, by 2020, 'rural women from marginalized communities and their collectives, in nine districts in four states of central India, will be able to raise their voice against violations and access their political and economic rights as mandated under central and state government policies'.

This project proposes over the next four years to mobilize women from 75,000 families in nine districts, forming over 5,000 self-help groups (SHGs). The project will build on earlier work of the implementing organization to mobilize women from disadvantaged communities into SHGs and their secondary and tertiary associations. This first phase will entail intensive engagement with 75,000 women in nine districts in the states of Madhya Pradesh, Orissa, Jharkhand and West Bengal. The programme anticipates a future second phase in which the project will be scaled up in over 24 districts in seven states, covering around 250,000 women.

Each woman in the selected districts will be supported to develop livelihood options enhancing her control over economic resources; effectively participate in local governance systems and build gender-sensitive accountability processes; negotiate intra-family issues that hinder equal access to rights for women and girls, including addressing domestic violence and accessing rights and entitlements enshrined in various statutes (including the National Policy for Empowerment of Women) and the Constitution. Intensive engagement will happen with the primary SHGs and their secondary and tertiary associations to enable women to enhance efficacy and develop sustainable livelihoods to increase their well-being and participation as complete citizens.

The intended outcomes of the programme are:

- 75,000 women increasingly exercise their right to participate in local governance structures, institutions and processes;
- 5,000 women's collectives at village and sub-block levels support women in facilitating expression, and addressing issues of inequality, discrimination and violations they face in their homes and outside;
- 75,000 women display an enhanced sense of equality as economic actors in the household;
- At least 1000 local self-governance representatives and government functionaries and officials (at various levels from the village to the state) in five districts in three states, exhibit more sensitivity to the demands of marginalized women under various constitutional requirements and entitlements including under the National Policy for Empowerment of Women (NPEW) and relevant state policies

DESTINATION AND ROAD MAP:
THE IMPLICIT 'THEORY OF CHANGE'

This section describes the implicit 'theory of change' in the programme based on the information contained in the logical framework prepared for the project. What is expected at the end of the process now being initiated is empowerment of rural women from marginalized communities. In turn, change is expected to be reflected along four axes, political empowerment, economic empowerment, social empowerment, and accessing entitlements.

With 'empowerment' as the destination or long term goal, several strategies are proposed. It is expected that interventions will be adaptive and responsive to emerging needs and opportunities. There are multiple components to the programme that are expected to reinforce one another, and that are likely to vary by location and social group. Key strategies are: mobilizing women, forming self-help groups, training and awareness building, and technical assistance to support livelihood strategies. It is expected that the joint impact of these strategies will shift women's prior beliefs around gender roles and norms, in a manner such that they are able to participate more actively in the political realm, with greater consciousness of their own contributions in the economic and care realm, and with self-confidence and awareness in the realm of accessing entitlements. Very importantly, their sense of self-worth will be enhanced allowing them to interrogate patriarchal constructions within their home.

What can realistically be expected to be achieved over the three-year project period are small changes rather than major transformations. The roadmap for the project allows for variations in the precise strategic choices in each location and the indicators that are used to guide the selection of interventions. The basic assumption being made is that continuous support to women in the form of access to information, making visible gendered norms, and practical support, will enable reflection and action by the women themselves.

IMPLEMENTING ORGANIZATIONS

The implementing agency is Professional Assistance for Development Action (PRADAN), a national level civil society organization working in eight states in the country. One of the pioneers of the SHG concept in India, it has to date mobilized almost 200,000 women (primarily belonging to Scheduled Tribe (ST) and Scheduled Caste (SC) social groups) into over 18,000 SHGs as mutual help based affinity groups, in seven states in the country. It is also a pioneer in rural livelihood promotion work in the country in the civil society domain. It collaborates with the government at various levels to draw on development finances and advocate policy changes. It enables poor rural communities to leverage several million rupees from the government every year to finance livelihood enhancement initiatives. Besides economic empowerment it has over the years broadened its mission to impacting the well-being of the poor families it works with. This has in part been driven by the poor women themselves, organized into SHGs and their secondary and tertiary associations. It is in this context that programming has been broadened to include other critical issues besides livelihoods and economic empowerment.

Jagori, one of the most well-known women's organizations in the country, is a partner in the project, and will bring in the conceptual framework, staff capacities and tools for training communities on women's rights and gender issues and will support women's leadership for policy advocacy. It will bring in expertise from various women's groups in the country and facilitate joint learning sessions with the community. This programme is supported by a UN organization.

Designing and Implementing a Baseline

The baseline was conducted after the broad contours of the project had already been defined and described; however, specific strategies formulated on baseline study findings could be incorporated into the project process. Institute of Social Studies Trust (ISST) developed a design, including sampling, draft questionnaires, Focus Group Discussion (FGD) guidelines, and an analysis plan, for the baseline, which were validated by the implementing organization and the strategic organization. Methods using participatory as well as quantitative ways to collect data from a randomly selected sample were used, this included a survey, FGDs and interviews. Data collection was done by the programme organizations. The training for data collection was conducted by ISST. ISST was responsible for coding and entering the data collected; and writing the baseline report. Some demographic and socio economic data was also collated by ISST from the Census and National Family Health Survey (NFHS).

The baseline study was intended to provide the information needed to assess, at a later date, the achievements of the project. It was intended to be used in tracking the progress of the project, noting challenges that may arise and be faced in the field, and providing both quantitative and qualitative data through which to understand the situation at the start of the project. Additionally, the baseline information was to help to provide a framework for planning detailed and location specific interventions.

Based on the objectives of the project the dimensions for the baseline included:

- Political and economic empowerment of women;
- Their enhanced understanding of patriarchy and gender discrimination;
- Mainstreaming learning and influencing the duty bearers to be more accountable.

Adopting a Collaborative Approach: The Motivation

Collaboration to us implies a process where decision-making as well as responsibilities for implementing the study are shared by the evaluator, and implementing agency. We decided to adopt a collaborative approach in this baseline with the assumption that the risk of bias on the part of programme personnel could be minimized, while potential gains were high. By choosing teams to collect data in areas different from those where they worked, we hoped to minimize bias. It was also felt that the risk of bias is substantially lower for a baseline, than for an endline, as the implementing organization and teams are in no way responsible for the situation at the start of the project. The socio cultural differences (language, communication, culture, access) across the poor and geographically dispersed settlements in several states in India, where the programme works with women, would have made it difficult to collect data without a strong participation of the implementing partner. We also expected the collaborative evaluation to produce richer/quality findings and the improved use of these findings by the implementing partners; and that through sharing knowledge and skills among the collaborators these experiences would contribute to building skills in evaluation.

Using a Feminist Lens

The objective of the baseline was to formulate an understanding of how gender inequality and discrimination operate in the project areas. The construction of the baseline for future evaluation was also seen as a process through which the project team would become sensitized to a context specific understanding of gender inequality and discrimination. It should be noted that this was the first time the implementing agency had undertaken a programme with a strong gender focus, and hence used the opportunity of conducting a baseline not just to gather information, but to enable discussion and clarity on alternative strategies and approaches that would best help to meet the programme goals. With these objectives, the process of constructing the baseline questionnaires, sampling and data collection was consciously reflexive and collaborative. Further, adopting this feminist approach that encourages reflexivity, introspection and contextualization in a collaborative evaluation enabled the very process of collaboration itself, added nuances to the data and helped to identify locally relevant pressure points for the programme organizations to focus on in their intervention. These benefits of the approach applied will be illustrated in the last section.

Collaborating Partners

The three collaborating partners included ISST, which is an action research organization focusing on gender and development issues; PRADAN, a national level civil society organization with a focus on livelihood promotion, which is also a pioneer of the Self Help Group approach; and Jagori, a national level feminist organization working for women's rights. Each partner brought in different perspectives into the process. ISST's main concern was to ensure that the data collected was reasonably representative of the population, and that the actual perceptions of people were captured; the implementing partner brought in immense experience of development projects and livelihood issues, as well as understanding of the project locations and questions that could be canvassed without discomfort; and the feminist organization brought in political commitment to feminist change processes.

At times, the three perspectives did differ in detail. For example, there was some discussion on what issues could be captured at the baseline and how. To illustrate, one of the programme goals was to enable women to speak about any violence they faced and to know about ways in which they could get support. Thus it would be necessary to know women's awareness of their rights, how they perceived violence against themselves and the extent to which they raised their voices against it and sought justice, at the outset. However collecting such data might have meant additional ethical processes and moreover there was some hesitation in asking such personal questions to women who were not yet programme participants. While all three parties were agreed on the importance of the issue, there were different views on whether direct questions could or should be asked on it, particularly within the format of a survey questionnaire. The feminist organization felt that it would not be an ethical practice to ask women about violence and then not support them once they expressed their views; the implementing organization's experience suggested that it was too early in the programme to canvass these questions, as supportive interventions were not yet in place; and ISST agreed that a more indirect approach might work better. Therefore, in the end it was agreed that information on violence against women would be captured through focus group discussions where women were encouraged to talk about not the violence they personally faced, but the larger issue of violence against women as it persisted in their communities, in particular its prevalence, causes, its perpetrators and the efficacy of the existing redressal system. This was felt by the feminist organization to be particularly important in order to offer appropriate services and train the staff of the implementing organizations to collect such sensitive data.

Another topic that the feminist organization suggested be included was about women's control over their bodies, their ability to negotiate spacing, etc. However, it was not measured during the baseline because the other two collaborators felt that it would be too early to talk about such a sensitive issue in communities where no intervention had been even initiated around traditional gender roles, let alone sexuality.

BASELINE METHODOLOGY: SAMPLING

The sample was distributed across districts so as to be proportional to the presence of the implementing organization as reflected in the number of SHGs in each district (in preference to the total population of the district). Stratified random sampling was used to select the sample hamlets. The first step was to list hamlets in each district along with basic information on the caste composition, years of presence of the implementing agency (fewer than or more than five years), its engagement in multiple/single activities and its distance from the block headquarters. From this list, villages were first stratified according to the remoteness of the village, and then the other characteristics. From the strata so defined one hamlet was selected from each revenue village so as to include remote and accessible locations, different caste composition, years of engagement of the implementing agency, and in this way introduce diversity in the sample. The decision on selection of the sample women members of SHGs in selected hamlets was taken by the programme organizations in consultation with the evaluation agency.

Data was collected for the baseline in four ways, sample survey, FGDs with a smaller sample, interviews with duty bearers and data collection from village records.

Survey

Given the sample of around 1200 women spread across nine districts and to ensure comparability across these, a questionnaire-based survey was conducted with each sample SHG, based on the log frame and areas in which it was expected that an intervention would be made in the coming three to four years. The challenge in designing the questionnaire was that of capturing the qualitative question: 'what is women's current level of awareness and attitude regarding their rights?' Below is an extract from the first draft of the more traditional survey schedule, which includes the questions that were formulated to capture women's awareness and exercise of their right to vote:

Do you have a voter identity card?
- Yes
- No
99. No response

Did you vote in the elections that were held last?
- Yes
- No
99. No response

If you did vote, did you decide to vote for the candidate of your choice on your own or were you guided in that decision by others?

• Own decision	2. Household decision	3. Spouse decided	4. Father/ father-in-law decided	5. Caste/ community decision
6. Had to vote according to the village leaders' direction	97. Other (specify)	98. N.A.	99. No response	

This original design of the survey tool failed to meet the needs of the programme partners because it only captured women's behaviour, in this case their exercise of their right to vote, and not the reasons for this behaviour or women's awareness and attitudes regarding gender and their rights.

After discussions with the programme partners ISST arrived at the final questionnaire. This version was designed to give an indication of the levels of awareness, attitudes and behaviour through a ranking. Ranks were averaged across SHGs/villages/districts, and across themes, to give us a baseline for each district and for each indicator as well as overall, so as to provide a point for comparison at the endline.

To illustrate, below is an extract from the final questionnaire that includes the questions that were posed to survey participants to capture women's awareness and exercise of their right to vote:

Did you vote in the elections that were held last?	Yes
If you did vote, were you guided in that decision by others or did you vote on your own? (*guided by family, neighbours, villagers, party workers, etc.*)	The whole village decided that one person will stand for Sarpanch from our village
If you did not vote, what was the reason?	N.A.
If your vote was guided by others or you could not vote, what can be done to address the above reasons and enable your vote?	No response

Based on a woman's responses, the investigator ranked her on a scale of one to five using the ranking below:

Did not vote OR did not know how to vote	Wanted to vote but was unable to vote due to lack of voter ID or ration card or other identification	Wanted to vote but was not allowed to vote by family or others in the village, disability, other reasons like Maoist groups, etc; OR compelled to vote by family, party, villagers; OR cast her vote but not based on her decision	Cast her vote based on her decision	Voted for the candidate of her choice, or chose not to vote because does not like the candidate and sees no benefit of electing him/her, and is politically aware and has thought about problems and how to address them
1	2	3	4	5

In this manner, this set of questions and the ranking enabled an understanding not only of women's present status on their awareness and exercise of their right to vote, but also of all the reasons for women's present behaviour. Moreover, it also captured whether and what thought these women had been able to give to how their vote could be enabled.

OTHER DATA

Data was also collected through interviews with a sample of duty bearers (Pradhan, BDO, District Collector, SDM, Anganwadi, ANM, ASHA and SHO). FGDs with a smaller sample of women were also conducted to get information on some issues that could not be incorporated in the survey, such as violence, marriage, disputes in the village, and alcoholism and gambling. Preliminary information from and experiences during the survey were used to inform FGD questions. FGDs with men were also contemplated, but were not conducted finally. Information was collected about records of sample villages.

In addition, notes from and discussions with the field team that collected the data were very important to be able to understand what the practical limitations of the whole exercise were and what the important issues were that needed to be kept in mind to understand and that could inform the programme, but were not being captured appropriately. This improved understanding not only informed the analysis of data and the formulation of recommendations, but also our future evaluations. These learnings and how they were applied will be discussed in the next section.

The overall design that informed the baseline largely corresponds to the prospective evaluation. Gertler et al (2011:13) define prospective evaluation as one that is developed at the same time as the programme is being designed, and is built into programme implementation. In such an evaluation baseline data are collected prior to programme implementation.

Implications for Evaluation Theory and Practice:
Challenges and Value Add

We conclude with a candid discussion on the challenges all collaborators had to overcome and the benefits of the approach that made this exercise worth everyone's while.

As already established, the main rationale for adopting the feminist collaborative approach was that it enabled an understanding of gender in the context of very poor and geographically dispersed settlements across several states in India, with accompanying socio cultural differences, that is, the continuous engagement of the implementing partner helped to check unrealistic formulations of questions.

Planning for the Evaluation

Adopting a feminist collaborative approach in evaluation of development interventions has its own advantages as well as challenges to overcome. One of the challenges we faced in this collaborative evaluation of a women-focused development intervention was in planning the evaluation process, which arose from a lack of understanding among the collaborators, the evaluator and the implementing partners, of what the other's work entailed. The implementing partners did not completely understand the time needed to be invested in such a collaborative process, and the evaluators were not able to anticipate the amount of time that would be available to the implementing partners for evaluation activities. This was an important learning that continues to inform our evaluations thereafter, in which we invest more in explaining upfront the process and demands of such collaborative evaluations to the programme partners and in understanding what they can invest in it, as well as build in more time for the back and forth and discussions that such collaboration entails.

Practitioners Investigate

Some of the contradictions that developed through the collaborative process of evaluation were a result of the practitioners adopting the role of investigators. It was observed that the practitioners were faced with an ambivalence in taking on the role of an investigator that tends to entail more distanced interaction with the community (even though it may be less than in a completely quantitative survey), given that their training and instinct was to organize people and develop actionable projects, rather than simply recording responses. The practitioners-turned-investigators had to constantly refrain from slipping into an action mode while trying to probe for answers to the survey or focus group discussion questions. There was also a certain level of discomfort among them with non-response to questions since, as they shared, they were accustomed to facilitating people into challenging their realities and articulating their needs and priorities. A strategy ISST employed to try and address this ambivalence among the practitioners was to explain during the training for data collection not just the methodology but also the rationale behind each of the steps to enable the practitioners-turned-investigators to internalize a researcher's role.

Another internal conflict that the practitioners-turned-investigators faced was the ethical dilemma that might surface if their responsibility as investigators meant that they ought not to engage with the issues articulated by the participants until the investigation/discussion was through. Moreover the programme itself had yet to put in place appropriate support services etc. After discussion it was agreed that all cases of violence were to be referred and supported and on this point it was agreed that data collection would not become an excuse for inaction.

Engaging the PRADAN team in data collection also helped them learn how to dialogue around women's issues and value women's statements, which was critical to the following four years of the intervention.[1] Before the baseline the team had always been the repository of knowledge and women the recipients of knowledge.

VALID AND USEFUL FINDINGS

This baseline study was a learning experience in many ways. The implementing agency had deep experience of livelihood promotion and was seeking to learn how to systematically address gender issues in ongoing work. The feminist agency was a mentor in this process. ISST's role was to develop a suitable design and analysis plan.

The collaboration that developed can be described, in retrospect, as a 'feminist collaborative evaluation'. A feminist understanding suggests that we all carry our own biases into the evaluation process, and that it is better to acknowledge them and state them upfront. Our experiences, similar to Brandon's (1998: 326-28), suggest that the reflexivity such methodology allows, enabled the production of more valid and useful findings through a contextualization of data that took place with the involvement of different stakeholders, and through a balancing of the evaluator bias against the stakeholder bias, in our case the implementing partners/programme personnel. Further, by engaging different stakeholders, the approach lowered the 'evaluator bias', for instance it checked our (ISST) tendency to try and fit women's realities into pre-conceived frameworks offering explanations of how gender and related discrimination operate.

Many participants in the baseline study did not understand some words that were used in the survey and FGDs or participants from different areas understood some words differently; and without the engagement of the implementing partners we may not have been able to identify these. 'Injustice' was one such concept that did not mean anything to the participants; and it was through our interaction with the implementing partners that we realized that this word needed to be deconstructed and illustrated for the investigation. 'Asset' was one word, the understanding of which varied across states. To participants in one district only something newly acquired qualified as an asset, whereas participants in other districts also counted kitchen utensils as assets.

Interrogating Categories

The approach employed, by engaging the implementing partners in the evaluation process, helped strengthen the programme team's understanding of gender and inclusion.[2] Before their involvement in this process, the lens the team used was of savings and credit, and livelihood promotion. Also, they were alert to caste-wise differences, but not to gender. How women are embedded in the household, in social relations, were aspects that had not really been considered. It was through this evaluation that we found that while over half of all women express awareness of the importance of their productive and reproductive work to the household, this is not accompanied by an ability to question the gender division of and gender discrimination in labour, to influence expenditure decisions or control over household assets.

Women's understanding of patriarchy and gender discrimination was also found to be low, it was seen that some aspects are more resistant to change than others. There was a greater willingness to acknowledge that girls as well as boys should study, go to school, that household chores should be shared by men and women, that women should have the right to control over their own earnings – even though meekness was seen as a virtue for girls. But on more fundamental issues around power and sexuality, respondents were reluctant to change the existing balance of power – thus a dominant majority agreed that menstruating women were 'impure', men must eat first, have the right to demand obedience and the right to beat their wives, and so on. Therefore, by strengthening the team's understanding of how gender operates in their regions this feminist collaborative process enabled the team to look at livelihood promotion as part of a larger intervention. Moreover, since the baseline questionnaire was designed collaboratively the PRADAN team continued to use the scale that was used to generate these findings for an annual measurement of women's attitude towards patriarchy and gender discrimination in the project areas.[3]

DEVELOPING STRATEGIES FOR INTERVENTION

The feminist collaborative approach helped the collaborating partners identify particular areas and pressure points for action.[4] For instance, the small proportion of single women in their self-help groups was a detail that they had not paid attention to yet. Another key finding in one of the states was that although women appear to be active and aware voters, they show very low participation in village level governance, which is partly due to social norms limiting women's mobility in public spaces. Therefore, a recommendation to the project was to expand the scope of the self-help groups and encourage them to enter this arena *as groups*. Moreover, since the baseline was designed and conducted collaboratively the implementing team felt more ownership over these findings.

Collaborative evaluation, by engaging the implementing partners in the evaluation process, not only contributes to the process of building their skills in organization assessment and in the identification of community needs and priorities; but since the team was directly involved in designing the tools, and collecting and interpreting the data, it follows that they identify more with the recommendations. This, consequently, is expected to enhance the use of findings in detailing project strategies, even where it may be preceded by an initial resistance. Such an approach further enhances the utilization of the evaluation findings by facilitating the identification of micro issues in the implementation process and administrative mechanisms and possible ways of addressing these.

Therefore, contrary to popular belief, the challenges we find to be associated with collaborative methodologies are not those of decreased validity of findings, but those of inadequate planning that arise out of a lack of understanding among the collaborators of what the other's work entails. This limited understanding can be more generally attributed to the nascent stage that collaborative evaluation is at in India.

A collaborative approach to evaluation is justified by the conditions surrounding the evaluation, its ability to produce both richer and rigorous findings by enabling the application of mixed methods designs, and the improved use of these findings by the implementing partners. Through sharing knowledge and skills among the collaborators these experiences contribute to building the field of evaluation. And if we are to make the most of these advantages and address the challenges associated with the approach, we must begin to pay more attention to, and engage more introspectively with such designs.

Acknowledgments

Without in any way implicating them in the product, we are grateful to Madhu Khetan, PRADAN and Suneeta Dhar, Jagori for their very useful comments.

Notes

1. As shared by Madhu Khetan.
2. Validated through interviews with Madhu Khetan and Suneeta Dhar, Jagori.
3. As shared by Madhu Khetan.
4. Validated through an interview with Madhu Khetan.

References

Batliwala, S. and A. Pitman. 2010. 'Capturing Change in Women's Realities: A Critical Overview of Current Monitoring and Evaluation Frameworks and Approaches', Association for Women's Rights in Development.

Brandon, P. 1998. 'Stakeholder Participation for the Purpose of Helping Ensure Evaluation Validity: Bridging the Gap Between Collaborative and Non-collaborative Evaluations', American Journal of Evaluation 19 (3): 325–337.

Brisolara, S. 1998. 'The history of participatory evaluation and current debates in the field', New Directions for Evaluation, 80: 25–42.

Brisson, D. 2007. 'Collaborative Evaluation in A Community Change Initiative: Dilemmas Of Control Over Technical Decision Making', The Canadian Journal of Program Evaluation 22 (2): 21–39.

Cooperrider, David L. and Suresh Srivastava. 1987. 'Appreciative Inquiry In

Organizational Life', *Research in Organizational Change and Development*, 1: 129–169.

Cousins, J.B. et al. 1996. 'Collaborative Evaluation in North America: Evaluators' Self-reported Opinions, Practices, and Consequences', *Evaluation Practice* 17 (3): 207–26.

Fetterman, D.M. 1996. 'Empowerment Evaluation: An Introduction to Theory and Practice', in Fetterman D.M. et al (eds.) *Empowerment Evaluation: Knowledge and Tools for Self-assessment and Accountability*. Thousand Oaks: Sage Publications.

Gertler et al. 2011. 'Impact Evaluation in Practice', The World Bank, Washington D.C.

Hay, K. 2010. 'Evaluation Field Building in South Asia: Reflections, Anecdotes, and Questions', *American Journal of Evaluation* 31(2): 222–231.

Hay, K., R. Sudarshan and E. Mendez (eds.) 2012. Special Issue: 'Evaluating Gender and Equity', *Indian Journal of Gender Studies* 19 (2), New Delhi: Sage Publicaitons.

Kabeer, N. 1999. 'Resources, Agency, Achievement: Reflections on measurement of women's empowerment', *Development and Change* Vol. 30, 435–464.

O'Sullivan, R.G. and A. D'Agostino. 2002. 'Promoting Evaluation through Collaboration: Findings from Community-based Programs for Young Children and their Families' *Evaluation* 8 (3): 372–387.

Patton, M.Q. 2008. *Utilization-focused Eevaluation*, 4th edition, Thousand Oaks, CA: Sage Publications.

Podems, D. 2010. 'Feminist Evaluation and Gender Approaches: There's a Difference?' *Journal of Multidisciplinary Evaluation* Vol. 6 (14), August.

Scriven, M. 1996. 'Types of Evaluation and Types of Evaluators', *Evaluation Practice*, 17 (2): 151–61.

Sielbeck-Bowen, K., S. Brisolara, D. Seigart, C. Tischler and E. Whitmore. 2002. 'Exploring feminist evaluation: The ground from which we rise', *New Directions for Evaluation*, 96:3–8.

6

Feminist Evaluation of a Gender-Neutral Voice Messaging Programme

Dilemmas and Methodological Challenges

RAJIB NANDI

Introduction: Why Feminist Evaluation

Gender gaps and inequalities continue to inform the characterization of India's economy and society despite the implementation of numerous programmes and policies over the years. Scholars argue that appropriate programme evaluation can bring out the inside stories about what worked and what did not and why. Such information is necessary for building new policies and programmes, The increased attention that evaluation has gained in last few years, could be used strategically to disseminate this information among policy makers (Hay et. al. 2012)

We often hear that the beneficiaries of one or other project include women. For many, this is enough to indicate that the project is gender sensitive. However, merely including women as beneficiaries does not mean projects address questions of equality, power structure and other social discriminations. This could be true also for programmes that are considered women specific and where all the beneficiaries are women. Such programmes are by default considered to be gender programmes. And yet, including women beneficiaries does not necessarily mean that the project addresses the questions of women's access to power and resources or equal social/economic treatment or recognition.

Feminist evaluation however directly questions the basic power dynamics in any project or programme. It tries to include all voices in the evaluation process. Hence it is considered as transformative by nature in bringing the hidden questions up front and in giving a voice to unheard people. Evaluation can be instrumental in bringing changes in organizational culture and policies to seriously address gender issues and marginalized groups. It can play a major role in bringing about such changes.

Programme evaluations often explore an intervention within some aspect of society and do so with a particular focus on specific human beings. Rarely simple, the situations they explore are often complicated, even complex and, more often than not, a combination of the three. Designing an appropriate evaluation that will provide empirical information in a multifaceted political, social and cultural environment, in a timely fashion and within a given budget, is challenging at best. Understanding a plethora of approaches enhances an evaluator's potential to develop a cultural, social and technically appropriate evaluation (Podems, 2014: 113–4).

Situating ISST as an Evaluating Agency

In 2012, ISST was visited by a couple of executives from one of the largest voice messaging services in India with a request to evaluate their programme which had been running for two years.

ISST, which grew out of the women's movement in India, has since 1980 been working on gender issues. Its research projects have focused on women at the lower end of the caste and class ladder, and have shown how they are highly disadvantaged in accessing education and other social and economic resources, as well as social protection and information. Indeed women at the lower rung of the ladder suffer from restrictions on physical mobility. They are at the receiving end of unequal benefits of development programmes. Over the years ISST has emerged as an important gender research centre and advocacy organization.

In 2011, ISST undertook a project to build evaluation capacity with a feminist lens or gender transformative lens among its researchers, professionals involved in programme implementation, civil society organizations, those interested in monitoring and evaluation, evaluators and donor agencies. Apart from developing a network of feminist evaluators ISST also encouraged reflective writings on gender transformative evaluations. By the middle of 2012, ISST had begun to consolidate gender transformative evaluation principles in order to apply these to their own evaluations. It was at this time that ISST was approached by the voice messaging company for an evaluation.

A Voice Messaging Service in India

The evaluation assignment that came to us was about a voice messaging service that is a free value added service on a particular mobile phone SIM card through tying up with a large mobile service provider in India. The implementing agency was to disseminate five pre-recorded voice messages in a day. Each of the messages was a minute long. The messages were delivered in the local language – or more accurately, the dominant state language. The content of these messages broadly focused on agriculture, animal husbandry, climate, market information, health, education, women's empowerment, financial inclusion, and government schemes.

The rural subscribers of that particular SIM card would get five calls a day from the implementing agency. A typical call would be like this:

> Good morning, I'm speaking from XX organization. Today we would like to provide you information on scholarship schemes for the students from BPL households. The scheme will provide a monthly scholarship of Rs 200 to schoolgoing students up to the age group of 15 years belonging to BPL category. The enrolled student also will get an amount of Rs 1000 each year at the beginning of the academic year. Both boys and girls between the ages of 9 and 14 years can apply for this scholarship. Please collect the required application papers from your school and get the form attested by your panchayat pradhan. Don't forget to attach your BPL ration card along with your application papers. For more information, please contact the school or the panchayat office in your village. Please dial 0 00 to listen the message again. Dial 111 to talk to our help centre. Have a good day.

The mobile service provider also made provision for the message to be listened to several times if needed. The implementing agency had put a helpline facility in place. The end-user could call the help centre to find out more. At the time of the evaluation, there were 1.5 million active subscribers of this service across 18 states in India. The implementing agency was in charge of SIM distributing and marketing, selection and development of content, forming groups and communities of subscribers at the regional level and providing helpline experts for further explanation of the issue to the subscriber, if required.

The mobile service provider or the technical support agency had the responsibility of manufacturing the SIM, providing all kinds of technical support in delivering the message to the subscriber and generating technical data on usage of the service for the implementing agency from time to time.

Description of Responsibilities

Implementing Agency	Mobile Service Provider
• SIM distribution/marketing	• Providing technical support
• Selection and development of content	• Manufacturing the SIM
• Forming groups/ user communities	• Delivering the voice message
• Helpline experts/helpline support	• Generating data on usage and providing data to IA

Broad Objectives

The programme objectives were to 'empower farmers and people living in rural India with pertinent and high quality information and services, through affordable communication networks, in a sustainable manner. To work concertedly to develop content and services which will improve informed decision-making by people living in Indian villages.'

The implementing agency, a part of a large farmers' cooperative in India, has been formed with an exclusive mandate to design, develop, source, and supply state of the art, economical, rural communication with value addition of content and services. Their focus was to take advantage of the latest in technology to address several issues faced by the farmer due to lack of information. Cooperative societies formed the core of the strategy and were enabled to act as catalysts for promoting these services and products in an economically viable manner.

The implementing agency had a long-term perspective in launching this programme. The broad objectives of the voice message service were part of the mandate of the implementing agency to extend IT enabled services in rural India. More specifically the idea was to disseminate high quality information using technology with an understanding that relevant and timely information would lead to informed decision-making. The ultimate goal was to enhance opportunities for livelihoods among rural communities and eventually to empower them.

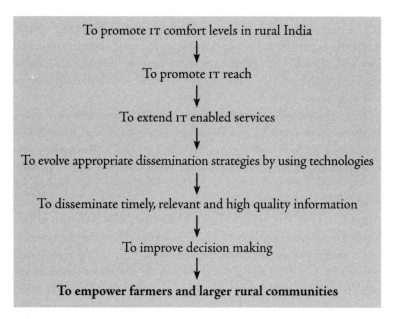

OBJECTIVES OF THE EVALUATION

The primary purpose of the evaluation was to provide the implementing agency and its partner organizations with useful information, analysis and recommendations, thereby enabling the implementing agency to engage in more effectively implementing the voice message service programme. It was assumed that, using the primary data collected from the primary users of the service, the evaluation process would be able to provide an assessment of the service by its stakeholders.

The implementing agency wished to engage ISST to evaluate the programme in two states, Punjab and Rajasthan, in order to get direct feedback from the actual users, primarily on (i) quality, timeliness, usefulness of the content; (ii) impact and effectiveness of the programme; (iii) further need and future expectations, (iv) to understand and enhance the use of the service in order to retain existing users and bring new users; (v) to know how to reach others who may need the information; and (vi) what improvements to make in order to reach others who may need the service and be more inclusive.

IA's Perception of the Programme and the Users

Initial discussions with the key officials in the implementing agency, and a thorough perusal of the documentation and materials provided by them, allowed the ISST team to get a sense of the agency's view of the programme and the users, more specifically those the programme was targeting.

ISST researchers noticed a strong gender bias in the perception of the implementing agency. A particular SIM card was marketed by the agency in the rural areas of 18 states in India. The agency also marketed and advertised this SIM in kisan melas in different parts of the country. However, the way the marketing was strategized, made it very evident that men were its primary targets. A follow up discussion with the agency clarified that they believed that mobile phones were used only by men (in rural India). The second major bias was a strong perception on the part of the implementing agency that agriculture is a male domain and women do not play any significant role in decision-making. As the implementing agency was a sister concern of an agricultural cooperative, their primary target was the farmers and their families. However, it was found that their strong bias deliberately excluded women from the target group. To include women in the programme the implementing agency constituted a few special women farmers' groups in Andhra Pradesh and Tamil Nadu. These comprised women vegetable growers of Andhra and fishing women communities of Tamil Nadu. The focussed communities would receive special messages geared to their requirements. Another strong perception was that women – who were not seen as primary subscribers – could in any case receive information that would be passed on to them by men. For example, information on health, which might be useful for the women, could be passed to them by their husbands.

ISST's Analysis of the Programme

Accessible information linked to one's occupation and other relevant social and economic aspects of life through telecommunication can be very essential for rural society in general and for small and marginal farmer households in particular. For the successful dissemination of the necessary information to the rural community, there are three main conditions to be fulfilled:

1. The content must be relevant for social and economic development. It must be easy to understand.
2. The information must reach everyone who needs it regardless of his/her social group, regional location, economic class or gender. The programme must be designed as an inclusive one and should not be exclusive or based on preconceived notions.
3. There must be a proper monitoring and feedback facility and an evaluation of the service at regular intervals.

Unlike small/marginal farmers, the large farmers have strong asset bases (economic, social and political) and can easily get farm related information through various sources. For any ICT programme to be successful, it becomes necessary to target small/marginal farmers as its primary stakeholders. Further, access to ICT becomes more important when, in the absence of a male member, the farm management is done by a woman. Therefore, digital (in relation to telecommunication) equality is a must in rural areas to reap the benefits provided by this service. In other words, there should be no digital divide on the basis of gender or scale. This latter effort towards women farmer inclusiveness will help move towards a digital gender divide free rural community.

The effectiveness of a programme depends on the geographical reach and information value for the listeners of the voice messages delivered. Such information can enhance listeners' knowledge on subjects like agriculture, animal husbandry, weather, input use, government schemes and skill development in any related aspect of livelihood. The majority of people in the rural sector are engaged in agriculture and allied activities; agriculture is a sector which is most vulnerable because of its dependence on rain and the general weather conditions. For this reason a voice message service through mobile phones to individual listeners which provides information on the weather, crop diseases, fertilizer use, product prices, input prices, etc., can prove to be the most effective medium for taking appropriate action. Not only can the mobile phone have a wider reach, but it is also an economically suitable option for farmers. In the long run farmers can work to make agriculture not only a viable income option but also a profit-making economic activity.

Past evaluation experiences from all over the world have shown that evaluation can be an essential tool to ensure that gender issues do not fade away during designing and implementing a programme. Evaluation can also be a key exercise for continuous improvement and accountability for the advances and challenges to gender equality (Rodríguez et al., 1999). In particular, gender sensitive evaluation frameworks, compared to other models of evaluation characterized by their 'gender-blindness' or so called 'gender neutrality', are critical to measure changes in gender relations, to foster greater and better equality between men and women; and thus, to promote equity as a strategy in development practice (Murguialday et al., 2008).

The use of the 'gender analysis' in evaluation generally means examining a set of gender dimensions throughout the phases of the evaluation. These are manifested in different forms in the family, the community, the market and the state and explain how deep gender inequality is entrenched and how it is structural. Gender and development theory and practice underlines a range of dimensions of gender analysis: from the sexual division of labour, men and women's private and public roles, the use and control of women's bodies, practical and strategic gender needs, how time is used by men and women, unequal access and control over resources, benefits and services for the community (Hunt and Brouwers, 2003; UNDP, 2001; Miller and Razavi, 1998; and Moser, 1995; Espinosa, 2013).

A feminist lens in analysis also focuses on other forms of inequality alongside its relationship with gender inequality. Gender inequality is often accentuated or softened depending on its intersection with other forms of inequality based on class, caste, ethnicity, educational level, religion and so on. In this sense, gender inequality is to be understood within a framework of multiple inequalities. (Espinosa, 2013) Overall, as indicated by Gonzalez and Murguialday, the incorporation of gender analysis in the evaluation involves a transformation of its philosophy and, thus, the adjustment of the tools and assessment processes (2004: 2).

As an evaluation organization ISST found serious flaws in the design and implementation of the programme, even before they went into the field. ISST also had some questions relating to the design and implementation. Their analysis of the situation was therefore different:

- to look at the rural community as a homogenous category could be totally misleading, as there are people/groups at the margins of rural society. The formation of a few isolated focussed communities does not resolve the issue.
- Gender blindness in a development paradigm can lead to the collapse of a programme.
- The cultural politics of difference can be coherently combined with the social politics of equality and economic injustices.
- Unequal access to information might create a sharper digital divide in society.
- Information should be regarded as a resource.
- By non-recognition of women's role in agriculture, other decision-making processes and by excluding them, the implementing agency was undervaluing women's roles and also perpetuating gender inequality.

The Evaluators' Dilemma

ISST has never evaluated a programme which is both gender insensitive and gender non-responsive. Once we had read the project documents and held some meetings with the top implementation team members, our evaluation team was in something of a dilemma:

should we accept the assignment or turn it away because it was gender blind?

The first issue for us was: if we did decide to take up the challenge, would we be able to develop an evaluation methodology with a gender lens for a totally non-gender responsive programme? There were other challenges too. First, to able to fulfil the expectations of the implementing agency. Second, to bring a feminist lens in designing the methodology in order to bring out some extra and relevant information and to use this to convince the implementing agency to redesign the programme as a gender responsive one in order to fulfil their broad objectives of empowering rural communities.

The questions that confronted us were how to present our analysis of the programme and how to introduce our evaluation approach. Sielback-Bowen, Brisolara, Tischler, Whitmore (2002) note that the word feminist invokes multiple responses. Using it may cause offence, and could hinder an academic and practical discussion on the approach. However, more commonly known evaluation approaches tend to use words like utilization-focussed, empowerment, etc., which do not immediately elicit defensive responses. From our past experience, we knew that when introducing the feminist evaluation approach, people start making judgments about what comprises feminism. The biggest challenge was to resist the attempt to discuss feminism at an academic or theoretical level, and instead emphasize the more acceptable issues, for example that men and women should have equal access to opportunities in all spheres of life, and put the agenda of equality on the table.

Both Pattons (2008) and Podems (2014) argued similarly. Podems argues that in order to bring feminist evaluation into the mainstream it is important to dissolve the widely held belief that you need to be labelled as feminist in order to implement feminist evaluation. Pattons writes that including 'feminist' and 'evaluation' in the same title is a challenge. Both words often evoke initial apprehensions or other strong emotions. Podems found that in order to address the challenge of labelling the evaluation approach, it helps to remove the feminist label. For example, introducing various feminist evaluation ideas while not using the word feminist can result in an approach that produces a useful process, a process that can lead to evaluation findings that the primary user finds appropriate and informative. Applying the feminist approach more directly can have a potential backlash or can result in its non-use. (Podems, 2014: 116–7)

In the present context it was more appropriate to bring out the added value of the particular evaluation approach that we intended to apply. However, we were aware of the consequences of hiding the labelling of feminist evaluation: if we did this, how would we bring out examples in the form of knowledge creation about feminist evaluation for wider users? Also we would be subjected to criticism for not bringing 'feminism' visibly in the forefront that was part of the evolving and upgrading of feminist evaluation over the time. Not using the 'feminist' label could also have larger implications for the approach in terms of a wider understanding of what feminist evaluation is, how it is different from common gender approaches and finally the public credibility of feminist evaluation in addressing the issues of power relations and deep rooted social discriminations.

A Feminist Evaluation Approach

Understanding the core principles of feminist evaluation is important. As Podems writes, feminist evaluation draws heavily on feminist research arguments that a story written based on a man's experience is missing half of the picture. Adding a woman's perspective enables a researcher to construct a picture with different perspectives. Feminist evaluation is often described as fluid, dynamic and evolving (Seigart and Brisolara, 2002, p. 2). Most feminist evaluation theorists describe the feminist approach as flexible and do not advocate a precise methodology. They define feminist evaluation as a way of thinking about evaluation without any precise approach. (Beardsley and Hughes Miller, 2002; Hirsch and Keller, 1990; Hughes 2002). Multiple definitions of feminism are another challenge. Podems finds the following best suited for feminist evaluation. 'A common belief that guides feminism is that gender bias exists systematically and is manifest in the major institutions in society.... Feminism examines the intersection of gender, race, class, and sexuality in the context of power.' (Mertens, 20015, p. 154)

Sielbeck-Bowen et al. (2002) defined the broad perspectives of feminist evaluation thus:

- Gender inequalities lead to social injustice and this is the central focus of feminist evaluation.
- Feminist evaluations are based on the understanding that gender bias is systematic and structural in social institutions.
- Feminist evaluation is a way of examining how gender and other social cleavages (race, caste, religion, sexuality, class) define and shape experience and exercise power in different contexts. This has enormous potential to contribute more deeply to development policies and programmes.
- Information/knowledge is a powerful resource in the context of the present programme.
- Evaluation is a political activity. The personal experiences, the perspectives, the characteristics of evaluation that the evaluators bring in conducting the evaluation reflect a particular political stance.

Minnich (1990) and Patton (2002) explain that feminist approaches recognize and give voice to multiple ways of knowing, including integrating reason, emotion and experience. Patton (2008) defines feminist evaluation as an approach that places a strong emphasis on processes that involve participation, encourage empowerment and advance social justice agendas.

Methodological Challenges and Limitations

After deciding to go ahead with the evaluation of this voice messaging service, we had another meeting with the implementing agency to design the broad evaluation framework and the evaluation methodology. There, more surprises were waiting for us. It had been pre-decided by the implementing agency that the present evaluation would mainly focus on a questionnaire based survey, which would be able to provide 'numbers/statistical figures' because they are 'easily readable' and 'presentable'. Therefore the implementing agency had come with a proposal of canvassing a questionnaire at the 'registered user level'.

Who is a registered user of a mobile phone? The answer is very simple – the person in whose name the SIM card is registered. During the purchase of a SIM card, an application form has to be filled by the subscriber with his/her basic data and they are required to provide a photo identity card. This can be a voter identity card, an Aadhar card, a passport, a driving licence, a bank passbook with a photo and address or a ration card with a photo etc. In many instances, it may not be possible for a woman to purchase a SIM card in her name from a male agent. Moreover, this particular SIM card was marketed in such a manner that not many women could purchase it. Also it is important to remember that in India, the original subscriber does not always use the SIM exclusively, and it can also be used by his/her family members and passed on to others who may use it as well.

ISST suggested canvassing the questionnaire at a 'user household level' rather than at the 'user level'. This suggestion was based on two reasons. First, if you move your sample base from 'registered user' to 'actual user/primary user' you perhaps may get a larger number of women in your sample. This was one way to include more women and young people. And second, by bringing the entire household in the purview of the sample, you include a number of other household members and can get their views on both mobile use and the particular service, as in rural India agriculture is more of a household occupation than a single person job. It was not difficult to convince the agency to make this 'minor' change. So a questionnaire was developed that tries to capture the household dimension of mobile use and the impact of the programme at the household level covering both men and women members. The control group was thus formed with 'non-user households' not just 'non-users' in order to include the entire household.

ISST also proposed to do focus group discussions, both with subscriber households and non-subscriber households. In addition, separate key informant interviews were also proposed. Both men and women members from user and non-user households were interviewed during the study.

A sample of 300 user households each from Punjab and Rajasthan (covering six districts across agro-climatic zones) was selected adopting a random stratified sampling technique. Selection was based on data (mobile number and address of the subscribers) provided by the implementing agency. About 150 non-user households were also selected from each state from the study villages with the help of the agency's field level workers. However, the sample does not pre-recognize the economic and other social categories of the households.

Policy Implications

USE OF MOBILE PHONE

The study found that 63.5 per cent of the population in the sample villages use mobile phones largely for making and taking calls. A higher percentage of men (70.6 per cent) use it than women (53.0 per cent). This disproves the common belief that only men use mobile phones. Interestingly both Punjab and Rajasthan are regarded as male dominated patriarchal societies. There are immense restrictions upon women in terms of their physical mobility in public spaces and gender roles are very clearly demarcated. However, it was possible for us to include existing female users as active participants in the programme, if the implementing agency wished to do so. More interesting findings were there in the young age group of up to 15 years. Here, the study found more young girls (10.7 per cent) than boys (1.5 per cent) as users of mobile phones. We argued that the chances were the study would find a larger number of women mobile users in the future. By simply not including them, the service provider was actually deepening the divide in people's future access to information related to their occupation and rural livelihoods.

ACTIVE MESSAGE LISTENERS

By including the user household, the study found that 18.6 per cent of the users of this service (not subscribers) were actually women. The registered women users were far less, almost nil at 0.3 per cent. Therefore, it shows that a good number of women are listening to those messages, though they were not included in the programme design. The study, however, found that only 20 per cent of listeners conveyed any message to anybody else. This was based on a question about how often they conveyed those messages to others in the family or the community. Therefore the assumption of the implementing agency that messages that were relevant would in any case be conveyed to the women by men does not really hold.

The study also found that both men and women users wanted to have value added services on their mobiles. A large number of men, 57.4 per cent, wished to have information on agriculture. But it is also true that in Punjab and Rajasthan 21.3 per cent women mobile users were also looking to have information on agriculture on their mobile phones. The number is not insignificant. Therefore, the implementing agency's idea that the need for agricultural information is gender related is not correct. The following table, however, shows that there are differences in the kind of information men and women require. For example, women – who have limited access to multiple information sources – require more information on health, employment, education and government schemes than men do.

People's Requirement for VAS on their Mobile Phones

Information	Men	Women
Agriculture related	57.4	21.3
Health related	11.2	37.2
Employment related	12.4	19.5
Govt. schemes etc	10.3	10.7
Education related	7.5	9.8
Any other	1.2	1.5
Total	**100.0**	**100.0**

Conclusion

Based on the findings, ISST recommended that the service provider needs to be responsive to the changing age/gender profile and should make an effort to ensure that women are included as primary users of the voice message service. ISST also recommended that this could be done by employing women as marketing and outreach agents and managers and encouraging them to develop better direct communication with women. At the same time, the nature of information being provided also needed to be changed and there needed to be more information on questions such as violence against girls and women, sexual harassment, reproductive and child health, women's rights and law and so on.

The implementing agency were happy with the evaluation report at the end. Their feedback on the initial report was encouraging and ISST's suggestions were accepted positively. We are not aware of all the changes that they brought in the second phase of the programme although we believe that some suggestions were accepted, in particular to include more women among their primary subscribers. About seventy more focused communities were formed in the next phase to include various marginal agricultural communities across the 18 states. They brought some changes in their messaging service by including other relevant social issues.

Finally I would like to say that feminist evaluation raises concerns regarding what an evaluation could be. Feminist evaluation effectively highlights the values of empowerment and social justice and is more about evaluation thinking beyond any particular evaluation approach. (See, for example, Podems, 2014; Beardsley & Hughes Miller, 2002; Hirsch & Keller, 1990; Hughes, 2002) Therefore, it could include principles and elements of other evaluation approaches. This inclusive thinking process adds extraordinary value to evaluation practice. These include wider applicability of findings and the transformative forces of the evaluation process. The present evaluation tried to draw the attention of the implementing agency towards making the programme more inclusive so that it gets closer to achieving its ultimate goal of social empowerment for all.

Acknowledgement

This essay is based on an evaluation experience conducted at the Institute of Social Studies Trust, New Delhi by the author along with Gurpreet Singh and Shalini Rani. The author acknowledges the contributions of Prof. A. Vaidyanathan and Ratna M. Sudarshan in designing the evaluation methodology. The author also acknowledges the comments and suggestions made by the members of ISST's feminist evaluation network on an earlier version of this essay.

References

Beardsley, R. and Hughes Miller, M. 2002. 'Revisioning the Process: A Case study in Feminist Program Evaluation', in Seigart, D. and S. Brisolara (eds.) *Feminist Evaluation: Explorations and Experiences*, New Directions for Evaluations (96), 57–70.

Espinosa, J. 2013. 'Moving towards gender sensitive evaluation? Practices and challenges in International development Evaluation', *Evaluation*, vol. 19, No. 2, 171–82.

Gonzalez, G.L. and M.C. Murguialday. 2004. 'Evaluate with gender.' in *Cuadernos Bakeaz*, No. 66, December. Policy Cooperation. Bilbao: Bakeaz.

Hay. K., R.M, Sudarshan, and E. Mendez. 2012. 'Why a Special Issue on Evaluating Gender and Equity?' *Indian Journal of Gender Studies*, Vol. 19, no. 2, June 2012. 179–86.

Hirsch, M. and E.F. Keller. 1990. 'Conclusion – Practising Conflict in Feminist Theory', in M. Hirsch and E.F. Keller (eds.) *Conflicts in Feminism* New York: Routledge, pp. 370–85.

Hughes, C. 2002. *Key Concepts in Feminist Theory and Research*, London: Sage Publications.

Hunt, J. and R. Brouwers. 2003. 'Review of Gender and Evaluation', Final Report to DAC Network on Development Evaluation. DAC Evaluation Series. OECD.

Mertens, D. 2005. 'Feminism', in S. Mathison (ed.) *Encyclopaedia of Evaluation* Thousand Oaks, CA: Sage Publications, p. 154.

Miller, C. and S. Razavi. 1998. 'Gender Analysis: Alternative Paradigms', in PNUD (ed.) *Gender in Development* Monograph Series, no. 6. Geneva: UNDP.

Minnich, E. 1990. *Transforming Knowledge* Philadelphia: Temple University Press.

Moser, C. 1995. *Gender Planning and Development Theory, Practice and Training* New York: Routledge and Kegan Paul.

Murguialday *et al.*, 2008. 'A step further: gender impact assessment.' Barcelona: Cooperacció and AECID.

Patton, M. 2002. *Qualitative Research and Evaluation Methods* Thousand Oaks, CA: Sage Publications.

Patton, M. 2008. *Utilization Focused Evaluation* (4th edition). Thousand Oaks, CA: Sage Publications.

Podems, Donna. 2014. 'Feminist Evaluation for Nonfeminists', in Sharon Brisolara, Denise Seigart and Saumitra Sengupta (eds.) *Feminist*

Evaluation and Research: Theory and Practice, New York: Guilford Press, pp. 113–42.

Rodríguez, G. *et al.* 'Taking the pulse of gender: Monitoring and evaluation systems that sensitive to gender', San Jose, Costa Rica: World Conservation Union and Arias Foundation for Peace and Human Progress.

Seigart, D. and S. Brisolara, 2002. 'Editor's notes' in Seigart, D. and S. Brisolara (eds.) 'Feminist Evaluation: Explorations and Experiences', *New Directions for Evaluations* (96), 1–2.

Sielback-Bowen, K.D., S. Brisolara, D. Seigart, C. Tischler, E. Whitmore 2002. 'Exploring Feminist Evaluation: The ground from where we rise', in Seigart, D. and S. Brisolara (eds.) *Feminist Evaluation: Explorations and Experiences*, New Directions for Evaluations (96), 3–8.

UNDP. 2001. Gender analysis: Learning and Information Pack. Gender in Development Programme.

7

Strengthening Systems for Prevention of Child Marriage

Insights from a Feminist Evaluation

RENU KHANNA and ENAKSHI GANGULY THUKRAL

Introduction

Child marriage in India has continued despite social reform movements and legislation against it. In 1929 India got its first law against child marriage, the Sharda Act. The Act prohibited the marriage of girls below 15 years and of boys below 18 years. After independence, the Sharda Act was renamed the Child Marriage Restraint Act. In 1978 the law was amended and the age of marriage was raised to 18 for girls and 21 for boys. In 2006, the Government of India passed the Prohibition of Child Marriage Act, 2006 (PCMA). The amended law is clear in its commitment to end the practice of child marriage, and moves away from mere restraint to complete prohibition. This legislation has enabling provisions to prohibit child marriages, protect and provide relief to victims and enhance punishment for those who abet, promote or solemnize such marriages.

The Integrated Child Protection Scheme (ICPS) introduced in 2009-10 is an additional mechanism to address child marriage as a child protection issue. A draft National Strategy on Prevention of Child Marriage (2013) and a draft National Plan of Action on Prevention of Child Marriage propose convergent and multi-dimensional strategic interventions. Several national level policies formulated since 2000 (the National Population Policy 2000, the National Youth Policy 2003, the National Adolescent Reproductive and Sexual Health Strategy) have advocated delaying the age of marriage and the age of conceiving the first child. Programmes such as SABLA and Beti Bachao, Beti Padhao are also geared to raising awareness about the issue and promoting preventive action. Annexure 1 presents the details of the Child Marriage Prohibition Act (2006). Annexure 2 describes components of the Integrated Child Protection Scheme.

Despite all these measures, child marriages continue. The Prohibition of Child Marriage Act, 2006, remains unenforced in most places. Child marriages continue to be looked upon as a social evil instead of a crime. It does not help that the Right to Education is guaranteed to children only up to the age of 14. Girls who finish elementary education are 'prime targets' for child marriage.

There are several reasons for child marriages. The main one seems to be control over a girl's sexuality. There is a fear of daughters getting into relationships and eloping with their boyfriends. There is also fear of not finding a suitable match later, once the girl is a little older. Families who face financial insecurity want to send the girl away, so they have one mouth less to feed. Dowry increases once the girl gets older. Over the years, trafficking of under-age girls for marriage, especially to areas and states where the sex ratio is falling (such as in parts Haryana, Rajasthan and Gujarat), has become a practice, thereby increasing violence against girls.

Child marriage results in inter-generational socio-economic impact on education, health and empowerment. It is both a symptom of and a contributor to gender inequality.[1] With early marriage and additional family responsibilities, children drop out of education; they are also deprived of any scope for skill development by taking away their right of choice and imposing family responsibilities beyond their age and capacity. Many times, girls become vulnerable to early marriages in the first place because of a 'lack of alternatives and constructive opportunities. Educational opportunities, which could support daughters' autonomy or employment skills, are frequently denied to girls, or the girls are withdrawn from school because of marriage. In addition, (inadequate) access to schools (especially) in rural areas, makes parents fearful of their daughters' commute and the potential for sexual assault or involvement with men.'[2] Child marriage leads to high maternal mortality rates, premature delivery and high mother/infant mortality and morbidity rates, as well as a greater susceptibility to gender based violence and sexual abuse and trafficking, increased number of miscarriages and low birth weight babies. Complications related to pregnancy and childbirth are among the leading causes of death worldwide for adolescent girls between the ages of 15 and 19.[3] To complicate matters further, 'if and when young women suffer from illness or die as a result of pregnancy and childbirth, this is rarely attributed to young age.'[4] Although girls are more vulnerable and affected much more, early marriage also impacts boys, vesting them with the early responsibility of fatherhood and having to take on economic responsibilities at a young age.

While social attitudes are an important reason for the continuance of child marriage, there are other reasons that contribute to its existence in India. Firstly, despite the formulation of laws, implementation mechanisms at the state and district level are weak and inadequate. In addition, gaps in such formulation, a lack of clarity about roles and inadequate capacities of the people implementing the various laws and programmes have led to their non-implementation.

A Critique of the PCMA

Several experts have commented on the contents of the PCMA and found it to be gender discriminatory and patriarchal, and something that allows religious forces to violate children's human rights. For example, the setting of different ages of marriage for girls and boys, 18 and 21 years respectively, can be construed as gender discrimination because Article 14 of the Constitution clearly states that all are equal before law.[5] Also, while the PCMA prohibits marriage of a girl under the age of 18 and a boy under the age of 21, child marriages per se continue to be legally valid unless one of the parties to the marriage wishes to nullify it. The Act defines 'child' and 'minor' differently. While child marriage is legally valid and can be nullified only after either party files a petition for an annulment, the law declares marriage of a 'minor' null and void if such marriage is solemnized by the use of force, kidnapping and trafficking and is a result of violation of an injunction order preventing the marriage. The law does not give a clear unambiguous message that can make implementation in the field easier.

The law also does not provide enabling conditions and support for girls who might choose to get out of the child marriage. A girl can file a petition for a decree of nullity within two years of attaining majority, that is, till she is 20 years old. A married girl will need either an agency, access to the court and/or support from the family if she wants an annulment. The custody of minor girls is also a major area of concern. If the girl is above the age of 16, which can also be considered as the age of discretion/maturity, she can refuse to stay with her parents. What kind of support is available for her if she chooses this path? The implementation framework for this clause is not satisfactory at this point in time.

There are several other contradictions between related laws. For example under the Protection of Children from Sexual Offences (POCSO) Act, 2012, sex with a girl under the age of 18 is considered rape. Boys under the age of 18, as well as older men, in consensual sexual relationships with girls aged below 18 can get booked for rape. However, if the same acts occur under the shroud of marriage they are considered legal under the IPC (Section 375 exception 2) and personal (religious) laws. According to the explanation in Section 375 of the IPC, sexual intercourse by a man with his wife without her consent or will was not rape if she was above 10 years old in 1860, which was later raised to 15 in 1949, the age that remains current today. Muslim personal law recognizes the age of puberty as the age of marriage and unless proved otherwise, the age of puberty is presumed to be 15 years for both girls and boys. The Hindu Marriage Act lays down 15 as the age of marriage for girls and 18 as the age for boys. It requires the consent of guardians for girls in the 15-18 age bracket. What is more, Section 18 of the Hindu Marriage Act provides for punishment of the bride and groom if a marriage is solemnised between a bride below 18 years or a bridegroom below 21 years. It however does not specify that failure to comply with the minimum age is grounds for making the marriage void or voidable. Hindu law gives a special provision for divorce if a girl has been married before the age of 15. However, legally, divorce and annulment are separate. Therefore, there is considerable lack of clarity.

Another contradiction is that no minor can be a guardian except under the cases of child marriage where the minor girl's guardian would be her minor husband. In addition, while defining the age of majority as 18, the Indian Majority Act also lays down that its provisions will not affect 'religion or religious rites and usages of any class of citizens of India'. It thus allows a varied definition of the age of majority based on religion. So here there is confusion between the PCMA, the Indian Majority Act and personal laws. All these, and other points of confusion and ambiguity, lead to practical difficulties in implementation and enforcement of the law.

THE PROJECT

This is the context in which Haq: Centre for Child Rights developed a three-year project proposal 'Strengthening Existing Systems for Prevention of Child Marriage'. This was a collaborative project with MV Foundation in Andhra Pradesh and Jabala Action Research Organization in West Bengal. The overall goal of the project was to work towards the prevention of child marriage by ensuring accountability of the child protection systems through implementation of the Prohibition of Child Marriage Act, 2006. The idea was to develop and demonstrate a model for addressing child marriage by strengthening them and enabling collaborations between existing legal and governance mechanisms. The project proposed to do this through strengthening of the existing state mechanisms/structures/ institutions through training and monitoring of their functions, and holding them accountable; interventions at the community level to prevent child marriages and change social norms; networking and collaborating with other organizations engaged in similar issues and policy advocacy.

The collaborative interventions with MV Foundaiton were conducted in three gram panchayats in two identified mandals of Warangal and Mahbubnagar districts in Telangana. With Jabala, the interventions were in two blocks each in Murshidabad and Birbhum districts of West Bengal.

SITUATIONAL ANALYSIS

In this section, we describe the context in which the project was implemented. This, we hope, will help us to understand why child marriages take place in the project areas. While there are issues that are peculiar to the states, what is common is that there is no official or detailed policy for rehabilitation of 'child marriage survivors' and there are issues with the implementation of the Right to Free and Compulsory Education Act (2009) which has a potential area for advocacy from the perspective of the prevention of child marriages.

More than half the girls in West Bengal get married before 18. West Bengal ranks sixth in the country with a child marriage rate of 54 per cent. The selected districts have a very high rate of child marriage. Apart from being listed as a backward district on the Human Development Index (HDI) Murshidabad ranks 17th out of 19 districts, and has also been classified as one of the most backward districts in India by the Sacchar Committee Report (2006). Apart from child marriage, Murshidabad has remained one of the source areas for trafficking of children for labour, marriage and prostitution. A long and porous border with Bangladesh facilitates cross border trafficking. Birbhum is a district with both minority and tribal populations. Because of the presence of Tagore and Shantiniketan, it has been a cultural hub of Bengal for almost a century since the 1800s. And yet child marriage and other regressive social and cultural practices remain.

The Kanyashri Scheme is said to be the Chief Minister's favourite scheme, and one of the major mechanisms in the state to delay the marriages of girls. Everything has been set up to make it a success and there is also substantial budgetary provision, including a Kanyashri Day on August 14 in which *melas* etc. are organized. The girls whose marriages are stopped are on the priority list of Kanyashri beneficiaries.

Jabala has been working on issues of abuse and exploitation of children, especially child trafficking, for almost two and a half decades. They work with different stakeholders in the community, building capacities of communities – especially the adolescent girls themselves – and undertake training and advocacy on child protection issues.

When the project was initiated in 2012, the selected state was Andhra Pradesh. The state and the districts were selected because of the high incidence of child marriage. In most districts of AP more than 50 per cent of women in the age group of 18–24 were married before 18. The two selected districts for the project, Warangal and Mahbubnagar, featured on the Planning Commission's list of the 170 most backward districts in the country. Some 50.7 per cent and 58.7 per cent of women in the age group 18-24 were married before the age of 18, in Warangal and Mahbubnagar respectively (DLHS III). In June 2014 the bifurcation of the state resulted in the project area falling in Telangana. The split resulted in the formation of a new government and a number of other changes which have impacted the implementation of the project.

MV Foundation has been working on the issue of child right protection with community involvement in Andhra Pradesh for two decades now. The organization focuses on eliminating child labour as well as empowering girl children and upholding their rights.

Determinants of Child Marriage

Discussions with various persons during the field visit revealed that there were several factors that influenced the decisions of families to marry their children young. All of these need to be considered when developing a strategy to prevent child marriage. These factors are listed below.

In West Bengal, poverty and more than one daughter feature as major determinants. If a man likes a girl and asks to marry her, it is likely that the family will not have to give a big dowry. Otherwise the dowry is anything between Rs. 800,000-10,00,000. For younger girls the dowry is less. If a girl is ill, or has some ailment, she should be married off, thus transferring the liability to someone else. If there is more than one girl in a family, the first has to be married early so that the dowry for the second one can be mobilized in time. When there is an unmarried older girl in the family, people suspect that something is 'wrong' in that family.

Girls aged 13-14 are not preferred, 16-17 year olds are preferred because their bodies have matured. Societal perceptions are: older girls are not beautiful – 'chehra kharab ho gayaa hai'. Beautiful girls can get away with a smaller dowry, grooms for not so beautiful girls have to be enticed with bigger dowries. One of the Block Development

Officers (BDO) told us that dowry is a tradition that no one questions. The rates are fixed.

The 'safety' of the girls is a major reason for child marriage. The understanding of 'safety' extends to girls choosing to have boyfriends or elopement. Parents are not able to trust their daughters, they fear that they will run away and get married, so best to get her married before she does that. Parents often migrate in search of work, and anxiety about the safety of their daughters ensures that they are married. In Murshidabad we were told that before fathers migrate to Saudi Arabia, they are keen to get their 10 to 12 year old daughters married, so that they are 'safe'. Any reason is good. For example, if daughters do not do well at school, marriage is used as a solution.

Muslim Shariyat law says that on menarche a girl can be married. She is an adult at 14 and can read the Quran, so she can be married also. Imams in Beldanga block said:

> Children are growing up faster now. There is attraction, love affairs. Parents feel these can damage the family's name… Children also want to get married to the person that they have chosen…so to avoid embarrassment, parents agree. Earlier parents wanted early marriage for their daughters. Now they would rather wait – but because of Facebook and internet the young people get into relationships and so parents feel that they might as well get them married.

Most boys from poor families are unable study beyond Grade 8 or 9 because they usually need to migrate for work. If girls are educated more than boys, the fear is that they will not get grooms. Boys themselves want younger girls for their fear is that older ones may have had affairs and not be 'pure'. Those boys who have 'good' jobs actually demand bigger dowries as a prize for the security they offer the girls. Among Muslims, early marriages also happen between cousins to strengthen family bonds. But the main reason seems to be that if there is a girl, one should not lose the opportunity to set up a match.

In Telangana poverty is the reason cited for child marriage by the Yadavas in Mahbubnagar district. The Yadavas are a shepherd community and they migrate with their sheep to Andhra Pradesh. Daughters are considered a burden they want to rid themselves of and the fact that 'there will be one less mouth to feed' is a primary driver for child marriage. Also, education is not valued at all, so many children drop out or are pulled out of school.

This view was echoed by the Child Development Project Officer, who held that child marriages happen because of financial backwardness as there are too many mouths to feed and educate. According to her, parents arrange the early marriages of their daughters because 'she may do the wrong thing so it's better to get her married,' and they often think that 'we can't afford the dowry so better to dispose of her at a low dowry' or 'let her be the second or third wife because then the dowry too will be low.' Basically the attitude is that it is better to get rid of 'the burden'.

If this was the view of the Child Development Project Officer, the Warangal Joint Collector held that child marriages happen because of low female literacy, poverty, high levels of migration. The short lifespan of people, because of illicit liquor, leads to insecurity and therefore to child marriage, the attitude being to pass on the burden of the girl. This has acquired the status of a custom so people accept it without question. According to another respondent, there is a 50-60 per cent decrease in child marriage as education is increasing. Such marriages continue to happen in poor families, or those where a parent is ill or has died and the family thus becomes vulnerable.

What the Project Achieved?

A Model for Addressing Child Marriage

One of the objectives that HAQ and its partners set out to achieve was to develop a model to address child marriages through a strengthened governance system and an empowered community that could hold governance accountable. At the inception meeting for the evaluation, the team members of the three partner organizations were asked to describe the elements of the model, specifically its mechanisms and processes. The discussions resulted in the conceptualization presented in Box 1.

The model shows:

- A two pronged approach was used: (i) working with communities to (a) change mindsets and social norms around child marriage and (b) build capacities to act as pressure groups for implementation of the law and to demand accountability.

ii) to activate the mandated government structures to prevent child marriages, and promote child protection.

The processes included mapping existing opportunities, both at the community level and at the official/administrative level. At the community level, the partners found that issues relating to youth aspirations and concern for girls' safety served as helpful factors for the project. At the official/administrative level, programmes/schemes that address children (like SABALA, NRHM, ICPS, ICDS) were congruent with the goals of the project and could be leveraged for convergent action. Campaigns and mass communication were used to disseminate awareness of the provisions of the PCMA.

- The project identified key stakeholders at the community level and worked with them. These included adolescent girls' groups, parents, youth, religious functionaries who solemnize marriages and uphold religious customs and rituals, caste leaders who influence social norms, political leaders, teachers, media and other service providers. The idea was to create change agents from among the stakeholder groups who could influence the other members of that group.

- Representatives from the groups mentioned above were organized into multi stakeholder platforms like the Child Rights Protection Forum (in Telengana), or the Village Child Protection Committee or the Child Marriage Prevention Committee, many of which were later turned into or merged with Village Child Protection Committees (in West Bengal). Capacity building activities were undertaken with these committees so that they could respond appropriately to prevent child marriages, or intervene if a child marriage was imminent. These committees were then amalgamated with the Village Level Child Protection Committees mandated by the Integrated Child Protection Scheme (ICPS), once this scheme began to be implemented in the states.

- The role of the facilitator was key to make all the above happen. Wherever the outcomes were positive it was realized that certain qualities of the facilitator were significant, such as, for example, the skill to negotiate with communities, families, officials without making them feel threatened, and the ability to strike a balance between community and duty bearers.

- Finally, documentation and evidence creation was an important ingredient of the model. Authentic and participatorily generated data helped in advocacy at all levels.

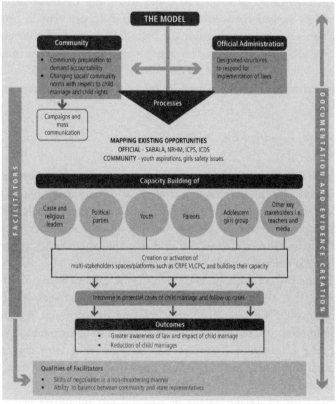

Note: CRPF- Child Rights Protection Forum; VLCPC- Village Level Child Protection Committee; CMPC- Child Marriage Prevention Committee; NRHM- National Rural Health Mission; ICPS- Integrated Child Protection Schemes; ICDS- Integrated Child Development Services

Outcomes of the Project

Increased Prevention of Child Marriages

From several sources of data (marriage data from the Imam's Kabilnama, which is the same as a Nikahnama) marriage registers, Sardere (Samajpati), Moyajjem (Purohits and Masjid Secretaries) in

West Bengal, it can be seen that there is a reduction in child marriages. The decline has been between 25 and 84 percentage points in the 12 gram panchayats that Jabala is directly intervening in. Khidirpur panchayat had 92 per cent child marriages in 2011-12 which reduced to 8.2 per cent in 2013-14.

In Telengana, between 2012 and 2014 the decrease in child marriages ranged between 61 per cent and 81 per cent in project and non-project areas through MV Foundation's work. Government officers too have noticed a decrease in child marriages even in non-project villages. The Mandal Education Officer of Amrabad told us 'child marriages have decreased by 60 per cent even in non-project villages.'

Marriages Registered with Panchayat Secretaries/Village Revenue Officers (VROs)

In both Telangana and West Bengal, marriage registers are being maintained by the panchayat secretaries and the VROs although this is only in the panchayats where the project is being implemented and is not universal to all blocks/mandals. In fact, a number of block and district officers interviewed said that that there is no system of registering marriages and this is not mandatory.

In the project areas of West Bengal, the Imams have collectively decided that they will not conduct any child marriages and have started asking for age certificates, refusing to solemnize marriages without seeing these. The age certificates are also being retained along with the kabilnamas. They are actively promoting later marriages through the Friday namaaz, events known as Jalsas, house to house visits, and influencing their colleagues.

Similarly in Telangana the priests will not solemnize marriages without seeing birth certificates or proof of age or getting the sarpanch's clearance. Around thirty photographers in Warangal District have decided not to provide their services to marriages of underage children. Both the priests and the photographers told us they were facing a reduction in incomes due to this decision.

In West Bengal in Khidirpur and Begunbadi gram panchayats (GPS) we saw that all marriages are being noted in a register. The panchayat pradhan of Begunbadi GP said that in every fourth Saturday meeting he gets the information on all marriages in the village from the ASHA workers, the Anganwadi (AWW) workers and the panchayat members. The pradhan believes that by and large the information is accurate.

Out-of-school Children/Dropouts Enrolled/Re-enrolled into Schools

In addition to preventing child marriages, both MV Foundation and Jabala, have consistently been enrolling children in schools. In Telengana, each year around 250 children were enrolled although in the first year (2012) the number was the highest – 267 – probably because there were more children out of school and in subsequent years the numbers evened out. In 2012 and 2013 the number of girls enrolled was more than boys, probably because girl dropouts were higher than boy dropouts. In both the states, where marriages could not be stopped, the parents or in-laws were encouraged and convinced to allow the girl to continue in school.

More Girls Enrolling for Higher Education

It is by now internationally accepted that one of the best ways to reduce child marriages and delay the age of marriage is to keep girls in school. In Telengana, in three years an impressive 930 girls were helped to transition to higher education, the highest number, validating this theory in practice.

Government Responses: Setting up Village, Block and District Level Committees

Child Protection Committees (CPCs) were formed at different levels (village, panchayat and block) in the intervention area in West Bengal. Although the project team facilitated the formation of these committees, they were organically formed by the communities themselves once they were convinced of their importance. After the initiation of ICPS, District Child Protection Units (DCPUS) were also formed. All these are under the Department of Social Welfare. The Social Welfare Officer at the block and district level is the Child Marriage Prohibition Officer (CMPO). Although under the ICPS there is no provision for a panchayat level CPC, Jabala has facilitated their formation. The committees meet regularly, minutes are kept. Panchayats have review meetings with grassroots functionaries from different departments every Saturday and child marriages are reviewed in these meetings. Phone numbers of different officers are displayed in the panchayats where information on child marriages can be sent.

The Block Development Officers (BDOs) conducted meetings with Imams and through their committees issued notices to all masjids and Imams to not solemnise child marriages. Bravery awards were given by the block administration for girls whose marriages were prevented. BDOs supported girls' education after their marriages by providing books, uniforms, bags etc. According to the Annual Report of 2013, the BDO of Hariharpara, Murshidabad 'provided Rs 2000 to Sonia Khatun (a child marriage survivor) for education and assured her that he would take the necessary action for her education support.' The village level CPC in Angarguria DP in Birbhum district organized an event in their village in December of 2014 where an adolescent theatre group was invited and all expenses were supported.

The DPO of ICDS in Birbhum district, invited Jabala to act as a resource group for ICDS supervisors and Block Coordinators/ PD facilitators. In three days more than 60 ICDS supervisors were trained on how to restrict child marriages. Jabala was then asked to do similar training for the police. In addition the DPO (ICDS) from both Birbhum and Murshidabad districts also issued circulars to all CDPOs that required them to send monthly reports on child marriages in the district. The officer in charge at the Hariharpara police station took the initiative to organize meetings with religious leaders, and events to raise awareness about violations of child rights. Also the Sub-Divisional Officer at Birbhum asked Jabala to intervene in a panchayat where child marriage was prevalent (Annual Report 2013).

In Telangana, Child Marriage Prohibition Committees (CMPCs) were formed in the villages in the intervention area. Child Marriage Prohibition Officers (CMPOs) were appointed at each level, including at the divisional level. The CMPOs (who are the Mandal Revenue Officers in Telangana) called all the departments (the Revenue Department, Police and Women and Child Development – these three are the main drivers for action against child marriage) to strategize together. At the divisional level the Sub Divisional Magistrate conducted such multi-department reviews.

DCPUs were formed, although staffing was a problem (the number of staff appointed were less than the sanctioned number and the appointments were contractual in nature). During the field visit at the end of March, we were told that the DCPU in Warangal needs to make 2500 VLCPCs because a new order had been issued that these had to be formed by a certain date. This method of formation of village level committees is problematic because the process of identifying the right persons in the community, who are motivated and take ownership of the agenda, is likely to be short circuited.

Village level committees as well as mandal level committees conducted their meetings and took required action. Panchayats reviewed child protection issues with all departments – with schools and the anganwadi workers for dropouts, with the Health Department for early pregnancies and so on. Convergence of all departments is now happening.

The Education Department especially realized its role in delaying child marriages. The Revenue Department, Police and the Women and Child Development Departments became the drivers for this project, taking responsibility especially at the gram panchayat level. During the marriage season, announcements were made to prevent child marriages, and rallies and campaigns were organized. Phone numbers of CMPOs were displayed in public places. The childline number (1098) was advertised for people to report child marriages and other child protection issues. Alternative channels were created for child marriage reporting – if the childline response was weak, the other channel for reporting was the CMPO – and the Mandal Revenue Officer's number was also displayed.

CMPOs who did not know what their role was, now understood their responsibilities and were taking increasing ownership of the issue and many, for example, spent their funds for wall writings and other IEC material.

MV Foundation had kept a record of the circulars and government orders issued by the administration. Many of these government orders were issued at the behest of the MV Foundation field team and their interactions with the concerned officials. These serve as an indicator of the extent to which the administration takes ownership of the issue as well as an indicator of institutionalization. Between May 2012 and September 2014, 57 circulars have been issued in the two districts by diverse government functionaries like tehsildars, panchayat secretaries and others on various subjects. These include forming CMPCs at village and mandal levels and also in non-project mandals, attending CMPCs, participating in regional coordination meetings, review meetings with priests, bands, tent house owners, participating in training programmes organized by MV Foundation, and round tables with political parties and principals of colleges to orient students to the PCM Act (2006) and so on.

During the field visits in West Bengal and Telengana, we met many officials who displayed a high commitment towards the issue. The police too took on the responsibility for stopping child marriages. Guidelines were given to civic police in the villages, along with the required training in which child marriage was one of the issues along with 'eve teasing' and other safety and crime issues. Parents were being counselled and asked to give undertakings that they would not carry out child marriages.

IEC MATERIALS DEVELOPED BY THE GOVERNMENT

In West Bengal wall paintings and 'miking' (announcements on a microphone carried on a rickshaw or any other vehicle) have been done by the panchayats. The DCPU has prepared leaflets for awareness on Child Protection. Between February 21, 2015 and March 24, the DCPU in Murshidabad conducted awareness programmes in 52 gram panchayats of 17 blocks and 5 subdivisions. The BDO of Mohammad Bazar was so impressed by a theatrical piece on child marriage created by adolescent girls that he had a video made and it has been widely shown. In Telangana several departments of the government were mobilized to contribute to IEC and campaign material around child marriage and the protection of child rights.

In addition, some budgetary provisions were also made. Panchayats in the project areas in West Bengal have begun to budget for child marriage related work. Two blocks in Murshidabad District had started budgeting for the rehabilitation of child marriage survivors. In Begunbari I gram panchayat, Rs. 2.5 lakhs were budgeted for 2015-16 for support for girls whose marriages are stopped. The BDO of Beldanga was promoting this. Other gram panchayats too had probably begun budgeting for child marriage related activities. There was also an increase in awareness about the issue. In West Bengal, everyone we spoke with during our field visit, believes that awareness of the PCM Act has increased. There is fear of the law. Police stations undertook awareness programmes on the issue. Awareness amongst girls was also high – girls in schools were directly approaching the appropriate authorities. In Birbhum, we were told that girls had gone directly to the SDO.

In all the melas at the block level, there were stalls on child marriage and the adolescent girls' group performed their anti-child marriage dramas. This was especially done in the Kanyashri melas. According to the Quarterly Report, 'All the Masjids of Hariharapara are making announcements to stop child marriages after Friday prayers through mikes and loud speakers. Leaders are also making door to door visits.' (*Ananda Bazar Patrika* December 2013 ((cited in Quarterly Report 2013)) The Annual Report mentions that 'in two gram panchayats viz. Humaipur and Swaruppur a day-long mass campaign followed by a cultural programme was held to raise awareness. More than 3000-4000 people including important stakeholders like Members of Parliament, the Superintendent of Police, the Additional District Magistrate, the Chief Medical Officer and other Block and Panchayat officials attended the programme.' (Annual Report 2013).

During our field visit in Telangana we were told that there was an increased awareness that child marriage was illegal. Apparently, while earlier no one thought twice about getting girls married at 13 or 14 now there was wariness and fear and people knew that it was wrong. Many understood the consequences of child marriages. Women in SHGs in Kummaronipalli told us, 'earlier child marriages occurred without any discussion, now they bring aadhar cards to the meetings to check out whether it is okay to marry their child.' There was also an agreement that the reason for stopping child marriages was a fear of social sanction rather than concern for child rights. Awareness among girls was high – girls in schools were directly approaching the appropriate authorities. Male youth groups had taken pledges not to marry before 21 and that they would only marry girls over 18. In addition, citizen groups and CBOs are now contributing to publicity campaigns and to the production of IEC material.

We also came across several examples of girls who described how their self-perception had changed as a result of Jabala's interventions. The Mohammad Bazar girls, members of the Drama Group, told us that their parents now recognized that 'we are becoming smart, they now allow us to go out. They listen to us now'. The Officer in Charge (Police) and the BDO had also publicly recognized them and this had contributed to parents' increasing respect for them. Social solidarity had also increased – we were told about a girl with a heart problem, who was helped by the VLCPC and the local media to access medical treatment. Adolescent girls were now playing an active role in reporting complaints against child marriages and seeking responses from the system.

The one big issue articulated by the girls whom we met is the fact that they were not given freedom to move around (Margram I and II). Some also mentioned that they needed support for higher studies. Below we provide some case studies of girls we interviewed during the field visit.

Uzma Khatun (Interviewed during field visit March 28, 2015)

Uzma is pursuing a BA Honours degree in Physical Education and is in her first year. Her parents have attempted to get her married five times, as she is the eldest child. Uzma has refused each time because she wants to study further and make something of her life. She sought help from the BDO and OC twice about her parents wanting to get her married. They came to her home and counselled her parents. Her younger sister got married before turning 18. Uzma says she was helpless and she could not stop the marriage. Her parents say Muslim girls must get married early and that sport has no meaning for girls like her (Uzma is the captain of the Hariharpada Hockey Team). She says that she is still subjected to physical violence by her parents.

Jaba (Interviewed on March 28, 2015)

Jaba has been in the football team for the last five years. She dropped out from school and stopped coming for practice some time ago as her family's financial condition is not good. Jabala kept her in one of the homes run by them so that she could get proper meals and a shelter. She has now been re-enrolled in class 10 with the help of Jabala. Now she works as a domestic help in seven households during the day and also attends school. She comes for the football coaching every week without fail as she likes playing.

In an attempt to change the lives of girls through sports, Jabala initiated a football team, the Hariharapada Girls Football Team, in 2006. The main aim of was to help girls, especially survivors of trafficking and those vulnerable to being trafficked, to develop a greater sense of self-esteem, self-discipline, and positive bodily integrity by using team sports as the means to accomplish this. This football team became an important element of this intervention on child marriage. This initiative is now being taken to some villages in the project area of Birbhum district.

Going Beyond the Project Area

The evaluation had shown how the work had spread into non-project areas which were calling on the team for support to stop marriages. MVF has taken the upscaling agenda forward within its own organization – because of its organizational mandate there has been an expansion of the intervention in two other districts. The staff in these non-project areas had come on 'exposure' visits to the project areas, in order to see if they could replicate the model in their project areas. District Coordinators of this Child Marriage project also went to orient volunteers/staff of MVF to the 'model'.

MVF had initiated discussions with the State Council of Educational Research and Training (SCERT), Hyderabad which led to the inclusion of the topic of child marriages in the textbook of Social Studies for Class IX. The textbook, both in English and Telugu, will reach around 11,00,000 children.

In addition, Jabala was invited as a member of a committee to formulate guidelines to set up a Village Level Child Protection Committee under ICPS by the State Directorate of Social Welfare. Jabala also initiated an 'Alliance on Protection of Child Rights' of state level civil society organizations working on girl child issues, along with selected representatives from the government.

Theory of Change and Possible Indicators

Discussions with the project teams of the three organizations through the evaluation process helped to concretise the Theory of Change.

The Theory of Change

Child marriage can be prevented and children protected by activating the mandated government structures through a two-pronged approach of working with specific community groups, as well as with representatives of the mandated systems through skilful facilitation ensuring institutionalization and sustainability.

Some indicators that can be suggested are listed below. These are based on what emerged through the project as well as those contained in a presentation by a HAQ representative at the 'Girls Not Brides' conference in 2014.

Two important principles to be followed in setting indicators for this work are that:

i.   they are gender sensitive, and
ii. they are grounded in a comprehensive vision of the task at hand, keeping the determinants of child marriage in mind.

The categories of indicators that emerged were indicators of results, such as:

- Increased identification, reporting and prevention of child marriages;
- Improved response from government;

Process indicators such as:

- Community engages in active dialogue on child marriage and implementation of laws;
- Adolescent girls' groups play an active role in accessing their rights including preventing child marriages;
- Youth take an active stand against child marriage, dowry and promote gender justice;
- Priests and other religious leaders engage in active dialogue and take steps to prevent child marriages;
- Government structures and functionaries become active and are held accountable in preventing child marriages;
- Village, block and district level mechanisms play an active role in preventing child marriages and monitoring implementation of the law;

- Increased awareness and publicity on the issue;
- Documentation of processes and results towards developing a model for addressing child marriage through the strengthening of governance systems and community mechanisms for implementation of the law.

(See Annexure 3 for a detailed list of indicators that emerged.)

Strategies, Challenges and Lessons Learnt

By refining capabilities and outcomes within the administration and communities, this model has sparked impactful, cost efficient, relevant, and sustainable transformations. Changes at this scale put this model at the level of the 'credible' and its successful approaches could be adopted as 'best practices'. Improvements have been visible in four major domains, and they can be used for impactful outcomes by other interventions:

1. Increased identification, reporting and prevention of child marriages;
2. Improved response from government;
3. Increased awareness and information on the issue;
4. Increased self confidence amongst girls.

Some of the ideas that worked were:

- *Interventions with religious functionaries.* In West Bengal, interventions with the help of religious leaders were useful. The secretary of the Qazis' Block Level Committee (Mohammed Bazaar) reported that there are 67 completely Muslim villages in the block. In the block level committee when he took up this issue, the other qazis debated it fiercely because the Quran allows/promotes marriages as soon as girls attain menarche. He was then able to put forth his own interpretation of what is written in the Quran and this resulted in influencing many qazis to rethink what they believed. According to the Officer in Charge (of the police station) Beldanga, 'Maulavis are coming forward and playing a positive role.' Since the Imams are paid by the government, they can be – and are being – used to promote government programmes like the prevention of child marriages.

- *Plugging in the child marriage prevention agenda in every existing mechanism of the government.* Child marriage prevention and related activities were made into an agenda item in the Saturday meetings between the different department staff and the panchayat members. Systematic minutes were maintained and it was easy to examine the discussion and action around the issue from these records. Gram sabhas, block melas and block level meetings are all used to draw attention to the provisions of the PCM law.

- *Meetings with Child Protection Committees at the village, panchayat and block levels.* Jabala staff members as well as field animators make it a point to be present in these meetings and facilitate them if required.

- *Working with adolescent girls.* This key strategy infused a tremendous energy into the project. Girls, even from the non-project areas, stopped marriages by going and talking to parents and families. They helped dropout girls resume their education, to get benefits of the Kanyashri scheme, get food and rations from the AWCS etc. The adolescent girls who were nurtured by Jabala as leaders, helped to educate and inform other peer group members. The training they received from Jabala, and the fact that they were able to come together frequently, helped them become more self confident and many began to conduct awareness generating programmes of their own. Interventions in schools also helped a great deal.

CASH TRANSFER SCHEMES LIKE THE KANYASHRI

Although not a project strategy, many people believed that the Kanyashri scheme is the best strategy to delay child marriages (Margam II Panchayat representatives). It was reported that many mothers came forward to delay marriages because of the Kanyashri benefits and there was a sense that positive messages around Kanyashri worked to motivate parents against child marriage. There are indications that girls who have got the money are deciding what to do with it. According to the Joint Block Development Officer in

Hariharpara block of Murshidabad district: 'About 178 girls have already received Rs 25,000 under the Kanyashri Scheme and 3672 girls are getting the benefit of Rs 500 every month as scholarship. This scheme has helped Hariharpara become a model for other blocks in West Bengal.'

MV Foundation reported that while many of the above mentioned strategies worked for them too, there were others that they regard as key to the success of the project. These include:

- Circulars from government offices as a means of institutionalizing activities and promoting ownership of the agenda.
- Intervening consistently at all levels, providing a strong push at the village level, creating stakeholder groups, training them, following up on issues, campaigning with them. Similarly at the mandal and district levels. Developing personal relationships with officers is an important ingredient identified by the MV Foundation team.
- Encouraging direct reporting of imminent child marriages to the district and mandal levels. Reporting at higher levels is strategic because then the entire system – the hierarchy – gets activated and the effect is seen at the village level. In Maddimagudu we were told 'people from the government – the CDPO, SI, MPDO – started coming to the village after being informed about a child marriage.'
- Creating awareness of law, persuading people to not do child marriages, enabling girls to take a stand. However, there is widespread recognition that this phase is now over. The focus needs to be more on booking cases, with CWC and at police stations.
- Using supportive structures like the Childline and Child Welfare Committees. The CWC Chairperson, Warangal (who had been there for a year) told us:

  Eighty seven planned child marriages and five cases of married girls, came to the bench in the last one year. Mamata, a 'child marriage survivor' stayed 1.5 years in the Swadhaar home – she was taught weaving and sewing. On January 23

2015, when she became a major, she was sent to her husband's home by the CWC with gifts of a sewing machine and a loom. Another girl was sent to the KGBV, three others were restored to their families, they are continuing with their studies.... I call them up regularly and they are asked to report to the CWC every three months. The parents are not happy with this, neither with the letter of undertaking that is required to be given by them.

The Chairperson told us that the Minister called her up to say, 'this is my constituency so allow this marriage to be performed.' She asked him to give these instructions to her in writing. 'We can't be scared with every phone call,' was what she said to us.

She looks at each case with a humanitarian lens. 'In our society girls can be stigmatised for life if marriage stops at the mandap.' She believes in talking to the boy, appealing to his better senses. She tells his parents, 'Keep this relationship, let them be engaged – only defer the marriage till the legal age.' She says that it is possible to achieve good results through this approach.

Generally, however, there is a low awareness of government schemes. In Pedanupar village, when she told people about the Kalyanlakshmi scheme, people were thrilled to know that the government would pay Rs. 51,000 if the marriage took place after the girl turned 18. She warned priests in two cases that she would call the SI and book a case against them if they went ahead with solemnizing the marriage. They apologized and said they were not aware of the PCM Act. She then called a big meeting of all the priests/pastors/qazis and oriented them and told them, 'now you know, you have no excuse to perform child marriages.' Similarly, she got all the marriage hall owners together in a meeting and gave them a written notification not to perform any child marriages. She told them that if they did they would be booked.

- Using MV Foundation's history and credibility and social capital from past projects on child labour. Many who have been active with MV Foundation for over two decades are now part of the citizen platforms against child marriage.
- Creation and use of platforms like the existing Child Rights Protection Forums, Teachers Forum for Child Rights, Photographers' Association. These are measures of

sustainability, of creating champions and change agents. Using credible voices to promote the agenda. Similarly identifying caste and community leaders has been an excellent strategy.

The Mahbubnagar District President of All India Yadav Mahasabha told us during the field visit that the turning point for him was a survey in 2014 by the district administration which showed that 75,000 children were not going to school and 80 per cent of them were Yadavs. This is a shepherd community. They consider land as a big asset which has to kept within the community and even within the family, so child marriage is a way of preserving community assets and also strengthening community bonds.

He was aghast at the high percentage of dropouts within his community and decided to work on this issue. He is committed to the cause of increasing education among the Yadavs. He feels that power and recognition come from education, and says that no one in the village will notice you for how much gold you have, but your status will increase if you have education.

In meetings of his community he now emphasizes that there should be no child marriages and that all children must go to school. He tells them that child marriage is against the law. People often call him if there is a child marriage and the family asks him to intervene and protect them, but he says 'no, I warned you'. He told us about the change within himself: He says that twelve years ago there was a Yadav child marriage and the family was caught. They asked him to intervene. He prevailed upon the Sub Inspector to let them off the hook. The child marriage went through. He told us, 'if this happens now, we stop the child marriage.'

He makes concerted district level efforts in 64 mandals. For the last few years there have been compulsory meetings. His message is 'Leadership is not only about money, it is about increasing the voice of the community and education is necessary for this. Educated children will provide direction to others.' In his community meetings, he gives examples of cross breeding of sheep to emphasize how they must marry outside of their areas to strengthen their breed. This is beginning to happen now. According to him there has been about 50 per cent change in the situation.

- In Telangana under the Kalyanalakshmi Scheme for SCs and STs a sum of Rs. 51,000 is paid to each girl when she marries after 18. Similarly for Muslims there was the Shaadi Mubarak Scheme. Kavitha, an ICDS Supervisor in Warangal district, told us that she persuaded ten girls to wait till they were 18 years old and got them the Rs. 51000. Another idea that emerged from the field visit was that BPL Yadavs should also be included in the Kalyanlakshmi scheme.
- There appeared to be one strategy that did not work. Taking undertakings from families that they will not go ahead with the child marriage does not necessarily stop it, they find newer and more devious ways of circumventing the law.

Challenges and Gaps

According to Jabala team members, the districts and blocks where they were working in West Bengal were riddled with political problems and lawlessness. It was quite dangerous to work in these areas against social customs like child marriage. Team members felt that the Muslim personal law and religious norms that actually supported child marriage presented a huge challenge to bring about a change in mindsets. Other problems were that people had begun to falsify birth records in most creative ways. Poverty and the fear of missing out on a good match and the prospect of having to pay a higher dowry are the reasons for child marriage and the law does not address these causes. Lack of political interest in the issue is another challenge.

According to a Block Development Officer, one of the obstacles that they have to face is that the police will not book a case without proof/evidence/witnesses. Panchayat members in Beldanga I block pointed out that under-resourced public systems hinder action: 'As the numbers of police staff are very low – only about 42 per cent staff are available and there are only two cars to cover 13 panchayats – this acts as a hindrance in getting police support quickly.' Rapid staff turnover both in the government as well as in Jabala has also been a challenge. There have been four different Officers in Charge of a particular police station since 2012.

In Telangana, some of the challenges mentioned by the MV Foundation team were the same as in West Bengal. Under-resourced public systems was a major constraint: the District Child Protection Unit in Warangal has only 8 of the 12 sanctioned staff, there were only 9 Panchayat Secretaries in Rayaparthy when 23 were required, the childline was without satellites, making it difficult to reach out to the entire district. There was no budget for implementation of the PCM Act – the Gender Committee members who go to stop marriages, don't even get their travel reimbursed. These were all the reasons that affect the replicability and scalability of this model. Frequent transfers of the block and district officers adversely affected the project. The fact that Andhra Pradesh has been in a state of flux due to the bifurcation into Telangana, added to the human resource instability and confusion in the project districts. Girls whose marriages were stopped needed to be placed somewhere. Some go to KGBVs, others need vocational training and a place to stay. Mandal level colleges and vocational training institutes with hostels are required for girls. In addition, other means of increasing access to higher education need to be improved.

The general public is reported to be afraid of booking cases in the police stations because of the attitude of the police personnel as well as threats from politicians, leaders and families. Political leaders come out for general campaigns against child marriages (to look good), but do not take a stand against individual and specific child marriages – they do not want to lose their vote banks.

Some of the gaps that we observed through the evaluation were:

- Whose responsibility is it to produce district level reports on the number of child marriages prevented, girls helped for school enrolment or higher education and so on? At the moment different organizations – Childline, District Child Protection Unit, MV Foundation – are producing their own reports, with some overlaps (same cases being reported by more than one organization). Who ensures that all cases get recorded and a consolidated report is produced?
- Accountability is not pinned down. Responsibilities and tasks are not formalized in job charts along with indicators. For example, who examines a Panchayat Secretary's record of

marriages registered and questions if these are low (compared to project villages)? Or, do ICDS Supervisors ask ANMs questions if no child marriages are reported from their villages?

- Through this project, stakeholders are trying to use the law for a social issue, using fear. And they are also trying to change the social norm around child marriages. But there is singular focus on child marriage, and no discussion on dowry which is so closely linked with the child marriage issue.

- The focus appears to be only on the girl child – what about working with boys? Can we dissuade them from marrying minors, and encourage them to respect girls/women, combat alcoholism and domestic violence?

- Another question that needs to be asked is, what are the girls' own issues? Can the Kishori Ballika Samoohs, girls' committees in schools, be facilitated to expand their purview to *all* rights issues (instead of only child marriage)? During our discussions with girls, they identified several needs. For example, girls in Amar Singh Tanda mentioned toilets; others, including teachers, spoke of the lack of high schools close by. Girls in Bommanpalli addressed the question of mobility; in Amar Singh Tanda, girls said that they paid Rs. 450 every month for autos to school, which they had to earn by working as agricultural labourers; girls in Kummaronipalli asked about career options (Minutes of meeting 10.1.2015).

LESSONS LEARNT

Several important lessons have been learnt that can guide future such efforts, as well as build on this initiative. These are categorised below.

System Related

- While it is critical to work with communities to change mindsets and social norms, it is equally important to build the capacities of duty bearers, to sensitize them to the issues on the ground, and to enable them to respond sensitively yet firmly. Duty bearers have to be systematically prepared to fulfil their roles. This requires consistent, careful and diplomatic facilitation by the NGO staff. This is a necessary investment and should be recognized as such.

- Recognizing government officials by providing them opportunities to present their work and achievements at the state and national levels works as a motivator and further increases ownership of the issue. It also provides a role model for other officials in similar positions, for example, block and district officers.

- Establishing formal interdepartmental committees for action on the issue is necessary for institutionalization but in the short term this may not always be possible. In the short term, bringing together individuals from different departments to work as a team for specific tasks also gives results and provides a model that can be followed – government officers begin seeing the value of collaborative action.

Political Factors

- Elected representatives take an active part in campaigning against child marriages but are reluctant to take a stand in specific cases. This may affect the functioning of the Child Protection Committees as a collective. However, it is possible to get members to act by approaching them individually.

- Caste and religious leaders can be powerful change agents and influencers for the transformation of social norms (although this may conflict with our feminist values of vesting further power in patriarchal structures).

Strategy Related

- Context is important. It determines the reasons for child marriages. Changing contexts also give rise to changing reasons. It is important to understand these and develop suitable strategies.

- Awareness raising strategies must be designed according to the target group for one size does not fit all.

- The single point agenda of child marriage does not appeal much to stakeholders. While dealing with it directly, it is useful for the team and the communities to keep discussing and acting upon other related child protection issues such as abandonment of new born girls, birth registration, personal hygiene, school dropouts and their re-admission etc.

Support for Human Rights Defenders

Adolescent girls groups are organized both in schools as well as in the community. Community based groups have faced threats from those who want to go ahead with child marriages. Anganwadi workers said they had been harassed while reporting child marriage cases. School headmistresses reported facing threats. It is important to recognize this as an issue that all those who work on child marriage and related issues are human rights defenders and they need support. This should be publicly proclaimed so that people are aware that their threats will be monitored.

OTHER LEARNINGS

One pattern that is emerging is that the successful stopping of child marriages has happened when the girls themselves take a stand against the marriage, or if the parents are against it (in case a girl chooses her own partner). The implications of this need to be unravelled and clearly girls' empowerment is important too.

There were 248 interventions to stop child marriages of girls in the two states. A follow-up study on the impact of the campaign to stop child marriages shows that the girls whose marriages had been prevented need some degree of emotional, moral and financial support to be able to continue with their studies and their lives. It is important that their families too understand that they must not be treated as if they were burdens on them and that their own community and society in general do not stigmatise them. To ensure this, families and communities too need to be sensitized and brought into the change-making process.

Discussion

Some dilemmas and conflicts: Some aspects of the enforcement of the PCM Act give rise to a degree of discomfort. The idea of community members turning 'informers', was a bit disturbing for us, initially. The role of NGOs like MV Foundation and Jabala and others like them has been to promote social harmony and bring communities together. And yet in this project an indicator of success appears to be community members – including young people – informing authorities about impending child marriages. This results in mistrust and tension in the village. While standing up for what is right is something that should be taught to young people, how would we look at informing on a friend who tells you that her parents are planning her marriage? Can this be construed as breach of confidence? What is the role of consent in such a case? In some ways, reporting on an impending child marriage is like reporting on domestic violence or child sexual abuse, or rape occurring in a neighbour's house. These are issues that have been considered as private matters, 'within the family' and have resulted in human rights violations. Similarly, how do we look at turning to priests and religious functionaries to enforce the PCM Act? Many of us find the idea of giving more power to religious functionaries who have controlled women and their bodies abhorrent. Religious leaders have been the toughest opponents when it comes to reproductive and sexual rights. Similarly, while we fight against the caste system, we also appeal to them to exert an influence and use their power on their communities to stop child marriages. Are these alliances dangerous? Or are they strategic and short term?

This project has also used the strategy of creating fear of the law and punishment (partly) to bring about social change. Is this the right thing to do? As we heard during the field visit, people are devising newer and more devious ways of subverting the law. Signatures and birth certificates are being forged. Duplicate Aadhar cards are being produced. Girls are being whisked away into the anonymity of big cities like Hyderabad and being married off there. Can social change come about through the enforcement of such laws?

The Conditional Cash Transfer Schemes are also being used effectively to delay marriages of the targeted groups of girls. Yet there are many points on which these schemes can be critiqued – there are others who are as vulnerable as the groups targeted by particular schemes and these vulnerable groups are excluded. Many of these schemes, while delaying the age of marriage, are still focused on marriage. Their underlying message is that the money can be used as dowry. How do the schemes ensure that girls have control over the money that comes their way?

The reason for highlighting these dilemmas is that these – and other points of discomfort that the implementing teams face – should be discussed openly. While an easy resolution of many of these may not be possible, discussion will help team members to deepen their understanding of the issues and sharpen their perspective.

CHILD MARRIAGE, EARLY MARRIAGE OR FORCED MARRIAGE? DIFFERING PERSPECTIVES

Child Marriage has largely been considered as a reproductive and sexual health and rights issue. This project addressed it as a child protection and governance issue. Communities insist that they are marrying their girls to 'protect them' and the project designers felt that this argument needed to be turned on its head to show the communities that in the long run, the girls become more 'unprotected' when married early, losing out on all opportunities of self actualization in any form. While this project looked at child marriage as a child protection issue, and worked with child protection mechanisms, it recognized that a gender perspective and a reproductive and sexual health perspective needed to be made explicit in order to expand alliances, strengthen collaborative work, and address the issue in a holistic way. We attempted to explore child/early marriage from multiple perspectives with the partners during the inception meeting and came up with the following schema.

- **Gender perspective.** This concerns the girl as well as the boy. It considers the differential consequences of child/early marriage from the girl's as well as the boy's point of view. Strategies to address the issue include not only the empowerment of girls, but also sensitization of boys to issues of the burden of early responsibility of caring for a family, the right to create your own life and future before taking on the responsibility of a family, issues of dowry and its exploitative nature, power relations that subjugate a new young wife in an alien household and family, caring sexuality, consent, and so on. A gender perspective would look at the dimensions of masculinity in relation to child marriage.
- **Adolescent sexual and reproductive rights** emphasize young people's right to age appropriate comprehensive sexuality

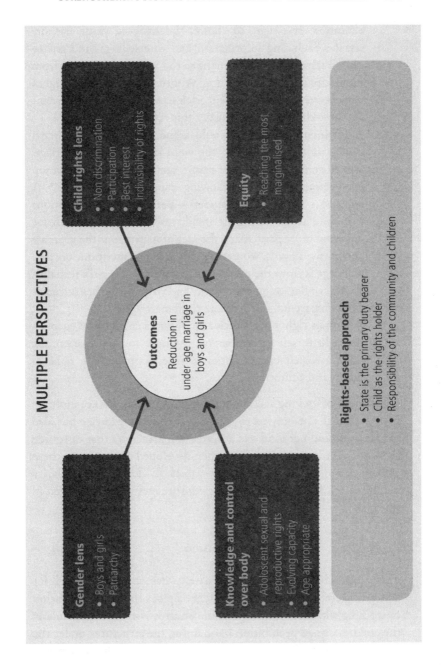

MULTIPLE PERSPECTIVES

Child rights lens
- Non discrimination
- Participation
- Best interest
- Indivisibility of rights

Equity
- Reaching the most marginalised

Gender lens
- Boys and girls
- Patriarchy

Knowledge and control over body
- Adolescent sexual and reproductive rights
- Evolving capacity
- Age appropriate

Outcomes
Reduction in under age marriage in boys and girls

Rights-based approach
- State is the primary duty bearer
- Child as the rights holder
- Responsibility of the community and children

education, the right to choice, the right to youth-friendly services including information and counselling, the right to reproductive self determination, the right to freedom from discrimination and violence. A broader adolescent rights' perspective would also look at adolescents' right to development and how child marriage violates this right.

- **A feminist perspective** would argue against the patriarchal connotation in the use of the word 'child' in 'child marriage', as well as the protectionist stance versus a self determination perspective within the 'evolving capacities' framework.[6] A feminist – as well as a gender – perspective also questions the entire notion of the inevitability of 'marriage' especially for girls, and more particularly the idea of marriage as the ultimate destiny for all girls/women. A critical feminist critique of child marriage is from the perspective of control of a girl's sexuality, the fear of her losing her chastity and virginity pushes society – through parents – to promote child marriages.

- **A human rights perspective** emphasizes the right to equality, the right to self determination, the right to participation, the right to equal opportunities and development, the right to health and education.

The idea of looking at child marriage through the lens of multiple perspectives is not only to engage in a theoretical exercise but also to create common ground and agreed upon principles that can guide the work. The strategies that are then developed are based on these principles and uphold the common values. By doing this, solidarity is created on the issue and a larger constituency is then engaged in this task.

Conclusion

The project has been able to create a demonstrable model for addressing child marriage. This model employs the twin approaches of working with the mandated administrative systems – particularly the child marriage prohibition mechanism, the structures under the ICPS and the school education system – as well as at the community level to create pressure both for accountability by the system towards child protection, as well as to change social norms related to girls. The model consists of processes and structures – capacity building activities both for communities as well as for service providers/duty bearers, facilitation for enforcement of provisions of the PCM Act and for transformation of mindsets and social norms.

The model has resulted in many positive outcomes: increased awareness of the PCMA in the project and non-project areas resulting in the prevention of child marriages and a substantial decrease in child marriages. There are increased efforts towards girls' education, both at the community level and at the policy level through schemes such as Kanyashri in West Bengal and Kalyanlakshmi in Telangana. Girls are empowered to take action to prevent child marriages. There has been creation and activation of structures mandated under the PCMA and the ICPS, increased action by duty bearers at all levels, ownership of the issue by the PRIS, campaigns by youth for girls' education and safety. Child marriage is being recognized as an issue by several departments and convergent action for prevention, is beginning to take place. However, action is not being taken *after* child marriages have been solemnized – complaints are not being filed, convictions not being done.

The strategies that have been powerful are: nurturing adolescent girls as change agents, sensitization of religious leaders, priests/ imams and those who solemnize marriages, ensuring that the committees at every level (Child Protection Committees/Child Marriage Prevention Committees) meet regularly and actions are followed up, mainstreaming the child marriage prevention agenda into every existing forum, getting various officers to issue circulars and government orders so that they take charge and the agenda is institutionalized, establishing broad-based citizens forums using credible personalities and champions, and drawing in schemes like the Kanyashri and Kalyanlakshmi to promote girls' education.

The challenges have been huge: under resourced public systems (which leads us to question how this effort can be made sustainable and replicable), political turmoil like elections, changes in governments and the bifurcation of Andhra Pradesh, turnover of staff within project teams as well as in the government, covert political pressures to condone child marriages. Some gaps in the current intervention relate to the perspectives and capacities of the project teams – an equity perspective that demands that we invest more where there is greater weakness – the out of school girls, areas where we have not worked before. The work with girls – and boys – needs to have a sharper gender perspective, needs to be more holistic (rather than the narrow focus on only preventing/delaying marriages till 18 years), it needs to be based on the affected group's own analysis of the problems (rather than top-down project oriented messages). NGOs need to become facilitators of institutionalization, the teams need to think strategically.

Important lessons have been learnt in relation to how to work with administrative systems, how political figures operate, what kind of strategies will work, the support required for human rights defenders. All these lessons can take the work to the next level of analysis and complexity.

Notes

1. International Center for Research on Women. 2011. 'Delaying Marriage for Girls in India: A formative Research to Design Interventions for Changing Norms, UNICEF p. 1.
2. Ibid. p. 3.
3. UNICEF The State of the World's Children. 2011. 'Adolescence an Age of Opportunity', February.
4. International Centre for Research on Women, Delaying Marriage for Girls in India: A formative Research to Design Interventions for Changing Norms, Unicef, 2011. p. 3.
5. Report of the National Consultation, 'Come Together' August 2014.
6. Mohanty, C. 1991. *Third World Women and the Politics of Feminism*. Bloomington: Indiana University Press.
7. The concept of 'evolving capacities' in the Child Rights Convention seeks to strike a balance based on capacity – between parental responsibility for protecting the child and the rights of the child to autonomy and decision-making.

Annexure 1: Prohibition of Child Marriage Act (2006)

The Prohibition of Child Marriage Act was notified in January 2007 to effectively deal with the problem of child marriages in India and to put in place a comprehensive mechanism to address the issue. It applies to all citizens of India irrespective of religion except the state of Jammu and Kashmir and the Union Territory of Pondicherry. The law makes marriage of girls below 18 and boys below the age of 21 an offence punishable with rigorous imprisonment of upto two years, or a fine of Rs. 100,000 or both.

The provisions of the law can be categorized under three sections: Prevention, Protection and Prosecution of Offenders.

Prevention. Under the law child marriage is a cognizable and non-bailable offence. Those who permit or promote child marriage can be punished. Those who know that child marriage is going to take place, have a duty to inform the appropriate authorities – failure to do so will be construed as abetting a child marriage and the person will be liable for prosecution. Child Marriage Prohibition Officers are to be appointed in every state to prevent child marriages, ensure protection of potential child brides/bridesgrooms, as well as prosecution of offenders. The courts are empowered to issue injunctions for prohibiting child marriages. Child marriages will be declared null and void if the injunction prohibiting child marriage is violated or if the child is taken away forcibly, or is sold or trafficked for the purpose of marriage. Under the law those who solemnize child marriages can be penalised. The CMPO and the District Collector are responsible for awareness creation in the community.

Protection. The law makes child marriages voidable by giving choice to the children in the marriage to seek annulment of marriage within a period of two years after the child has attained majority. It provides for maintenance and residence of the female contracting party. Children born from child marriages have a legal status and the law makes provisions for their custody and maintenance. The law provides for support – medical aid, legal aid, counselling, rehabilitation – to children once they are rescued. The CMPO is empowered to provide all necessary aid to victims of child marriage and can produce the children before the Child Welfare Committee or a First Class Judicial Magistrate.

Prosecution. Offenders can be: guardians/parents of both parties, priests, relatives/friends of both parties, neighbours, community leaders who give patronage to such marriages, marriage bureaus, traffickers, bridesgrooms if over 18 years of age, caterers and other service providers. The law clearly states that women offenders in any of the aforesaid categories cannot be punished with imprisonment – they can be penalized by the imposition of a fine. The authorities identified for prohibiting child marriage under the present law are: CMPO, District Magistrate, First Class Judicial Magistrate, Police, Family Courts, any person called upon by the state government to assist the CMPO. Any person can report a child marriage either before or after it has been solemnized. The report can be made to the police, the CMPO, Child Line, District Magistrate or a member of the CWC or the First Class judicial Magistrate. In case of mass marriages the District Magistrate has the powers to stop the solemnization of child marriages. A complaint about child marriage has to be made at the nearest police station and the police have to make an entry in the Daily Diary and register an FIR. A complaint can also be filed with the First Class Judicial Magistrate. Complaints can be oral or written, by phone, telegram, fax, email. They need to be signed by the complainant – whose identity has to be protected to avoid repercussion

Annexure 2: Integrated Child Protection Scheme

In 2006 the Ministry of Women and Child Development (MWCD) proposed the adoption of the Integrated Child Protection Scheme (ICPS). In 2009 the central government gave the scheme its approval and has begun the extensive task of providing children with a protected and safe environment to develop and flourish. The purpose of the scheme is to provide for children in difficult circumstances, as well as to reduce the risks and vulnerabilities children have in various situations and actions that lead to abuse, neglect, exploitation, abandonment and separation of children.

The specific objectives of the scheme are: to institutionalize essential services and strengthen structures, to enhance capacities of all systems and persons involved in service delivery, to create a database and knowledge base for child protection services, to strengthen child protection at family and community level, to coordinate and network with government institutions and non-government institutions to ensure effective implementation of the scheme, to raise public awareness about child rights, child vulnerability and child protection services.

Within care, support and rehabilitation services the scheme will provide CHILDLINE services, open shelters for children in need in urban and semi-urban areas, offer family based solutions through improving sponsorship, foster-care, adoption and after-care services, improve quality institutional services, and general grant-in-aid for need based/innovative interventions. Within statutory support services the scheme calls for the strengthening of CWCS, JJBS, SJPUS, as well as seeing to the set up of these services in each district. Beyond this ICPS also outlines the need for human resource development for strengthening counselling services, training and capacity building, strengthening the knowledge-base, conducting research studies, creating and managing a child tracking system, carrying out advocacy and public education programmes, and monitoring and evaluation.

In order to ensure the objectives and approaches of ICPS are met, the scheme also calls for the establishment of new bodies within a service delivery structure. At the district level there are: District Child Protection Society (DCPS), District Child Protection Committee (DCPS), Sponsorship and Foster Care Approval Committee (SFCAC), Block Level Child Protection Committee, Village Level Child Protection Committee. At the state level there are: State Child Protection Society (SCPS), State Adoption Resource Agency (SARA), State Child Protection Committee (SCPC), State Adoption Advisory Committee. At the regional level there are: Child Protection Division in the four Regional Centres of National Institute of Public Cooperation and Child Development (NIPCCD), Four Regional Centres of CHILDLINE India Foundation (CIF). And lastly at the national level there are: CHILDLINE India Foundation- Headquarters, Child Protection Division in the National Institute of Public Cooperation and Child Development (NIPCCD), Central Adoption Resource Agency (CARA).

The Childline website outlines a specific implementation plan. It discusses the need for convergence of services to give the child the integrated plan. This is achieved through coordination of all departments and ministries and NGOs involved. The annexure of the scheme lays out guidelines on how to achieve each service provided in the scheme.

Annexure 3: List of indicators

Indicators of Results

1. Increased identification, reporting and prevention of child marriages
   - Number of marriages reported (Male/Female);
   - Number of marriages registered (Male/Female);
   - Number of potential child marriages (Female/Male) reported by stakeholders;
   - Number of child marriages stopped at that point in time (Female/Male);
   - Number of child marriages delayed (till 18/21 years);
   - Number of child marriages that could not be prevented (Female/Male).

2. Improved response from government:
   - Number of committees/structures created at each level (as mandated by law and programmes/schemes);
   - Number of committees/structures that are active ('active' will have to be defined – there will be progressive indicators as the programme matures);
   - Number of circulars and government orders issued;
   - Number of officials involved in direct/indirect interventions in child marriage prevention and community outreach. (This will need to be backed by a qualitative analysis of the kinds and intensity of involvement for example, timely response, initiative taken and so on.);
   - Number of/range of/quality of IEC materials developed and disseminated by the government – material against child marriages, for child protection, and related gender issues;
   - Degree and quality of convergence and coordination of services;
   - Initiatives taken to mainstream prevention of child marriage agenda in existing forums.

Process Indicators

1. Community engages in active dialogue on child marriage and implementation of law:
   - Formation of mothers'/self help groups;
   - Formation of male youth groups;
   - Periodic meetings of mothers'/self help groups and male youth groups;
   - Child marriage and related gender and child protection issues become part of the agenda of mothers'/self-help/male youth groups;
   - Community members begin taking action against child marriages.

2. Adolescent girls groups play an active role in accessing their rights including preventing child marriages:
   - Adolescent girls groups are formed;
   - Groups meet regularly and identify and discuss their own issues;
   - They are aware of their rights and protections under the law;
   - They are aware of whom to approach and how for reporting on violation of rights;
   - They begin taking action on child marriages and related issues;
   - They are able to intervene in individual cases;
   - They initiate or participate actively in awareness programmes against child marriage and related gender issues;
   - Girls get linked to higher education and vocational training;
   - Girls get toilets and other basic facilities in school to make education a viable option;
   - Girls access basic services, all entitlements (SABALA, Kishori Shakti Yojana, ARSH services) and other forms of support.

3. Youth take active stand against child marriage, dowry and promote gender justice:
   - Youth take personal and collective action against child marriage;
   - Youth demonstrate and promote gender sensitive behaviour;
   - Youth are able to negotiate with political leaders for social justice.

4. Priests and other religious leaders engage in active dialogue and take steps to prevent child marriages:

- Religious leaders initiate or get involved in spreading awareness against child marriage;
- Priests develop their own measures to keep a check on child marriages;
- They stop solemnizing child marriages;
- They actively report possible/potential/prospective child marriages.

5. Government structures and functionaries become active and accountable in preventing child marriages and are held accountable:
   - Key government structures, officials and functionaries, police and administration are aware of their roles and responsibilities in implementing the child marriage law, rules and regulations;
   - Key departments, officials and functionaries take necessary measures to stop child marriages;
   - Local police take initiative in community outreach, verification of information of possible/prospective child marriage and respond effectively;
   - Specific cases receive timely response;
   - Increased maintenance of school records and follow-up of girls dropping out of school;
   - Increased follow-up with girls and ensuring their re-enrolment in school;
   - Increase in number of girls accessing cash transfers and other entitlements.

6. Active involvement of gram panchayats (village level local self-government institution) in preventing child marriages and promoting child rights:
   - Child marriage and related gender issues become part of agenda for gram panchayat meetings;
   - Members of gram panchayats initiate or participate in awareness drives;
   - Members of gram panchayats are part of task force/child protection committees/child marriage prohibition committees;
   - Marriages are registered by gram panchayats as per law;
   - Gram Panchayats make budgetary provisions for child rights.

7. Village, block and district level mechanisms play an active role in preventing child marriages and monitoring implementation of law:
   - Child marriage prohibition committees/child protection committees at village, block and district level are formed with various stakeholders represented on these committees such as local-self government bodies, revenue officials, child marriage prohibition officers, health workers, government functionaries schools, religious leaders, women's self-help groups, adolescent girls and youth groups etc;
   - These committees have an official mandate to act and intervene
   - The committees meet regularly and their meetings and actions are documented and records properly maintained;
   - The committees develop action plans, execute those plans, directly intervene in stopping child marriages, monitor implementation of law, child protection schemes and government circulars and orders issued from time to time, undertake periodic review of their actions and chart out future course of action;
   - Regular information flow between community and government is ensured.

8. Increased awareness and publicity on the issue:
   - Mass awareness drives are undertaken with participation of all stakeholders in the project;
   - A clear message is communicated about seriousness of implementing the law;
   - The issue receives increased media coverage.

9. Documentation of processes and results towards developing a model for addressing child marriage through the strengthening of governance systems and community mechanisms for implementation of the law:
   - Clear indicators are set before the project;
   - Simple baseline studies are done based on the indicators;
   - Indicators are understood by the implementing teams;
   - Reporting systems (MIS) are designed based on the indicators;
   - Capacity building workshops on documentation are held periodically;
   - Mid Term review is done.

8

Using a Feminist Lens to Deepen Communication for Development Evaluation Approaches

VENU ARORA

Introduction

I have been leading a communication for social change organization based in India for over fifteen years. Some of the early work we did was around Behaviour Change Communication largely in response to the HIV pandemic in the mid to late nineties and with a view to increasing awareness and promoting safer sexual practices. As an organization we believed in working closely with communities for designing their 'messages' and communication materials and as we evolved our practice of community engagement, a certain tension started to emerge between donor expectations and our process driven approach to communication design. It is in this context after several years as a practitioner that I stepped into academic research to look at theories around communication and relate these to practices on the ground. However, on the battlegrounds of implementation, when communication programmes are rolled out, the demands for showing 'numbers of people reached' and 'impact achieved' and 'behaviour change accomplished' becomes hard to contend. Most impact assessment indicators are in direct conflict with what can be achieved in the limited life cycles of the several projects we worked on and there was no way to reflect, at least in the formal reporting, the learning we were gaining on the ground, especially those insights which conflicted with the dominant development paradigm. I felt strongly that there needed to be alternate ways to look for the impact that our work was having.

For this essay I am treading two parallel themes: reviewing communication for development theories and exploring evaluation theory and practice in order to make the case for a new articulation for evaluating Communication for Development (C4D). This essay explores the discordant notes in communication evaluation and then focuses on some emerging work on participatory evaluation and the key tenets of feminist evaluation. I do this in order to reframe and re-imagine a way of evaluating Communication for Development. I have used this opportunity to revisit two communication initiatives that were implemented by my own organization – Ideosync Media Combine – as well as review other large-scale communication for social change evaluations in the South Asia region to ground the ideas I am putting forward.

A Brief History of C4D in Its Myriad Avatars

Theorizing on communication for development has adopted ideas from a variety of other disciplines, including sociology and pedagogy. Communication theories have evolved in most part based on development models with global political underpinnings. In the early post war thinking, the problem of underdeveloped regions was believed to be an information problem; communication was presented as the instrument that would solve it. Daniel Lerner (1958) and Wilbur Schramm (1964) theorized communication as a transmission of information. Exposure to mass media was thus considered a key factor in bringing about modern attitudes. This knowledge-transfer model defined the field for many years. In the same vein Shannon and Weaver (1949) proposed the Transmission model of communication where communication was seen as a linear process of information flow from mass media to individuals.

Later the Diffusion of Innovation model conceptualized an individual's ability to move linearly from a point of no knowledge to a point of positive action. Variations of this model guided Behaviour Change Communication programme designs for several decades including guiding evaluation questions around the effectiveness of messages.

Diverging from the media-centrism and 'magic bullet' theory of affects that underpinned earlier analyses, Rogers (2010) and subsequent 'diffusion' studies concluded that while media was important to increasing awareness, interpersonal communication and personal sources were crucial in guiding decision making.

By the mid 1960s a strong Latin American critique of 'vertical' approaches of information transmission led to the adoption of horizontal projects emphasizing access, dialogue, and participation. Dominant paradigm scholars acknowledged the value of community participation in development and recognized the new uses of media to unlock local energies.

Since early 2000, participatory communication has gained momentum and interpersonal communication is achieved often through the use of community media. Participatory theories of development communication rearticulate communication as being people centric rather than media centric. Participatory theories take their inspiration from Paulo Freire and his ideas of a 'dialogical pedagogy' where equity in distribution and active grassroots participation are central principles. The role of communication is therefore redefined as one of providing a sense of ownership to participants through sharing and reconstructing experiences.

Community-based forms of communication such as songs, theatre, radio, video, and other activities that required group intervention thus became valid ways to communicate. More than mechanisms to disseminate information, these could provide opportunities to identify common problems and solutions, to reflect upon community issues, and mobilize resources. Community members, rather than 'professionals', could be in charge of the decision and production processes.

Due to these movements in theories of development communication several varied avatars came into practice ranging but not limited to social marketing, media advocacy, interpersonal communication, health promotion and education, infotainment, social mobilization. Most, despite changes in nomenclature, reflected one or other dominant idea and while several used notions of participation, they lacked definitional clarity.

Several organizations like the Rockefeller Foundation and the Johns Hopkins University have been trying to reach some form of consensus. One such attempt at defining the key tenets of a communication for social change model include:

- Sustainability of social change is more likely if the individuals and communities most affected own the process and the content of communication.
- Communication for social change should be empowering, horizontal (versus top-down), give a voice to the previously unheard members of the community, and be biased towards local content and ownership.
- Communities should be the agents of their own change. Emphasis should shift from persuasion and the transmission of information from outside technical experts to dialogue, debate and negotiation on issues that resonate with members of the community.
- Emphasis on outcomes should go beyond individual behaviour to social norms, policies, culture and the supporting environment

Over the last decade, implementers of programmes have interchangeably used Communication for Development, Communication for Social Change and Participatory Communication as terminologies to describe their work. However, the dominant top down structures of the modernization theory and diffusion theory continue to seep into implementation designs.

What is even more frustrating is that while participatory evaluation methodologies have been evolved, oftentimes participatory projects are evaluated using the old formula for reach and efficiency (read effective social change achieved through individual positive action undertaken by members of target community). There is an underlying tension where nomenclatures of participatory communication are co-opted while programme implementation as well as evaluation practice continue to embody power dynamics of the top down approach.

The Case for an Evaluation Turn

I believe that the ways that we evaluate our work informs its practice and what we are able or unable to document, as learning from our work. If despite a plethora of articulations around Communication for Development and Social Change there continues to be a predisposition in implementation towards a top down development paradigm and a gap in assigning an 'impact value' to rights based, social justice, accountability and transparency principles, then our evaluation approaches are yet to incorporate ideas of power and the imbalances thereof which are increasingly being recognized as the key issues to be addressed in most developing nations.

June Lennie and Jo Tacchi (2010) have clearly articulated the need for a different evaluation frame for Communication for Development programes

> Alternative, participatory approaches to development, complexity theories and whole systems approaches understand social change as unpredictable and emergent. Social change is unknowable in advance, something to learn from and adapt to. The former instrumentalist approaches prioritize evaluation that is based on the categorization of abstract concepts, control of planned activities and inputs, and pre determined measures of success; the latter prioritize evaluation that captures relationships, openness, emergence, innovation and flexibility. The former are mainstream, considered rigorous, and largely based on standardized methods; these are alternative, considered (by proponents of the former) to lack rigour and based on a range of approaches, methodologies and methods selected according to each initiative and its context.

Nobuya Inagaki (2007) refers to three blind spots in existing research in Communication for Development

i.   The majority of the empirical evaluations report positive impacts of Communication for Development projects. It is often pointed out that published studies tend to deal with projects that had significant outcomes, with an effect of under-reporting failed projects (Hornik1988; Bauman 1997; Morris 2003).

ii. The issue of power is a common cause of unsuccessful outcomes in c4d interventions; power imbalances in political, economic, occupational and gender domains have created blockages to communication across social boundaries. *Another commonality is that these failed experiences were identified through qualitative evaluation methods.* (Italics mine)

iii.   The most invisible part in the recent empirical literature is the effort to understand the long term effects of communication. Most project implementation schedules are too short to do so.

An absence of theorizing around failure leads to stasis as has been seen in the Communication for Development space. It stunts learning and retards knowledge building and understanding of the complexities of the social, political and economic fabric in which we live and function.

In 'Equity based Evaluation' (2012), Katherine Hay talks about how evaluators are asking for a shift away from questions of impact and attribution to new questions in assessing how effective the strategies are in particular contexts or whether outcomes are in line with the needs of beneficiaries. She further discusses how evaluations need to value process results and unintended outcomes and study how dominant discourses guide policies and programmes and question whether the implicit assumptions behind these discourses resonate with the ground experience of marginalized communities.

What Feminist Evaluation Offers

Figuring out whether something works or not often entails first articulating what 'working' or success, means. How success is defined, where success is seen to reside, what is measured, and by extension often, what is done.

As part of the process of exploring ideas of feminist evaluation for designing a different framework for c4d and in preparation for writing this essay, a roundtable was held with academics and practitioners, writers and filmmakers in India who have been thinking about issues of evaluation, equity and gender, feminist discourse and social justice. Participants spoke about the need to break hegemonies of knowledge and to be certain that research does not fall into the trap of recreating hegemonies while paying lip service to bottom-up approaches for monitoring and evaluation. Participants also discussed the need to question inherent patriarchal biases that exist in policies, especially policies for sexual and reproductive health. Another key concern at the round table was the preoccupation of development programmes to be scaled up and the strong likelihood of iterative and learning approaches being abandoned in favour of large-scale reductionist approaches that provided numbers

'It becomes important for us to go beyond the numbers of scale and access and look for ways to demonstrate subjective experiences that contribute to the larger pool of change stories,' said one participant at the round table.

Certain forms of communication in historical and political contexts at a particular point of time become more acceptable than others. Instead of making communication products for consumption, give the communities the technologies and capacities to tell their own stories and see them engage themselves. Considering the importance we give to participatory approaches for the creation of media content and handling the media tools, we should look for building capacities of communities in creating their own grammar of a media form. The internet and the democratisation of media have changed the meaning of communication so evaluation frameworks need to look at communication and media as appropriate resources/infrastructure. Such an ownership oriented – theoretically contemporary – approach to communications and media can generate insights in evaluation that move the relationship between communication and positive change in directions that are truly transformative and based on the autonomy of the most marginalized.

The idea of changing the measuring yardsticks to look at *contribution* rather than *attribution* was presented and discussed as was the notion of thinking about evaluation as a means to give economic validity to project outcomes, thus making the notion of evaluation utilitarian and reductionist. Participants of the roundtable also emphasized the need to make evaluations accountable to people and ensure ethical guidelines for data usage now that data also means audio and visual data.

Feminist analysis brings to evaluation, recognition that this process is constructed and political. Podems has outlined six key tenets for feminist evaluation where discrimination is seen as structural; knowledge and values are seen as being culturally socially and temporally contingent. And most importantly for evaluators to acknowledge that knowledge is filtered through the knower. There are multiple ways of knowing; some ways are privileged over others.

Mohanty (1991) problematises singular notions of development, and I would hazard that this is the case in most communication for development projects, especially those addressing women's health and reproductive and sexual health. A privileging of certain kinds of 'progress' over others assumes that all third world women have the same desires, problems and needs. Mohanty points out that development policies do not affect all groups of women in the same way. I would broaden this to say that communities construct and deconstruct communicated ideas and actions based on cultural, ideological, historical as well as social, educational religious, caste and class based frameworks.

REVIEWING RECENT BCC EVALUATIONS

In order to seek out the gaps and ascertain the contention that behaviour change communication programmes and evaluation designs are unable to address the critical issues of power, inequities and the larger complex canvas of social cultural political and economic contexts within which communication is practised, we explored six evaluation reports from India and South Asia that were readily available online or through organizations and agencies who had commissioned them. We limited our sample to evaluations done over the last decade to see whether in the most recent work in the C4D field, there is a movement towards capturing reasons behind social change or an attempt towards complex indicators that discuss structural inequities or issues of power. The studies were both large and medium sized in terms of scale, ranging from multi country to national and state level as well as smaller studies that looked at segmented communities, in particular slum based populations.

The findings from a review of these evaluations led to some critical observations:

- The larger the scale of the initiative, the greater the homogenization of the communities.
- The evaluations reveal a set of assumptions that value certain knowledge and practices as more privileged over others. For example institutional deliveries are privileged over home deliveries and therefore communications are directed towards changing home delivery practices.
- Complex marginalization like the gendered burden of contraception and sterilization are not taken into account when designing BCC to promote contraception and smaller family sizes, nor when evaluating these programmes.
- In none of the six evaluations studied was there a clear value based, political articulation of the programme or evaluation except for one, the Meena project by UNICEF which articulated a gender equality based discourse.
- Success indicators are based on knowledge, attitude and practice; access, exposure and recall of media and message; community influencers and their role, self efficacy of 'target audience'.
- The purpose of the evaluation is to show the success of the BCC intervention. Most are published as documents and reports. There is no evidence of tracking how these get used for further programme design by the implementing organizations or communities where these were implemented.
- Participatory communication initiatives do not seem to be evaluated in a participatory way.
- The evaluations do not explicitly link social justice, rights, voice, power and are not constructed self consciously as political.

RE-IMAGINING THE EVALUATION FRAMEWORK FOR C4SC

Evaluations are thought of as distinct from programme implementation. More often than not donors ask for external evaluators because there seems to be a fear of bias if implementers undertake evaluations. However if the purpose of evaluation is to learn what we are achieving and how to improve upon it, rather than prove in pure economic and quantitative terms whether the project was 'successful', then it may be useful to include, through a high level of participatory decision-making, all the key players, including implementing partners and community members in the evaluation process.

Further, if in practice the kind of participation that is valued is one where the power to accept or reject processes and results lies with partners and community members, it facilitates sustainability and long term learning as it fosters an ownership of the entire evaluation.

In process oriented participatory evaluation, knowledge and learning is created while doing the evaluation and in many ways it overlaps with the communication process. Therefore it may be critical to an evaluation methodology to articulate the points of intersection where the evaluation processes feed into programme implementation and vice versa. These 'intersections' are important to identify in order to provide clarity and rigour to the participatory evaluation process.

Along with colleagues at Ideosync Media Combine, we undertook a participatory evaluation of two initiatives, Chahat Chowk and Radiophone. Using participatory research tools adapted from the action research toolkit by Jo Tachhi, we were able to chart multiple conversations that the communication projects initiated within the community and identify conflict zones where power and hierarchies retarded dialogue or created vertical pathways.

Some similarities between both evaluations included:

- Programme officers at the donor organizations were invested in valuing bottom up knowledge and were not singularly focused on demonstrating the success of projects.
- There were several points of intersection where the research process contributed to programme outcomes, for example the researcher's community engagement helped gather the stories that were then used by the community radio stations as part of their progrmmes. This practice therefore collapsed distinctions between formative and evaluatory research.
- Despite overall partcipatory design and the learning that it contributed, as the evaluation reports were being finalized, there remained a consistent push to also show and prove success through numbers.

Given that no evaluation, whether external or internal, is free from bias, when the political positions taken within evaluations are clearly articulated, it contributes to the overall strength of the outcome analysis. Such recognition of points of intersection between programme implementation and evaluation that mutually enhances outcomes is also a way to be reflexive about the evaluation process itself. It leads to newer insights and allows for the tensions between programme design and expected results to be discussed. For example in the evaluation of the Chahat Chowk initiative, it was easier to have a dialogue with the donor and evolve processes where the numbers being sought from the evaluation could be more meaningful.

Based on the reflections from the two participatory evaluation initiatives and in keeping with feminist evaluation principles, I would like to propose the following inward looking four Ps for Evaluating c4d: Power, Politics, Purpose, Profit.

Power: The feminist proposal of locating the researcher is the first step in locating power within the evaluation frame. This inward looking P demands that before any evaluation process begins, it be clearly identified and articulated who has the decision-making powers in the process. Very often even in participatory evaluation initiatives, communities contribute to data collection but analysis and interpretations of data are not open or shared. Participatory processes for co-evaluation and co-interpretation of data with communities and partners need to be evolved for undertaking a horizontal sharing of power in the evaluation project. It may be useful to work out how the relationships between those commissioning the evaluation and the evaluators, implementing partners, and communities can be made horizontal. Simultaneously all evaluation partners must be watchful and aware how power dynamics shift during the project or older hegemonies resonate during the process. These must then be reflected upon and documented.

Secondly, as part of the inward looking P of Power, an evaluation design must explore the ways in which it deals with knowledge: whose knowledge is being valued and why; what spaces for negotiated knowledge are available and how the knowledge gained through the evaluation will be discussed and shared.

Politics: All evaluations must chalk out a political identity where the core assumptions and desired outcomes are mapped. What are the lenses with which activities and discourses are being viewed? Social justice, equity, agency, gendered, feminist, accountability based, historical etc. Framing the politics will enable evaluations to articulate and visualize what the success of the project would look like or mean. This would also help articulate what to look for, to be able to find the cues for such successes. An open exchange that facilitates the creation of shared meanings of success will enable all evaluation partners to be better prepared in understanding the evaluation outcomes and reshaping the next phase of implementation.

Purpose: Perhaps one of the singularly obfuscated elements of evaluations are their purpose. Sometimes evaluations are carried out to justify the existence of certain agencies or organizations. More often than not, they are undertaken to showcase success and garner extension on projects or explore more funds/grants or negotiate greater allocation of resources to certain sectors. Sometimes they may also be undertaken to learn about certain new practices. Hardly ever are evaluations undertaken to explore and locate failures and seek what is not working. Perhaps exploring failures should become a central focus of a lot of c4D evaluations and I would not be surprised if the very things we have been finding successful year after year over the past two decades turn out actually to be failures. It will all depend on the frames of reference and what is being termed as success.

I am therefore asking for all c4D evaluations to clearly state any overt or covert agendas and purposes for which they are being commissioned. These purposes need to be articulated by those commissioning the evaluations as well as those undertaking the evaluations. It should also be stated in consent documents of evaluation partners and communities why they are agreeing to partner and what purpose they see the evaluation fulfilling in their own contexts.

Profit: Lastly, the evaluation must specify who is likely to benefit from the findings and how. This articulation of the likelihood of profit must include profit in economic and non-economic terms. For example in the case of the community learning Project Chahat Chowk, the evaluation helped establish Ideosync Media Combine's credentials as an organization capable of undertaking a complex participatory research initiative and of course paid for research team and staff time. It benefitted Gurgaon Ki Awaaz community radio through capacity building of the CR team on communication research as well as reproductive and sexual health issues and it benefitted the community by creating a local movement for demanding better services and by creating social spaces in the village Mullaheda where such issues may be voiced or discussed. The evaluation also enabled the creation of successful showcase stories that Gurgaon Ki Awaaz could use to find funding to continue the project through support from other local donors. The data on numbers of people reached that emerged through the evaluation enabled Gurgaon Ki Awaaz to have the audience numbers in hand for any possible local advertisers, which contributed to enhancing the overall sustainability possibilities for the CR station. The evaluation reports however do not document these profit motives and possibilities in any way and there is also no knowledge among implementing and evaluation partners about how the donors profited from this evaluation or were likely to profit from it. Bringing out these profit motives and profit possibilities will help refine evaluation methodologies as well as reduce any unnecessary tensions and discordant notes between evaluation partners.

Outward Actionable Evaluation Frames

Along with the inward looking Ps, I propose a few outward actionable frames for C4D evaluations. These frames take forward the work of June Lenni and Jo Tacchi's framework for evaluating C4D, which has discussed seven key components and concepts of evaluating C4D. These seven framework components elaborate that the evaluation must be participatory, complex, emergent, learning based, realistic, critical, and holistic.

In addition and based on the review of BCC initiatives presented in this essay as well as on the learning from the two participatory evaluations elaborated earlier, I propose that all evaluations undertake research using the following broadly defined frames:

Probabilities for Change: Communication can only create possibilities for more openness towards dialogue, new negotiated knowledge and possibilities for action. Therefore it would be erroneous to treat outcomes through absolute indicators for knowledge, attitude, and practice. It may be more useful to think in terms of whether a particular set of communicative actions created greater probabilities or retarded existing probabilities of change.

Intersectionalities: As noted earlier, when undertaking participatory evaluation, the monitoring, evaluation and research process intersects with the communication implementation process. Additionally within the complex socio-cultural, economic and political contexts there are a myriad intersecting and overlapping spaces and planes that impact the outcomes and either enhance the probabilities for change or retard them. As part of these frames, evaluations must define and map these intersections including those of caste, class and gender identities with structures and systems. The greater the links and networks in such a mapped frame of intersectionalties, the higher the probability of positive outcomes. The leaner the network, the more the schisms, the less likely that the communicative action is facilitating dialogue or learning.

Probabilities for change and *intersectionalities* are therefore interlinked and interdependent variables in a participatory communication for development evaluation project.

Framing new and disrupted hegemonies: Lastly, evaluation must look for how existing hegemonies are being broken, reinstated or new ones created through the communication projects being evaluated. It is important to locate such disruptions of hegemonies – of knowledge, social and cultural hegemonies – as well those created through contextual politics and economies. The more hegemonies a communication project disrupts, the more the probabilities for change it creates. The more the project reinforces existing hegemonies, the fewer the probabilities for change. In case new hegemonies are being created, these could retard or enhance the probability frame.

The idea of framing the success of a communication project through probabilities based on intersectionalities and networks and through disruptive hegemonies may provide the complexity to evaluations that has been missing thus far in the linear more absolute terms in which c4d and bcc are being currently evaluated.

TABLE I

Sl. no	Title of Evaluation	Who is Evaluating? (Donors and Partners)	What is being evaluated	Target Population	Assumptions if any	Values (Rights, equality, social justice, etc.,)	If indicators used how are they selected
1	What Influences Maternal health Practices in four countries?	BBC Media Action with funding from the UK Department for International Development (DFID)	Understand Maternal health care practices; Ante natal care and birth preparedness among four countries - Bangladesh, India, Ethiopia and South Sudan	Young women their husbands and mother-in-laws	Traditional deliveries at home were seen as unhealthy and risking life; unsupportive family attitudes (strained relationship between mother-in-law and daughter-in-law); calls for neo-natal medical care and institutional deliveries.	–	Birth preparedness Ante natal Care Unsupportive attitudes and norms around health facility deliveries.

SL. no	Title of Evaluation	Who is Evaluating? (Donors and Partners)	What is being evaluated	Target Population	Assumptions if any	Values (Rights, equality, social justice, etc.,)	If indicators used how are they selected
2	The effect of Behaviour Change Communication (BCC) interventions on maternal neonatal and child health (MNCH) knowledge in urban slums of Bangladesh	BRAC, supported by Bill and Melinda Gates Foundation	The purpose of this study was to assess the selected MNCH related knowledge and practices among the urban slum women in relation to the *Manoshi* BCC intervention and explore the acceptability of BCC tools among the target audiences as well as community members and the association between exposure to different Behaviour Change Communication (BCC) approaches and changes in MNCH knowledge.	Urban slum women, their families and community: The evaluation was carried out in three urban slums of Dhaka city with only women who gave birth to a child one year prior to the interview. Age, literacy, religion, education, occupation and income were the chief demographic characteristics taken for the study sample. The results/ findings were in relation to the demography	–	–	Knowledge on selected maternal health messages; on selected Newborn and Child health care indicators; Maternal health care practices Neonatal and child care practices; exposure to different BCC channels of *Manoshi* program

Sl. no	Title of Evaluation	Who is Evaluating? (Donors and Partners)	What is being evaluated	Target Population	Assumptions if any	Values (Rights, equality, social justice, etc.,)	If indicators used how are they selected
3	Participatory Communication Campaign Approaches in improving Health Practices in India: An Impact Assessment of DFP's Programme for Improving Mother and Child Health in Selected States	Department of Communication Research, IIMC. Supported by Directorate of Field Publicity, Ministry of Information & Broadcasting Government of India	To evaluate the effectiveness of the communication campaign that is aimed at promoting change in knowledge, attitude and practice and uptake of services in the area of JSY (Janai Suraksha Yojana) institutional delivery, family planning and exclusive breast feeding. The study was done across 4 states, Assam, Jharkhand, Madhya Pradesh and Rajasthan	Responses for evaluation were gathered from women beneficiaries, micro level health functionaries, DFP officials and opinion leaders. Demography of the study sample did not have caste and religion – only age and gender	Institutional delivery is safe delivery. Family planning and small family as ideal. Attempts to promote contraceptive choices, does not recognize the burden of family planning and birth control eventually falls on women.	Community ownership of development programmes	Knowledge and Practices around Institutional delivery, exclusive breast feeding and family planning. No indicators for ownership

Sl. no	Title of Evaluation	Who is Evaluating? (Donors and Partners)	What is being evaluated	Target Population	Assumptions if any	Values (Rights, equality, social justice, etc.,)	If indicators used how are they selected
4	Increasing Postpartum Contraception in Rural India: Evaluation of Community based Behaviour Change Communication Intervention	International perspectives on sexual and reproductive health – Guttmacher Institute	To increase the knowledge and use of lactational amenorrhea and postpartum contraception through counselling by community workers. This intervention was done complementary and integrated to the government's initiatives on contraception and family planning	Women from rural Uttar Pradesh, Meerut. The study was with pregnant women and the elder women in the household (mother-in-laws)	Lack of knowledge among the Indian couples on birth spacing. Does not acknowledge the burden of family planning and sterilisation methods on women	–	Increase in knowledge and use of lactational amenorrhea and postpartum contraception
5	Kyonki Jeena Isi ka Naam Hain	UNICEF, Centre for Media Studies	Aims to provide parents and other caregivers with the information they need to save and improve children's and mother's lives.	Parents and other care givers to improve children's and mother's lives among the six Hindi speaking majority states of	–	–	The broad areas covered in this survey are: Timing Births; Safe Motherhood; Breastfeeding;

Sl. no	Title of Evaluation	Who is Evaluating? (Donors and Partners)	What is being evaluated	Target Population	Assumptions if any	Values (Rights, equality, social justice, etc.,)	If indicators used how are they selected
			To estimate the reach and background characteristics and media habits of the audience of the series. To understand the direct and indirect effects of exposure to the TV drama and how audience identify with the characters in the series. Measuring the level of impact on the target audience and change in their knowledge, awareness, efficacy, norms, behaviour and action in comparison to the baseline and midterm data.	Bihar, Uttar Pradesh, Madhya Pradesh, Chattisgarh, Rajasthan and Jharkhand. DD viewership was a pre-requisite and the demography included age, gender, level of education, occupation, Socio economic status and access to health systems.	–	–	Nutrition and Growth; Immunization; Health and Hygiene; HIV/AIDS; Gender and Social Norms; Interaction with the health system; Access to Communication; Roles and Responsibilities of secondary audiences

Sl. no	Title of Evaluation	Who is Evaluating? (Donors and Partners)	What is being evaluated	Target Population	Assumptions if any	Values (Rights, equality, social justice, etc.,)	If indicators used how are they selected
6	Meena ki Duniya: Impact Assessment Summary Report (Uttarpradesh	CMS; UNICEF, Drexel University - School of Public Health	Entertainment education programmes in schools for enrolment, retention and completion of education. For child friendly schools, life skills and gender; hygiene, sanitation, health and nutrition.	Primary audience are children attending school. Gender, Caste and Religion were discussed on demography but were not explored further	–	Gender equality	The first section examines specific elements of program exposure. The second section compares groups of respondents to examine effectiveness of the Meena Intervention. Mapping Exposure and Recall. Section 2: Measuring Impact – Knowledge, self efficacy, attitudes and level of importance

TABLE 2

Sl. no	Title of Evaluation	Findings	Who were they finding for?	How were they disseminated?
1	What Influences Maternal health Practices in four countries (Bangladesh, India, Ethiopia and South Sudan)	Low self-efficacy and assertiveness of young women and dominance of older women in the family stand as unsupportive attitudes to maternal health care. Pregnancy is seen as normal process and women are forced to continue household work and other heavy work for normal delivery. Assumptions that such attitudes are harmful. Target population (Bangladesh and India) seems to have a myth that disclosing pregnancies at early stage to people outside the family might lead to complications and miscarriages. Such cultural beliefs are sought to be broken rather than understanding why they resonate with communities.	The findings were designed to inform the future communication interventions of BBC Media action on maternal and child health practices.	BBC Media Action Research portal
2	The effect of Behaviour Change Communication (BCC) interventions on maternal neonatal and child health	Most of the study participants considered BCC materials (posters and stickers) as being essential and the images of healthy mothers and children presented in these materials were well accepted by them. Cultural practices of general approval are not accounted for.	Though the study was conducted in urban slums of Dhaka, the findings were correlated to the larger urban slum context of Bangladesh.	MANOSHI Working Paper Series.

Sl. no	Title of Evaluation	Findings	Who were they finding for?	How were they disseminated?
	(MNCH) knowledge in urban slums of Bangladesh	Despite these barriers, study participants stated that BCC materials influenced them to change their MNCH care seeking behaviour in many ways. Need to attribute change to the intervention seemed core driver for evaluation	The findings of this research paper provide comprehensive feedback to the BCC intervention and to improve communication materials suiting the needs and contexts of the target population.	
3	Participatory Communication Campaign Approaches in improving Health Practices in India: An Impact Assessment of DFP's Programme for Improving Mother and Child Health in Selected States.	Higher is the exposure to the intervention and for longer duration, higher is increase in the knowledge level of the population. Considering the contextual factors, knowledge thereby can also be related to attitude (though the relationship is not straight) and practice. Campaign Messages should be in sync with the needs and desires of the community and in their context and languages hence an extensive formative study is required for better programme implementation The findings and recommendations call for a participatory approach in designing the intervention and campaigns and by bringing the PRIs and organising meetings which will provide a forum for discussion and feedback.	The women from poorer districts of the states in which the evaluation was carried out. The findings are aimed at providing DFP – to encourage service utilisation through JSY; to encourage more coordination among frontline health workers, block level health officials, important community organisations and PRIs; and to spread activities of NRHM.	Report – Directorate of Field publicity. No documentation of creating an enabling environment for uptake of learnings by the various players that the report says the findings are for.

Sl. no	Title of Evaluation	Findings	Who were they finding for?	How were they disseminated?
		It suggested community participation in programme planning, implementation and monitoring, so that community takes ownership of development programmes.		
4	Increasing Postpartum Contraception in Rural India: Evaluation of Community based Behaviour Change Communication Intervention	Targeted BCC using community workers is an effective and feasible strategy for promoting postpartum contraception. Women in intervention group, those with higher knowledge of healthy spacing practices and or two or more spacing methods were more likely to be using contraceptive method. Use of modern contraceptive methods was higher in the study group.	Women from rural Uttar Pradesh, Meerut. The study was with pregnant women and the elder women in the household (mother-in-laws). The evaluation was successful and the government departments scaled up the activities to other blocks of Meerut district.	Published as a research article by Guttmacher Institute (available in JSTOR). *Source:* International Perspectives on Sexual and Reproductive Health, Vol. 38, No. 2 (JUNE 2012), pp. 68-77.
5	Kyonki Jeena Isi ka naam Hain	Significant increase in all the indicators stated from baseline to endline. Significant exposure leading to significant recall and thereby change in the attitudes (indicators)	Target population who is exposed to the TV series. The effectiveness of the programme was measured. (There is no information on how the results were used or interpreted)	CMS Reports.

Sl. no	Title of Evaluation	Findings	Who were they finding for?	How were they disseminated?
6	Meena ki Duniya	The positive findings on exposure and liking for the show also translate into high levels of message recall with virtually every respondent recalling at least one message from the show an on average respondents remembering some 7.2 messages. Not only do the students recall the messages but also indicate that the messages they received from the show were new for them. Sustained exposure leading to better recall and there by influencing practice	Target population (school going children) who is exposed to the radio series The effectiveness of the programme was measured (**There is no information on how the results were used or interpreted**)	CMS Reports

Note

I would like to acknowledge the contributions of Himabindu Chintakunta to this work. Himabindu assisted in convening the round table organized by Ideosync Media Combine and was a diligent rapporteur. She also helped with collating the materials for the evaluation table presented here as well as contributed to reviewing appropriate literature.

References

Ailish Byrne. *Pushing the Boundaries: New Thinking on How We Evaluate.* Accessed from http://www.communicationforsocialchange.org/mazi-articles.php?id=399.

Ajzen, I. and M. Fishbein. 1980. *Understanding Attitudes and Predicting Social Behavior*, Englewood Cliffs, NJ: Prentice-Hall.

American Public Health Association Workgroup on Public Health Promotion/Disease Prevention. 1987. 'Criteria for the Development of Health Promotion and Education Programs'. *American Journal of Public Health*, 77: 89–92.

Arnst R. 1996.'Participation Approaches to the Research Process', in Servaes, J. and T. Jacobson, S. White (eds.) *Participatory communication for social change*, New Delhi: Sage Publications, pp. 109–126.

Bandura, A. 1977. *Social Learning Theory*, Engleood Cliffs: NJ: Prentice-Hall.

Becker, M. 1977. 'The Health Belief Model and Prediction of Dietary Compliance: A Field Experiment', *Journal of Health and Social Behavior*. 18(4): 348–66.

Bell, C. and H. Newby. 1971. *An Introduction to the Sociology of the Local Community*, New York: Praeger, p. 32.

Berlo, D. 1960. *The Process of Communication*, New York: Holt.

Biber, S. (ed.) 2014. *Feminist research practice: A primer*, Thousand Oaks: Sage Publications.

Bowes, J. *et al.* (1978), 'Communication of Technical Information to Lay Audiences,' Report of the Communication Research Center, University of Washington.

Bracht, N. 1990. (ed.) *Health Promotion at the Community Level*, Newbury Park, CA: Sage Publications, p. 47.

Breckon, D., J. Harvey and B. Lancaster. 1994. *Community Health Education: Settings, Roles and Skills for the 21st Century* (3rd Ed.), Gathersburg, MD: Aspen Publications, p. 123.

Brisolara, S., and D. Seigart. 2014. *Feminist Evaluation and Research Theory and Practice*, New York: Guilford Publications.

Carlow, R. *et al*. 'Organization for a Community Cardiovascular Health Program: Experiences from the Minnesota Heart Health Program', *Health Education Quarterly*, 11: 243–52.

Caserta, M. 1995.'Health Promotion and the Older Population: Expanding our Theoretical Horizons', *Journal of Community Health*, 20: 283.

Chaffee, S. and J. McLeod.'Sensitization in Panel Design: A Coorientational Experiment', *Journalism Quarterly*, 45: 661–69.

Chaffee, S., J. McLeod and J. Guerrero. 1969. 'Origins and Implications of the Coorientational Approach in Communication Research' (Paper presented to the Association for Education in Journalism Convention, Berkeley).

Dervin, B. and B. Greenberg. 1972. 'The Communication Environment of the Urban Poor', In G. Kline and P. Titchenor *Current Perspectives in Mass Communication Research*, Beverly Hills, CA: Sage Publications, pp. 210–33.

Dewey, J. 1946. *The Public and Its Problems*, Chicago: Gateway Books.

Elder. J. *et al*. 1986. 'Organizational and Community Approaches to Community-wide Prevention of Heart Disease: The First Two Years of the Pawtucket Heart Health Program', *Preventive Medicine*, 15: 107–17.

Enghel, F. and F. Wilkins. 2012. 'Mobilizing communication globally', *Nordicom Review*, 33(2012) Special Issue, 9–14.

Farquahar, J. *et al* 1977. 'Community Education for Cardiovascular Health', *Lancet*, 1192–95.

Farquahar, J., N. Maccoby and D. Solomon. 1984.'Community Applications of Behavioral Medicine', in E. Gentry (ed.) *Handbook of Behavioral Medicine*, New York: Guilford pp. 437–78.

Field, M. 1996. (ed.) *Telemedicine: A Guide to Assessing Telecommunications in Health Care*, National Academy Press: Washington, DC.

Fine, S. 1981. *The Marketing of Ideas and Social Issues*, New York: Praeger.

Flora, J., N. Maccoby and J. Farquahar. 1989.'Communication Campaigns to Prevent Heart Disease: The Stanford Community Studies'. in R. Rice and C. Atkin (eds.) *Public Communication Campaigns* (2nd edition), Thousand Oaks, CA: Sage Publications, pp. 240, 251.

Foote, D. *et al*., 1985. The Mass Media and Health practices Evaluation in Honduras: A Report of the Major Findings. A report by Stanford University and Applied Communication Technology to the US Agency for International Development (USAID), p. 7.

Freire, P. 1970. *Pedagogy of the Oppressed*. New York: Herder & Herder.

Gibson, Cynthia. n.d. Strategic communications for health and development.

Gantz, W. 'Seat Belt Campaigns and Buckling-up: Do the Media Make a Difference?' *Health Communication*, 2(1): pp. 1–12.

Green, L. and M. Kreurter. 1992. 'CDC's Planned Approach to Community Health as an Application of PRECEDE and an Inspiration for PRECEDE', *Journal of Health Education*, pp. 40.

Grunig, J. 1989. 'Publics, Audiences and Market Segments: Segmentation Principles for Campaigns', in C. Salmon (ed.) *Information Campaigns: Balancing Social Values and Social Change*, Belmont, CA: Sage Publications, p. 207.

Harding, S. 1987. 'Is there a feminist method?' in *Feminism and Methodology: Social Science Issues*. Milton Keynes: Open University Press.

Hay, K. 2012. *Evaluating Gender and Equity*. New Delhi: Sage Publications.

———. 'Strengthening Equity-focused Evaluations through Insights from Feminist Theory and Approaches', *Evaluation for Equitable Results*, UNICEF.

Hein, K. *et al.* 1993. 'Adolescents and HIV: Two Decades of Denial', in S. Ratzan (ed.) *AIDS: Effective Health Communication for the 90s*, Taylor and Francis: Washington, DC: Taylor & Francis, pp. 215–32.

Hennessy, B. 1981. *Public Opinion* (4th ed.), Monterray, CA: Brooks/Cole Publishing p. 21.

Hillary, G. 1955. 'Definitions of Community: Areas of Agreement', *Rural Sociology*, 20: 111–23.

Huesca, R. 2008. 'Tracing the history of participatory communication approaches to development: A critical appraisal', in J. Servaes (ed.), *Communication for Development and Social Change*, New Delhi: Sage Publications, pp. 180–99, doi: http://dx.doi.org/10.4135/9788132108474.n9

Hyman, H. and P. Sheatsley. 1947. 'Some Reasons Why Information Campaigns Fail', *Public Opinion Quarterly*, 11: 413–23.

Inagaki, N. 2007. *Communicating the impact of communication for development recent trends in empirical research*. World Bank: Washington, DC.

Israel, B. *et al.* 1995. 'Evaluation of Health Education programs: Current Assessment and Future Directions', *Health Education Quarterly*, 22(3): 364–89.

Janz, N. and M. Becker. 1984. 'The Health Belief Model: A Decade Later', *Health Education Quarterly*, 11(1): 1–47.

Katz, E. 1991. 'On Parenting a Paradigm: Gabriel Tarde's Agenda for Opinion and Communication Research', *International Journal for Opinion*.

Klapper, J. 1960. *The Effects of Mass Communication*, New York: Free Press.

Lennie, J., & J. Tacchi. 2013. *Evaluating communication for development: A framework for social change.* Milton Park, Abingdon, Oxon: Routledge.

Learner and Schramm. 1976. *Looking forward: Communication and Change, The Last Ten Years – and the Next* Honolulu: East West Centre, p. 343.

McAlister, A. *et al.* 1982. 'Theory and Action for Health Promotion: Illustrations from the North Karelia Project,' *American Journal of Public Health,* 72: 43–55.

Mertens, D. 2013.'Mixed Methods and Credibility of Evidence in Evaluation' *New Directions for Evaluation, Number 138.* Wiley.

Mohanty, C. 1991. *Third World Women and the Politics of Feminism.* Bloomington: Indiana University Press.

Podems, D. 2010. 'Feminist Evaluation and Gender Approaches: There's a Difference?' *Journal of MultiDisciplinary Evaluation,* Volume 6, Number (14).

Rhinegold, H. 1993. *Virtual Community: Homesteading on the Electronic Frontier,* Reading, MA: Addison-Wesley.

Robinson, J. 1976. 'Interpersonal Influence in Election Campaigns,' *Public Opinion Quarterly (fall).*

Rogers, E. *Diffusion of Innovations* New York: The Free Press.

Rogers, E. and D. Kincaid. 1981. *Communication Networks: Toward a New Paradigm for Research,* New York: The Free Press, pp. 79–142.

Rogers, E.M. 2010. *Diffusion of innovations,* New York: Simon and Schuster.

Rothman, M. 1983. *Hierarchical Comparison of Structural Equation Models: An Application to Models of Health Behavior.* (Ph.D. Dissertation, College of Education, University of Washington, 1983), p. 7.

Rotter, J. 1954. *Social Learning and Clinical Psychology.* New York: Prentice-Hall.

Shannon, C., and C. Weaver. 1949. *The Mathematical Theory of Communication,* Urbana, IL: University of Illinois Press.

Shibutani, T. 1966. *Improvised News: A Sociological Study of Rumor,* Indianapolis: Bobbs-Merrill.

Smith, D. 1987. *The everyday world as problematic: A feminist sociology.* Boston: Northeastern University Press.

SRI International. 1995.'Exploring the World Wide Web Population's Other Half' Palo Alto, CA, June, Internet resource on URL: http://future.sri.com/vals/vals-survey.results.html.

Stamm, K and J. Bowes. 1990. *The Mass Communication Process: A Behavioral and Social Perspective,* Dubuque, IA: Kendall-Hunt, p. 227.

———. 'Communication during an Environmental Decision,' *Journal of Environmental Education,* 3: pp. 49–56.

The National Rural Health Assn., Internet resource, URL http://www. nrharural.org/ (10/11/97) and *Rural Health Futures: Integrated Rural Health Information Networks*, Internet resource, URL http://www. pageplus.com/~ruralfut/doc5.htm (9/26/97).

Thomas, P., and E. Fliert. (n.d.). *Interrogating the theory and practice of communication for social change: The basis for a renewal.*

Tones, K., S. Tilford, S. and and Y. Robinson. 1990. *Health Education: Effectiveness and Efficiency*, London: Chapman & Hall.

US Congress, Office of Technology Assessment. 1955. *Telecommunications Technology and Native Americans: Opportunities and Challenges*. Washington, DC: USGPO, p. 2.

US Congress, Office of Technology Assessment. 1990. *Health Care in Rural America*, Washington, DC: USGPO p. 11.

US Congress, National Technology and Information Administration. 1995. *Falling Through the Net: A Survey of the "Have Nots" in Rural and Urban America*. Washington, DC: USGPO. July p. 1–7.

US Congress, Office of Technology Assessment. 1995. 'Bringing Healthcare Online: The Role of Information Technologies' OTA-ITC-624 Washington, DC: USGPO, pp. 96–97; 127.

US Congress, Office of Technology Assessment. 1996. *The Impact of Health Reform on Rural Areas*, Washington, DC: USGPO p. 1.

Westley, B. and M. McLean. 'A Conceptual Model for Communication Research', *Audio-Visual Communication Review*, 3: pp. 3–12.

9

Equity Focused and Gender Responsive Evaluations

Viewing Mainstream Evaluations in the Irrigation Sector through a Feminist Lens

SEEMA KULKARNI and SNEHA BHAT

Section 1: Introduction

Inequities across caste, class, gender, religion, tribe and more characterize our society and can be seen in access to resources, education, decision-making, employment etc. Undoubtedly the forms they take have been changing as societies have changed. Recent incidents of violence against dalits, women and other discriminated groups are evidence of inequities. Increased inequities can be interpreted as either disempowerment of different social groups or as a backlash against groups finding spaces to empower themselves, negotiating the spaces and opportunities created through years of struggle. Both these processes are inherently linked with each other. A continuing process of action, research and evaluation and analysis is thus important to map the shifts in society and chart the course of future change.

GENDER AND WATER: THE MALE AND FEMALE DOMAINS

The water sector is usually divided as a) domestic water, which includes drinking water and sanitation and b) productive water which includes irrigation, industries or, more broadly, water for production.

The former is largely within the domain of welfare or nurture and the latter within the productive sphere. The dominant construction of women in the water sector largely revolves around the domestic sector, leaving the men to handle the production. The creation of the male and the female domains in the water sector is an obvious extension of how different gender roles are perceived by society. Provisioning of domestic water for the health of their families thus becomes a key area where women's role is thought to be important and women's role in the conservation of water becomes the stated goal of the water sector. This is, however, not true in the case of water used for productive purposes. Notions of women as nurturers of their households dominate and thus inform how policies and programmes get designed in this sector. This would apply to most other sectors as well.

Irrigation involves the use of water for production. The production of a commodity that can be exchanged for money or for other produce, thus gets characterized as 'male'. Women labour on irrigated fields and yet the 'malecentric' view dominates irrigation thinking and practice (Kulkarni 2011, Zwarteveen 1998).

Objectives of the Study

In this essay we focus on evaluation as a tool with a potential for change. We look at feminist evaluation as an approach and focus on the water sector, more specifically the irrigation sector which we argue to be a 'male' sector. We analyse and compare two sets of evaluations in irrigation a) those done by the irrigation department and b) those done by a pro-people, feminist organization SOPPECOM to which we belong. The two sets of evaluations are quite diverse, the government evaluations are of the entire sector and specific programmes within it, the SOPPECOM evaluations are of very specific programmes in the irrigation sector. So in a sense they are not the same evaluations that are being compared. The attempt here is thus to point out how the state looks at the progress in the irrigation sector so differently from organizations like SOPPECOM that would look at it from an equity and social justice point of view. We conclude that if such an exercise is done as an ongoing process the analysis will help in mapping changes that are taking place in the sector from a gender and social justice point of view.

Section 2: The Framework for Assessing Evaluations

Feminist evaluation as we understand it, is an important tool that can be used towards policy advocacy, practice and theorizing for social justice. Through an assessment of policies, programmes and practice/people's movements, feminist evaluation can help us get a better understanding of how a particular sector is thinking or acting. Further, this understanding can help us in planning for corrective interventions. For example, an evaluation of the Panchayati Raj system in terms of its policy and practice will tell us whether there is a gendered understanding of the process or not. Ongoing evaluation will help us monitor the impacts and changes, over a period of time, of different interventions.

Feminist evaluation as an approach is important to specifically map the above in the context of genders divided across diverse social groups. The starting point of such an evaluation would be an understanding of feminist and social justice research and theory. It has been argued by feminist researchers that knowledge based only on the lived experiences of men, or particular communities, presents only half the story and therefore a distorted perception of reality. Feminist evaluation has its roots in this understanding, and emphasizes participatory, empowering and social justice agendas (Podems, 2010).

Various feminist evaluation theorists have listed the following characteristics of feminist evaluation:

1. Feminist evaluation has a central focus on gender inequities that lead to social injustice.
2. It supports the belief that inequity based on gender is systematic and structural.
3. Evaluation is a political activity. The contexts in which evaluation operates are politicised and the personal experiences, perspectives and the characteristics evaluators bring to evaluation lead to a particular political stance.
4. Knowledge is a powerful resource that serves an explicit or implicit purpose.
5. Knowledge should be a resource of and for the people who create, hold, and share it. Consequently the evaluation and research

process can lead to significant negative or positive effects on the people involved in the evaluation/research.

6. There are multiple ways of knowing, some ways are privileged over others.

A feminist evaluation framework would seek to recognize and give voice to different social, political and cultural contexts that privilege some ways of knowing over others and importantly it is an attempt to bring about change (Podems, 2010).

The irrigation sector is both male and technocentric and completely misses out on understanding social justice and equity specifically in the context of gender and its intersection with various social groups like caste, class, ethnicity, race etc. It projects itself as a neutral sector with similar impacts on all users.

Drawing on literature on feminist evaluations discussed above we detail below the framework we have developed to review the evaluations done in the irrigation sector. We find four components to be an important part of the evaluation framework

1. The conceptual frame;
2. The methods used to collect the data and the sources of collecting information;
3. The process by which the studies were done and, finally
4. The outcomes.

THE CONCEPTUAL FRAME

The conceptual frame is useful to guide the evaluators in assessing a particular programme whether for its impact or otherwise. The evaluator lists out the key components that she/he needs to assess in a particular programme. For example an evaluation of an irrigation programme would consider efficiency, performance, participation, access as the key components to be assessed. However, how the evaluator understands these components is largely determined by the perspective/lens or the conceptual frame she/he believes in or has internalized. For example an irrigation engineer may not think of going beyond irrigation efficiency and performance as understood purely in terms of yield per drop of water, for a financial manager this may mean how much revenue per drop of water and for a feminist it might mean what is the overall labour of men, women and other toilers to yield the crop per drop of water.

Thus knowing and understanding the conceptual frame that has guided a particular evaluation is, we argue, a very important first step. It plays a critical role in determining which way the evaluation progresses and this finally reflects in the outcomes as well. In this study we will thus explore the conceptual frames that have guided the evaluation processes.

METHODS

One of the compelling questions for many of us engaged in working with women is whether there is a unique feminist method of enquiry and if so what is it? Does it really distinguish itself from the other methods such as quantitative surveys, interviews, and group discussions which are commonly used in different kinds of research? What is now of course part of received wisdom in feminist studies was also reaffirmed through years of research, largely action oriented research, that it is not the methods but alternative formulation of the questions and their explanations that turn the tables around. That is the reason why we feel the first component of any evaluation whether it is a need assessment one or an impact assessment, should be the perspectives or the conceptual frame that guides an evaluation.

The methods used for the enquiry range from observations to interviews, structured questionnaires, gathering histories etc., and can range from being both qualitative and quantitative and at a scale which can be large or small. Similar methods can however yield very different results if the conceptual frame is different.

THE PROCESS

The process of actually conducting the evaluation is also very important in determining the outcomes. For example it is important to know whether the process has been a top down one, with little or no participation from the people involved with the evaluation; or whether the process focused on sharing of the data collected and the insights of the researchers around that and the subsequent feedback from the people involved. Sampling is another important aspect in the context of process in terms of whether it was representative or not, who was contacted and spoken to.

The Outcomes

Articulation and presentation of outcomes also gives insights into what the evaluator was looking for, in other words, the mandate of the evaluation. Thus a detailed study of the outcomes and a reflection on that has also been an important part of the present reflection.

Section 3: Findings, Analysis of the Evaluations

In this section we discuss the findings of our study using the framework outlined in the previous section.

Review of the Government Evaluations

Maharashtra is credited with being among the states with the highest number of irrigation projects. The water resources department data shows that by the end of June 2010 the state had a total of 3452 irrigation projects with an irrigation potential to the tune of 47 lakh hectares. Large investments have been made by the WRD until the end of 2010. Given the scale of investments and the infrastructure that has been created, the water resources department has been doing annual evaluations to monitor progress.

Recently the department came under heavy scrutiny with several scams being brought to light and which essentially pointed out that despite the huge investments that had been made, the benefits measured in terms of the extent of irrigation have been very minimal. However the scope of the current review is not to critique the scams in irrigation but rather to understand how irrigation as a sector has completely missed out the question of social and gender equity. This we shall see through the evaluation reports that the department brings out annually.

The Water Resources Department of the Government of Maharashtra brings out three or four reports annually that highlight the different dimensions in irrigation performance. Only one of these is an evaluation done by a semi-independent committee and the rest are done by the staff of the department. Before going on to discuss the limitations of these evaluations from the point of view of social and gender equity we shall discuss the content of these reports and their framework.

We have looked at three important reports of the WRD which are brought out annually. These are as follows

1. Sinchan Sthiti Darshak Ahwal (The irrigation status report which is in Marathi)
2. Water Auditing of Irrigation Systems in Maharashtra
3. Benchmarking of Irrigation Systems in Maharashtra

The irrigation status report basically discusses irrigation statistics in terms of the extent of area irrigated in the state. Thus it provides information on the total number of irrigation projects to include major, medium and minor, water availability and use across the sectors of irrigation and non irrigation, the potential created for irrigation and the actual irrigation against that, area under major crops and their production, water tariff levied and the collection against that, total o&m charges and how they match up with the tariff charged and collection done. There is also a database on the water users associations registered and those that are functioning, the extent of saline and waterlogged lands, areas under drip and sprinklers etc. However there is very little information on how the water users groups are functioning, what their problems are and the support needed by them.

The report on Water Auditing of Irrigation Systems in Maharashtra is described as a systematic and scientific examination of water accounts of the projects. It is an intelligent and critical examination by an independent organization called Maharashtra Water Resource Development Centre (MWRDC) and does a critical review of the system of accounting. A water audit determines the amount of water used in different sectors, lost from the distribution system due to leakages and the cost of this lost utility. This was started in 2003–04 with 1229 projects and currently 2298 projects are being water audited. The total number of projects in Maharashtra in the year ending 2010 are 3452 of which 2298 are being audited, i.e about 65 per cent of the total project. Maharashtra is perhaps the only state that comes out with such a report annually. It looks at nine different parameters to compile the water audit report. These broadly cover details of storage, evaporation, water use, irrigation system performance and canal conveyance efficiency. It gives a detailed profile of the distribution system and water users, thereby facilitating easier and effective management of resources and improved reliability.

The report on benchmarking of irrigation systems in Maharashtra was initiated according to the guidelines issued by the Indian National Committee on Irrigation and Drainage (INCID) in 2002. In Maharashtra it was first done in the year 2001–02 for 84 irrigation projects with 10 indicators. However for 2010–11 it has been done for 1335 irrigation projects with 12 indicators. So currently about 39 per cent are being covered under this assessment. Broadly speaking benchmarking covers system performance, that is, measuring the performance against the norms set by the state for the volume of water and area irrigated; agricultural productivity is covered as output per unit irrigated area or water supply; financial aspects are covered as cost recovery ratio, unit costs per ha of O&M revenue generated per unit of water supplied; environmental aspects cover the land damage index which is the percentage of land damaged to irrigable command of the project and finally there is a social assessment which looks at equity performance in terms of the ratio of the total area irrigated to the projected irrigable command area in the head, middle and tail end reaches of the canal.

EVALUATIONS BY SOPPECOM

The Society for Promoting Participative Ecosystem Management (SOPPECOM www.soppecom.org) is a nonprofit organization working around water and rural livelihood issues since 1991. Its main work has been in the area of decentralized water management through the formation of water users associations on state owned and operated irrigation projects. However it has since then expanded its scope of work and also its depth in the area of conflicts around water, watershed development, gender and water, sanitation etc. As a small feminist group within SOPPECOM, we have been consistently making efforts to do research and action differently by asking questions that would make a difference to the question of gender justice within the water sector. One of the main tasks that we set ourselves was to understand how women are portrayed in the water sector and use this understanding to change the discourse in favour of social justice with an emphasis on gender and caste. Unpacking the dominant images and constructions of what constitutes women, dalits and tribals in the water sector helped in doing policy advocacy in a different way.

Over the years we have looked at the irrigation sector from a gender and social equity lens and made an effort to bring in those aspects in irrigation thinking and practice in the state of Maharashtra. Our first effort was way back in the mid 1990s when we organized a landless women's collective to claim their rights over irrigation water through an arrangement of leasing in land. A detailed documentation of this effort can be seen at http://soppecom.org/pdf/khudawadi-article.pdf

Further SOPPECOM continuously engaged with the government through dialogue as well as through a critical evaluation of the various programmes and policies through a gender and social justice lens. The three most recent studies around irrigation were:

Water Rights as Women's Rights

This was an evaluation of the decentralization process in irrigation and its impact on women and other socially discriminated groups, specifically in Maharashtra and Gujarat. The evaluation studied both the policies and programmes on decentralized water governance and did a field level evaluation to assess the impact in terms of access to water, decision-making related to technology, water pricing, water allocations and use. It also looked at whether governance which is closer to home actually benefits women and other socially discriminated groups. For details of this study see the policy brief on http://soppecom.org/pdf/policy%20brief%203.pdf.

Social and Gender Equity Gauge

Through its study on the social and gender equity gauge SOPPECOM made an effort to develop an evaluation framework for the water sector from a gender and social equity point of view. The full report can be referred to on http://soppecom.org/pdf/final_GEG1.pdf

It involved intensive field work in Ahmednagar district in northern Maharashtra, India and a few villages in Nepal. Apart from indicators such as access and control over resources and decision-making, it also highlighted the amount of unpaid work done by women that went into drawing and utilising water resources. It clearly highlighted that current evaluations did not go beyond households and did not touch upon the contribution of unpaid labour to water related work.

Situational Analysis of Water Users Associations in Maharashtra:
A Rapid Assessment

This evaluation was to assess the governance in irrigation management done through the involvement of 14 organizations in Maharashtra and co-ordinated by SOPPECOM. The objective was to do an assessment of key indicators broadly in the area of governance and participation and use the findings to a) do collective thinking towards alternatives b) lobby for change with the water resources department.

The evaluation looked at both the technical and social aspects of water. Thus inequities in access and decision-making were highlighted and so was its link to the technical management of the resource shown. What was, however, a more significant component of this evaluation was the process of taking the findings to the water users and the irrigation department and lobbying for change. In a very real sense then, evaluation was being used as a tool for policy advocacy.

The detailed study report can be found on http://soppecom.org/ pdf/6-%20Situational%20Analysis%20of%20Water%20Users%20 Associations%20in%20Maharashtra.pdf

---

Section 4: Assessment of Evaluation: A Comparison

Having looked at both the sets of evaluations in this section we compare them using the four components that we have outlined as part of the evaluation framework.

To compare we would broadly require that the same programme is being assessed, however the only available evaluations of irrigation by the government were of the sector as a whole. As against these, the three assessments that SOPPECOM did and discussed looked at three specific programmes within the irrigation sector. So although one could argue that this is not a fair ground for comparison, we feel that the value in the comparison needs to be seen in the broader context of a critical comment that can be made with regard to the priority of the irrigation department and how that priority reflects a certain kind of a bias against the agenda of social justice, specifically gender justice.

The Conceptual Frame

All the three reports view the irrigation sector from a single lens of irrigation performance or its efficiency, with the aim of ensuring that every bit of investment leads to an increase in revenue and increased area under irrigation. It is of course not within the scope of the review to point out the anomalies and the flaws in the methodologies to assess irrigation performance, but a few words on that would help us locate the gender question better.

The mandate of the status report is limited to looking at irrigation efficiency and performance which is outside the ambit of people and those who toil on the farms. The entire focus is on irrigation as a neutral resource provided by the state government through public investments without the recognition of women's work in making irrigation and agriculture possible. Increasingly efficiency is also being equated with revenue generation. Thus every drop of water needs to fetch maximum returns, a logic which allows for a policy to free up water for better revenue-generating options like industry.

The key words in the report refer to resources like land and water as commodities not linked to the livelihoods of people. Gender of course receives no place within this framework. Efficiency, the report stresses, can only improve with the use of modern technology and refers nowhere to people's understanding of the resource and the value system of its sustainable and equitable use.

Apart from missing out on the social and gender equity agenda, the irrigation status report has also been critiqued for its very lopsided view on irrigation efficiency, for basing its reporting on assumptions rather than actual field work. The ISR is thus a mechanical exercise that is carried out year after year without connecting with grassroot level realities. Rapid changes are taking place in water use, cropping patterns and modes of irrigation, all of which contribute significantly to the performance data in irrigation. None of these ground checks is done by the WRD before compiling its annual reports (Purandare 2012). Irrigation reviews done by the WRD Maharashtra are largely based on incomplete data and half truths. Most of the data used to assess irrigation outreach and expansion is based on assumed data and thus cannot be relied on (Purandare 2012). Purandare's article discusses in detail the gaps in the presentation in the irrigation status reports of Maharashtra. The data hides the figures of irrigation efficiency which according to him is as low as 20-25 per cent and not the 40-48 per cent as claimed by the department. Moreover there is complete silence of the ISRs on water theft and unauthorized use of water which has a serious impact on water equity. This aspect is in fact not discussed in the water audit and benchmarking reports either.

Social and environmental concerns are completely absent from any of these evaluation reports. The benchmarking report claims to take cognizance of social and environmental concerns through a cursory mention of the land damage index and distribution of irrigation across the different reaches in the canal. However neither looks at the impact of irrigation or the lack of it on people's livelihoods or their well being. Gender and other marginalized groups are out of the evaluation frame in these statistical reports.

SOPPECOM's work is based on the three principles of equity, sustainability and democratic and informed participation of people. These are thus the three conceptual gateways to our work which have informed our research and evaluations.

Equity as we understand it in the water sector is a matter of a) minimum assurance of resources and rights to all the water required for livelihood needs irrespective of their ownership of assets. Equity also has implications for water use prioritisation. Broadly the priority in most areas would be: drinking water, water for domestic use and for cattle, water required for ecosystem regeneration, water required for livelihood activity, surplus water that could be used for commercial crops. Gender is a dimension that is routinely added on as a component to most of the programmes. Gender and equity in drinking water and sanitation is about basic human rights – the right to water and sanitation has been well stated and women, like men, are adequately covered in principle at least. At the same time, you have water rights linked to land ownership which again is largely unfavourable to women. So the equity question in irrigation and water for livelihoods begins with the de-linking of access to water from land ownership, for women, poor and the landless; equity in the rule making process or allocations around water (who gets how much); the authority that comes with membership to water institutions from the micro to the macro levels.

Sustainability refers to the use of water within renewability limits where we restrict our uses to water that can be recharged. Thus it is important to minimize importing of water after a clear assessment of the local water resources is done along with the livelihood needs of the community. Sustainable use of the resource is also closely linked to equitable sharing as it curtails unbridled use of water by a few and opens up possibilities of sharing saved water.

Democratic, Informed Participation

Typically, participatory approaches have been dichotomised into 'means' and 'ends'. Participation also remains within the realm of the unitary, undifferentiated community. Such conceptualisation overlooks social difference and relations of power and exclusion underlying access and entitlements to resources, conflicts and processes of negotiation or the complexity of cooperative action. Our understanding of participation thus recognized the diversity and also the fact that local knowledges need to be combined with that which is not local for informed choices to be made around the resource. In terms of understanding women's participation, Bina Agarwal's typology of participation which typifies participation in six degrees, moving upwards towards more effective and empowering participation, has been useful.

Methods: In terms of the research methods we find that the Department evaluation was largely based on a lot of assumed data with no field-based studies involving user feedback. Statistical analysis was done based on these data sets which also formed the basis of introducing changes in the programmes and policies within the sector.

Methods used by SOPPECOM combined the use of qualitative and quantitative methods with an emphasis on participation of the people involved. In general they included a) focus group discussions b) in-depth interviews with men and women and different stakeholders c) discussions with officials d) walk through in field areas to assess the irrigation situation e) quantitative surveys where necessary. All of this was of course backed by homework on policies and programmes, government documents and a reading of the literature by state and non state actors.

Process: The process used by the Department has been non-participatory, top down and very hierarchical as would be expected of a bureaucracy. None of the data were shared in the public domain for discussions either in terms of the methodologies or initial findings.

SOPPECOM, however, used a participatory process to the extent that people were informed about the evaluation, different sections of the population were spoken to, and an effort was made to understand the views of the marginalized mand vulnerable groups. There was no hierarchy of relations between the researchers and the researched and all the findings and insights from the study were shared with the local groups by publishing the documents in Marathi.

In collaborative evaluation such as the one on the assessment of WUAS, the process was a long drawn one as 14 different organizations had to be consulted to prepare the research design. The actual process of evaluation was spread over a period of three to four months and it was conducted in a decentralized manner. Although this meant that the styles of collection of data varied with the people and organizations conducting the evaluation, it brought in an important element of building collective pressure through a participatory evaluation process. This entire process was a very important learning to all of us and brought out both the values and limitations of collective evaluations.

Outcomes

The main outcome of the evaluation done by the department was of course reports that gave the status of programmes within the sector, and very little assessment in terms of what it had set to achieve and what it finally did achieve. As we have seen, the frames of analysis and the mandates were different and hence the outcomes too were different.

The evaluations by SOPPECOM highlighted inequities in voice and access to the resource to women and other socially discriminated groups. They also highlighted the amount of unpaid work women across social groups engage in to productively use water. Moreover they highlighted how undemocratic the processes of decision-making were and that despite representation on committees, women and dalits weren't able to exert their influence over water related decisions.

This understanding has been useful for us in advocacy related to ensuring water access in an equitable manner to all social groups and women.

TABLE: Comparisons between the Two Sets of Evaluations

	Government Reports	SOPPECOM
Conceptual frame	Efficiency, performance	Participation, democratization, equity and social justice
Methods	Based on assumed data and no ground truthing, no direct dialogue with farmers	FGDs, in depth interviews, multi-stakeholder discussions
Process	Non participatory, uni-linear, no feedback and sharing with concerned people	Participatory, reflexive, non hierarchical
Outcomes	Gives the status of the achievements, but there seems little effort to plan for corrective actions	Effort is made at the end of every assessment to engage with both people and the government to make change possible

Section 5: The Way Forward

In this final section we make an effort to suggest a way forward at two levels a) widening the scope of some of the current criteria used by the irrigation department such as efficiency, performance etc., and b) including new criteria to further the social justice and equity agenda.

WIDENING HORIZONS OF UNDERSTANDING

Efficiency and performance: Irrigation is charecterized by a very technocentric approach but over the years we see a change in terms of shifts towards a more institutional approach. The view that institutional and economic reform along with technology will be able to address the problems in the sector assumed currency in the last two decades. In some ways this has opened up spaces for looking at water as more than a technical resource, however it is now dominated by the mainstream economic view that both the pricing of water and the decentralization of management will bring about water use efficiency. Mainstream economics assumes efficiency to be gender neutral. It does not look at women's non-paid labour, which is viewed as outside the purview of the economy since it is in the non-monetised sector. Irrigation looks at efficiency as expanding irrigated area with every drop of water. If this is not achieved then the sector is labelled as inefficient. Thus performance is entirely measured on the basis of a narrow understanding of efficiency. Also women are not seen as contributing to this efficiency and hence would not qualify to be in the sector in key decision-making processes. The understanding that women's domestic labour is critical in sustaining the labour force whether in irrigation or elsewhere receives little attention.

Challenging belief systems and notions around women: We need to see women's work as beyond care and nurture and as contributing significantly to production. We need to see women's roles as dynamic and not static. For example, they may be collecting water and using it for domestic purposes in the current context, but policy plans need to imagine a new world for them which goes beyond the collection of water and its utilisation for domestic use.

We also need to challenge our notions of women as a homogenous category, seen as ready to ally for a common cause. Feminist studies, black feminism, dalit studies have all pointed out the need to understand the gender question within the diversity of caste, class race etc. Similarly it is also assumed that the household is a site of co-operation and thus a homogenous unit with common concerns and common joys. Again, feminist studies have shown that a household is both a site of conflict and co-operation and intra household differences that discriminate against younger women and children are known and need attention.

Rethinking goals in water sector: We need to rethink how the goals of the water sector are defined. Are they geared towards social justice and sustainable use? This is a question we must not forget to ask. Sustainable water use needs to be understood from the point of view of the environment as well as social justice.

A minimum assurance of water for meeting livelihood requirements of all therefore becomes the central programme in livelihood security. It goes without saying that for every human being life becomes more meaningful if he/she has access to assets and skills to engage meaningfully in certain activities to fulfil livelihood needs.

Indicators such as access to water, access to decision-making in water institutions, voice in decisions etc., need to be assessed in this broader context of the desired change in locating feminist understanding in the irrigation sector.

References

Government of Maharashtra.n.d. 'Report on auditing of irrigation systems in Maharashtra state, from 2000 to the present.'

———. 'Irrigation status reports from 2000 to the present.'

———. 2012. *Rajyatil Sinchanachi pragati v bhavishyatil vatchal, Shwetpatrika-khand 1.*

———. 'Report on benchmarking of irrigation systems in Maharashtra state, from 2000 to the present.'

Kulkarni, Seema. 2011. 'Women and Decentralised Water Governance: Issues, Challenges and the Way Forward', April 30, vol. xlvi, no. 64, 18.

Podems, D. R. 2010. 'Feminist evaluation and gender approaches: there's a difference?' *Journal of Multidisciplinary evaluation*, Vol. 6, No. 14.

Purandare, Pradeep. 2012. 'Canal irrigation in Maharashtra: Present Status, in Dams, Rivers and People', July–August.

Zwarteveen, Margreet. 1998. 'Identifying gender aspects of new irrigation management policies in Agriculture and Human Values', 15: 301–312, 1998.

10

Gendering WASH Evaluations in India

VASUNDHARA KAUL and NEHA SANWAL

Introduction

With an increasing global focus on issues of Water, Sanitation and Hygiene (WASH), the number of programmes and projects addressing these are also expected to rise. In such a scenario it becomes critical to understand the manner in which WASH interventions have been monitored and assessed in the past. Monitoring and evaluation provides information and facts that, when accepted and internalized, improve the overall performance and the quality of results. Hence, the indicators employed for monitoring and evaluation of WASH projects are vital to ensuring the success of not only ongoing but also future programmes, projects and strategies.

This essay undertakes such an analysis by looking at WASH evaluations that were conducted for programmes/projects being implemented in India from 2005-2015. Our primary focus is to look at the extent to, and manner in which, the evaluations have incorporated gender as a key indicator. As pointed out in the 2014 update report on the 'Progress on Drinking Water and Sanitation' by UNICEF and WHO, national level household surveys in WASH often do not collect information on the use of facilities within a household and hence overlook certain dimensions of inequality such as those related to gender. This is extremely problematic given that the impact of the availability of adequate clean drinking water and adequate and appropriate sanitation facilities is not solely biological but also has a direct bearing on the self-esteem and dignity, vulnerability to violence, economic empowerment, and education of women and adolescent girls. The view adopted by most interventions wherein incorporation of gender is tantamount to making resources available to women, is not only narrow but also incomplete.

Gender refers to socially constructed roles, behaviour, activities and attributes that a particular society considers appropriate and ascribes to men and women (Water and Sanitation Program, 2010). The differentials in power and authority in determining access to resources arising from the prescription of different roles, behaviours, activities and attributes give rise to gender inequity. Therefore, it becomes essential to understand the extent to which a programme/project recognizes such structural inequalities and tries to address them.

Methodology

The method employed for this study is 'document analysis' wherein evaluation reports pertaining to WASH have been analysed and interpreted to understand the gender inclusiveness of WASH evaluation designs. This process of document analysis involved two main pre-analysis processes: (a) online data collection, and (b) coding.

Online Data Collection: For this study, data collection involved the identification of evaluation reports of WASH programmes in India. Only those reports available in the public domain serve as the purposive sample for this study since the reports were collected through an online search. Two rounds of searches were conducted between 4 June and 15 June, 2015 as described below.

At first, a preliminary search for the phrase 'WASH evaluations in India' on the Google search engine yielded 74,40,000 results (as on 6 June 2015). A majority of these results were related to evaluations of health programmes in the country, but very few were on WASH specifically. To further refine the search, key organizations engaged in WASH evaluations in the country were identified and a search was conducted in their web portals. These organizations are the World Bank, WHO, UNICEF, UNDP, BMGF, UN Women, Arghyam and

Government of Karnataka. The filters employed for the searches were: Country: India; Theme: Water and Sanitation.

A second round of search was undertaken via the Google Scholar search engine for the following key words: Water, Sanitation, India, Evaluations. These key words were used in conjunction with the same organizations that had been identified in the previous search, resulting in multiple permutations and combinations. For example, one of the search phrases employed for BMGF was 'BMGF evaluations on water and sanitation in India'. It is important to clarify that the period of publication for these evaluations was restricted to 2005–2015. The only exception was made on account of a UNICEF report published in 2000 as it was mutually decided upon by the team as being important for this research study.

Prior to the commencement of the coding process, a third search was undertaken using the same criteria 'to ensure that no reports had been missed out. The search did not yield any new reports.

At the end of the search process, a total of 20 evaluation reports were identified. However, when the team started reading the reports for the purpose of coding, four reports had to be deleted from the list since they were not M&E reports. In addition, it was also discovered that in some cases different reports were related to different phases of the same evaluation. For instance, for the impact evaluation of one programme, one report presented the baseline findings, one presented the midline findings and the last presented the endline findings. Thus, a total of 16 evaluation reports covering 13 distinct programmes serve as the basis for the analysis reported in this study.

Coding: The codebook was created as the online data collection was in progress. This involved identification and delineation of different codes through an iterative process. The multiple iterations are particularly important because it ensures that the definition of the codes as understood by the team is the same. The first set of codes that constituted the codebook was identified on the basis of reading of past literature. These codes evolved and were modified based on the information that emerged from the reports. Some codes were also incorporated based on the objective of the study. Since the study involves analysing evaluations, codes that cover the objective, design, methodology and funding of the evaluations are also taken into consideration.

The final codebook comprised of 54 indicators with each code detailed out such that one is able to assess whether gender/women are incorporated as a variable or not. During the process of reading and coding each report, a separate note-sheet was constructed to maintain a record of excerpts from the reports. The primary purpose of these excerpts is to allow for a better understanding of the codes and findings that emerge from the reports.

The indicators can be broadly classified under three main themes: (a) Structure of the Evaluation Design (8 codes); (b) Content (45 codes); and (c) Funding of the Evaluation (1 code). The content theme comprises of 6 sub-themes focused on water, sanitation, hand-washing, impact on health, waste disposal, and power relations and entitlements.

Analysis

For this research study, each of the evaluation reports was studied under two broad heads: (a) structure of the evaluations, and (b) content of the evaluations.

A. *Structure of Evaluations:* Of the 16 reports that constitute the sample, none had the word 'gender' in their title and for a majority (81 per cent, n=13), data was collected at the household level while the remaining 19 per cent (n=3) were at the community level. None of the evaluations focused primarily on intra-household variations between men and women of a household with regard to access to water, sanitation and hygiene. Furthermore, gender only found mention in the objectives of one study where it was recognized that 'Their [the communities'] role is central in planning and implementing improved sanitation, taking into account the needs of diverse community members, including vulnerable groups, people with disabilities, and women and girls'. Hence, for most WASH evaluations the variable of gender or women does not constitute a focal point.

An analysis of the study design reveals that 31 per cent of the evaluations were programmatic evaluations and another 38 per cent were purely experimental impact evaluations. Quasi-experimental studies accounted for 19 per cent of the sample and process evaluations were the least in number at 13 per cent. It is interesting to note that all three evaluations that were conducted at the community level are programme evaluations. All the impact evaluations and process evaluations were conducted at the household level. Further, only two (two rounds of process assessments of the same project) out of 16 reports were process monitoring evaluations which look at the processes followed under a WASH intervention.

The types of tools that are employed for data collection also provide insight into the nature of data that the evaluation attempts to collect. Of the total, 14 evaluations adopted a mixed methods approach including PRA exercises, case studies and observations. The remaining two evaluations that did not use close ended questionnaires, utilised a mix of Key Informant Interviews (KIIS) and Focus Group Discussions (FGDS). All the reports gathered primary data for analysis and then arrived at their findings.

While the dominance of mixed methods indicates that there is an attempt to capture a multiplicity of perspectives and experiences, none of the 16 evaluations attempted to gather feedback from the community and incorporate it in their recommendations. This is problematic because 50 per cent of the reports are for programmes under the Total Sanitation Campaign (TSC) which is based on the principle of community-led total sanitation (CLTS), wherein community led methods are employed to propel people into action. The omission of feedback in such situations results in limited insight into what works best with a community. For instance, in one programme (covered by two reports) the intent was to look at sanitation solutions desired by the people but the ability of the programme to achieve this was not assessed in the evaluation reports.

Nevertheless, 81 per cent of the sample reports (n=13) did provide recommendations based on the evaluation findings. Out of the three that did not provide recommendations, two were baseline reports and one a midline report of impact evaluations, for which recommendations are usually not required. The recommendations in these 13 reports ranged from suggestions on programmatic remodelling to scope for advocacy. A majority of the recommendations are either programmatic (69 per cent, n=9), i.e. how to improve the structure and implementation of the programme further, and looked at measures to improve the impact of the programme (31 per cent, n=4) or how to scale up (31 per cent, n=4).

THE CONTENT OF EVALUATIONS

This section examines the various facets of WASH that have been included in the evaluations and the extent to which they display gender sensitivity.

Incorporation of Gender: Analysis of the content of the report revealed that the words 'gender', 'woman' or 'female' do not find mention in 25 per cent (n=4) of the evaluations. The remaining 12 reports either mentioned or defined the words 'gender' or 'woman'. A majority of the evaluations (50 per cent) only mentioned the word 'woman' in their content. Clearly, most evaluation reports incorporate gender analysis at the very rudimentary level of man-woman comparison without exploring power relations in any depth.

Results indicate that in a majority of the evaluations, caste details (75 per cent) and income details as proxy of class (87.5 per cent) are recorded at the household level. With regard to caste, 44 per cent of the evaluations took all caste categories into consideration while 31 per cent only looked at outcomes/impact for marginalized caste categories. Similarly, 69 per cent of the evaluations took all income stratifications into account whereas 19 per cent only looked at results for those belonging to the Below Poverty Line (BPL) segment. Gender inequities are often further enhanced when the variables of caste and class are included. For instance, access to toilets for women from well off families is significantly different from the access levels for women from more economically vulnerable backgrounds. Hence, evaluations should ideally attempt to assess the impact of a project/ intervention along caste and income lines as well. While this data is collected by most evaluations, their interplay with gender was not explored by any.

Water, Sanitation and Hand Washing: When discussing water, sanitation and hand washing practices, the study tries to understand the extent to which evaluations go beyond the basic issues of awareness and access to include the behavioural component of practice adoption. This is primarily with the intention to assess whether evaluations are cognizant of intra-household differences between men and women not only on issues of awareness and access but behavioural practices as well.

Before proceeding, it is critical to differentiate between the comparison of men and women at a community level and looking at intra-household differences. The first approach aggregates findings across the community for both men and women and then draws comparisons. The second approach looks at differences within each household and then attempts to come to a more nuanced understanding of inequity.

Drinking Water: A clear pattern across the awareness-access spectrum emerges in evaluations on drinking water. While 63 per cent (n=10) of the reports identified the different primary sources of drinking water for their sample populations, 50 per cent (n=8) assessed the time spent on water collection activities. Of these eight, only two evaluations reports discussed the time spent on water collection by different genders. The level of drudgery involved in water collection is measured by the time spent and the effort expended on it. However, only 19 per cent (n=3) of the reports attempted to assess the effort expended on water collection activities, of which two did so based on gender.

A similar pattern is observed with regard to water quality. While only 38 per cent (n=6) of the reports took awareness of water purification methods into consideration, even fewer (13 per cent, n=2) collected data on the time spent on water purification activities. Similarly, only two reports (13 per cent) measured the effort expended on water purification activities. None of them looked at the awareness level of their sample populations around water quality. This stands in stark contrast to the fact that 69 per cent (n=11) of the evaluations measured the water quality in the sample geographies.

These results clearly illustrate how a majority of the evaluations focus more on issues of access as opposed to awareness of and adherence to different practices. Furthermore, even access is primarily looked at in terms of availability of drinking water sources and time spent on water collection activities, instead of other issues such as drudgery or availability of water purification material. Such a limited understanding is further constrained by the absence of any discussion in all of the reports on the factors influencing behaviour related to water collection and water purification. In a country where it is the women of the household who are primarily responsible for water collection and purification activities, omission of such variables reflects the absence of a gendered approach which results in an incomplete picture of the impact of the programme on different beneficiaries. It is particularly important to take the opportunity cost of these activities into consideration since it leaves women with less time to engage in remunerative employment and adolescent girls with less time to study. However, barring one report, none of the other 15 evaluations attempted to capture any such information. Furthermore, out of the 16 evaluation reports, only one spoke about decision-making around drinking water resources, that too across gender lines as the extract below shows:

> The focus group discussions made clear that the men in the community take the decisions on the water systems. Women had little or no voice e.g. in suggesting the sites of handpumps or taps. Very recently, e.g. in Lalawundi in the UNICEF-supported district women have also started demanding suitable sites for their water points. They said that the government officials talk only to the village leaders or local politicians about the proposed construction or installation of water systems and that the women are not even approached for consultations, leave alone that they have a say in decisions.

Such insight is critical because it is primarily women who are engaged in water collection and purification activities and who are more directly affected by decisions around them. However, more often than not they are excluded from decision making because of power hierarchies.

Sanitation: Sanitation looks at the promotion of health through prevention of human contact with wastes of all kind. Of the 16 reports, 81 per cent (n=13) captured the number of toilets constructed in their sample geographies; nine looked at the total number of toilets constructed, three looked at toilet construction by caste category and one looked at it by class. Almost all the reports (93 per cent, n=15) measured the level of toilet usage; 56 per cent (n=9) using a yes or no binary; 6 per cent (n=1) by different household members, 25 per cent (n=4) by different genders and 13 per cent (n=2) by different social groups. In addition, 9 out of the 16 evaluations (56 per cent) discussed the factors influencing toilet construction in their sample demography while 10 (63 per cent) incorporated behavioural change; i.e. factors influencing the use of toilets. Therefore, while the focus still remains on access to toilets, there is a higher degree of recognition by evaluations of the behavioural and gender component in the uptake of sanitation facilities.

Decision-making is also discussed in greater detail with regard to sanitation as opposed to drinking water. Forty four per cent (n=7) of the reports looked at how decisions are made with regard to improvements in sanitation. While only one report looked at decision-making across different genders and one looked at decision-making across different household members, three reports discussed whether improvement in sanitation is the responsibility of the government or individual households. The focus on government provision by evaluations also emerges when looking at expenses incurred for maintaining sanitation. All five reports that took these expenses into consideration also focused on whether the burden should fall on individual households or government bodies.

Although not to a great extent, the sanitation component in WASH evaluations is more cognizant of varying influences on different beneficiaries and the factors motivating their behaviour. The focus on gender is primarily limited to access, possibly because many problems arising due to the absence of sanitation facilities are specific to women.

Hygiene: Good hand washing practices have shown how to reduce the incidence of many diseases, particularly waterborne diseases like diarrhoea, cholera, etc. and hence form a critical component of hygiene. This component of WASH also includes menstrual hygiene and hygiene maintained at the community level. All these facets have a direct bearing on the susceptibility of individuals to a multitude of diseases.

Results indicate that 94 per cent (n=15) of the evaluations did not take into consideration either the awareness levels about hand washing or the factors influencing the adoption of hand washing practices. Furthermore, none of the reports included information on the decisions related to hand washing material purchase, infrastructure, etc. A majority of the evaluations (75 per cent, n=12) reported only the hand washing practices being followed at the household level. Of these 12, 50 per cent (n=6) did so at the household level, 42 per cent (n=5) looked at intra household differences and 6 per cent (n=1) looked at gender level differences at the community level. Since hand washing practices are likely to vary from one member to another in a household, inclusion of gender analysis within the household is critical. This is particularly so because the behaviour of children is strongly influenced by their caregivers who tend to be the women of the household. However, omission of awareness levels and decision making indicators is reflective of a very rudimentary understanding of hand washing practices and factors influencing it.

With menstrual hygiene only finding mention in two out of 16 reports, it emerges as an indicator that is largely overlooked. Such an absence is problematic because it reinforces societal taboos surrounding menstruation that silence the needs of women and adolescent girls. By not giving the issue adequate focus, evaluations fail to emphasize the strong impact it can have on the psychological and physiological development of women and adolescent girls and its critical role in all WASH programmes.

The study also attempts to understand the extent to which evaluations factor in waste management. Results indicate that waste management (solid waste disposal or waste water disposal) is discussed in very limited cases and that too primarily at the household level instead of the community level. In fact, only one study (6 per cent) assessed waste water disposal at the community level. Furthermore, none of these indicators looked at intra-household variations, i.e. who is responsible for waste disposal, their awareness levels, and factors influencing their behaviour. Since it is women who are viewed as being responsible for taking care of the house, this responsibility also usually falls on them. However, their participation in decision-making is usually limited.

Impact on Health: This section on health studies the extent to which evaluations attempt to capture awareness about diseases arising due to poor hygiene, the appropriate treatment for these, and the type of treatment facilities sought for such diseases.

Only 31 per cent (n=5) of the reports evaluated the knowledge levels of their programme beneficiaries on diseases arising due to poor hygiene, whereas 25 per cent (n=4) looked into knowledge levels about the treatment of such diseases. Only one out of the 16 evaluations captured information about the nature of health facilities sought out for diseases due to poor hygiene, that is, whether people go to a private clinic, government hospitals, Primary Healthcare Centres (PHC), etc. In fact, intra household variations were not accounted for in any of the indicators.

Such a low level of importance accorded to assessing awareness on WASH related diseases is a cause for concern because while access to safe water and sanitation facilities, and awareness about proper hygiene practices, has a significant impact on the incidence of diseases, it is also critical to be able to identify these diseases and access quality healthcare in response. Furthermore, differential awareness and access levels for men and women of a household make it even more critical to account for variations in these indicators, particularly since it is the women who are the primary care givers for newborns and young children. In four reports, the key respondent was the primary care giver of children but their ability to influence decision-making was not taken into consideration.

Power Relations and Entitlements: This section captures the extent to which evaluations are cognizant of power relations between men and women at the community level. It involves looking at factors such as discussions of WASH at community level meetings, attendance and participation of women in these meetings, the presence of water and sanitation committees in the community, and awareness and implementation of WASH related schemes and campaigns.

Out of the 16 reports, 81 per cent (n=13) did not assess the prevalence of discussions around WASH in community level meetings while none of them looked into whether discussions related to WASH conflicts take place on formal/institutional platforms or not.

Further, only two evaluations measured the attendance of women at community level meetings and only one of those two mentioned the level of participation of women. None of the evaluations reported the involvement of women in the decision-making process related to WASH at community level meetings. Hence, discussions around WASH at such meetings, particularly with regard to the involvement of women, are often overlooked by evaluation studies.

Results indicate that 69 per cent (n=11) of the evaluation reports did not attempt to identify the presence of water and sanitation committees in the community. Out of the five that did, none discussed the presence of women leaders. Water and sanitation committees play an important role at the community level by ensuring that focus is maintained on WASH activities. The presence of women in such committees is even more important as it ensures that the needs of women and adolescent girls are voiced on an institutional platform.

In the absence of such committees, local NGOs and government schemes often help bring to notice problems related to WASH. In fact, issues around WASH are often taken up by organizations working on women's issues due to the large impact it has on their health. However, only one evaluation reported on the presence of organizations working on women's issues in their beneficiary community. In addition, only 44 per cent (n=7) of the reports attempted to assess awareness about schemes and campaigns related to WASH and even fewer measured the nature of implementation (31 per cent, n=5) and utilization (38 per cent, n=6).

Concluding Remarks

Findings from this study are clearly reflective of the global trends related to WASH wherein there is more focus on issues of access and quality as opposed to drivers of behavioural change. This dominant trend also influences the manner in which a gendered approach is adopted in evaluations. Analysis that usually takes place around gender is at a very rudimentary level of man-woman comparison without taking into consideration the facets influencing different behaviour patterns because of variations in power and authority exercised by women (versus men) for basic necessities related to water and sanitation. As is evident in the results, behavioural variations are accounted for to a certain extent with respect to toilet utilization, but are largely absent in discussions of drinking water and maintenance of hygiene.

Such an oversight implies a lack of recognition of the power relations that underlie the focal point of WASH discussions as well as access to knowledge and resources. A more direct indicator of the failure of WASH evaluations to take cognizance of power relations is that the participation of women in decision-making, both at the household level as well as in community level platforms, is often overlooked. Such omissions are a cause for worry because village level social politics can often constrain women and residents from marginalized groups from participating in community forums such as the 'pani sansad' in Rajasthan (Subramaniam, 2014). This can not only be an extremely disempowering process for such groups but they also happen to be the worst affected in the absence of water and sanitation resources. The absence of disaggregation has a negative impact on the programming since there is no feedback on how to contextualize it to the differential needs of the community.

These findings also have implications for policy making. Rather than adopting a 'supply' model, agencies may want to consider generating a demand for water and sanitation as basic needs. Generating a demand will involve time and effort to raise awareness and educate the local community, especially women, to involve them in community decision-making processes.

Acknowledgements

We would like to thank Dr Mangala Subramaniam (Purdue University), Nitin Rao (Catalyst Management Services), Urvashi Wattal (Catalyst Management Services) and Siddhi Mankad (Catalyst Management Services) for their guidance and inputs in this study.

References

Fisher, J. 2006. *For Her It's the Big Issue: Putting women at the centre of water supply, sanitation and hygiene.* Water Supply and Sanitation Collaborative

Council (wsscc) and the Water, Engineering and Development Centre (wedc).

Kumar, A. 2015. 'Discrepancies in Sanitation Statistics of Rural India'. *Economic and Political Weekly, L* (2), 13–15.

Lala, S., and M. Basu. 2012. *Consolidated Reply: Ensuring Inclusion and Equity in wash Programming – Experiences; Examples.* New Delhi: United Nations Solution Exchange.

Lala, S., A. Cronin, and M. Basu. 2014. 'Collating Field Experiences to Inform Structured Approaches for Gender and Equity in wash in India', *sawas Journal,* 4 (2).

Panda, G.R., and T. Agarwala. 2013. 'Public Provisioning in Water and Sanitation: Study of Urban Slums in Delhi'. *Economic & Political Weekly, XLVIII* (5).

Reddy, V.R., and N.J. Kumar. 2011. *Financing the wash Sector in India: Cost of Provision and Budget Allocations.* Centre for Economic and Social Studies, wash Cost (India) Project, Hyderabad.

Smits, S., T. Schouten, and C. Fonseca. 2015. 'The Sustainable Development Goals for water and sanitation; what is new? What is different?' *Background note prepared for the IRC event.* The Hague, The Netherlands: IRC.

Subramaniam, M. 2014. 'Neoliberalism and water rights: The case of India'. *Current Sociology,* 62 (3), 393–411.

un Women. 2014. *Remarks by John Hendra at a side event on Women and Water: Multipliers of Development.* Retrieved from www.unwomen. org: http://www.unwomen.org/en/news/stories/2014/3/remarks-by-john-hendra-at-a-side-event-on-women-and-water

Water and Sanitation Program. 2010. *Gender in Water and Sanitation.*

Woodburn, H. 2015. *Where Do We Go From Here? wash in the sdgs.* Retrieved from www.huffingtonpost.com: http://www.huffingtonpost. com/hanna-woodburn/where-do-we-go-from-here-_2_b_7490146. html?ir=India&adsSiteOverride=in

Notes on Contributors

Venu Arora is Co-Director and Founder of Ideosync, an organization that works on Communication for Social change, Freedom of Speech, Media Access and Rights. She has a post-graduate degree in Mass Communications from Jamia Millia Islamia University, Delhi and an Advances in Health Communications from John Hopkins University's Bloomberg School of Public Health. Venu has been working in the development sector for last two decades. She headed national and international projects for DFID-India, UNDP, Plan India, Equal Access International, CHF, and UNAIDS, among others. She has also worked with UNDP as a communication specialist; and with Equal Access International, leading their work on establishing communication for change projects in Nepal, Cambodia and Tajikistan. She is currently working on her PhD on new pathways for assessing participatory communication and communication for development.

Sneha Bhat works with Society for Promoting Participative Ecosystem Management (SOPPECOM), Pune, as a Research Associate. Her work focuses on issues of gender, water and livelihoods, and she is involved in research and training. She has worked on issues of gender, water, participatory irrigation management, decentralization, sanitation, and single women.

Pallavi Gupta is pursuing her PhD from the Department of Geography at the University of North Carolina. Previously, she has worked as a trainer on gender, law and human rights. She has over eight years of experience in working on issues that lie at the intersection of law, social justice and human rights. She has designed and delivered numerous training programmes targeting various demographic groups including college students, professionals, civil-society organizations, government agencies and corporate houses. She has worked with Asmita Resource

Centre for Women, Hyderabad, a leading women's rights group, in various capacities, including as Director.

Vasundhara Kaul is a graduate student in the Sociology Department at Purdue University. Previously she was a Senior Consultant with the Impact Evaluation and Research team at Catalyst Management Services, Bangalore. Her main research interests are in the areas of gender (and its intersections with caste and class), development, and water and environmental justice. With over four years of experience in conducting impact and programme evaluations in India, she has worked across multiple thematic areas, from gender and education to issues of water and sanitation.

Renu Khanna is a founder trustee of SAHAJ-Society for Health Alternatives based in Vadodara (Gujarat), a community based action research and advocacy organization working on social accountability issues in the areas of Maternal Health, Child Rights, Adolescent Development. As a trainer, researcher and evaluator, she has also mentored several grassroots organizations as well as women's and community health organizations in India. Renu is actively engaged in several pro-peoples' networks, like the Jan Swasthya Abhiyan (Indian chapter of Peoples Health Movement), CommonHealth – Coalition for Maternal-Neonatal Health and Safe Abortion, COPASAH (Community of Practitioners on Accountability and Social Action in Health), Medico Friends Circle, and others.

Seema Kulkarni is one of the founding members of Society for Promoting Participative Ecosystem Management (SOPPECOM), Pune. She is presently working as a Senior Fellow in SOPPECOM and coordinates gender and rural livelihoods activities within the organization. She has headed various studies and programmes on decentralization, gender and water and sanitation. She has published several articles/book chapters around issues of gender, water, sanitation and rural livelihoods. She is associated with the movement for the rights of single women in western Maharashtra and is actively involved in the coalition of women's groups in Maharashtra, Stree Mukti Andolan Sampark Samiti.

Ranjani K. Murthy has had a long engagement with research, training, and evaluations on gender, equity and development. She has been involved in a number of evaluations for government, NGOs and UN agencies within and outside India since 1994, wherein she has adopted gender and equity sensitive participatory methods, and quantified the results. Of late, she has engaged in meta-evaluations of the National Rural Employment Guarantee Scheme, and of the International Fund for Agriculture Development, Rome. She is one of the members of the Advisory Committee of Engendering Policy through Evaluation Project of the Institute of Social Studies Trust, India. She is on the editorial board of the international journal, *Gender and Development* brought out by Oxfam and Routledge.

Rajib Nandi is a Research Fellow and Office-in-Charge at the Institute of Social Studies Trust, New Delhi. He has 20 years of experience in research and evaluation and a doctoral degree in Sociology from Jawaharlal Nehru University, New Delhi. His areas of work cover gender and development, the solidarity economy, information and communication technologies, the environment, HIV/AIDS, social movements, programme evaluations, and evaluative studies. He is a founder and core group member of the Evaluation Community of India. Presently, he is in the board of directors of the Community of Evaluators–South Asia.

Srinidhi Raghavan is a gender and disability rights advocate and a sexuality educator and trainer. She has worked with feminist non-profits for more than five years. Her work focuses on enhancing the rights of women, particularly women with disabilities and adolescent girls. She writes non-fiction essays and reported pieces for several news websites and magazines.

Neha Sanwal is currently working as a Portfolio Manager with Catalyst Management Services. A post graduate from Institute of Rural Management, Anand (IRMA), Neha has been involved in multiple evaluations employing mixed methods across various domains such as education, nutrition, rural development, and livelihoods. She brings the capacity of undertaking both quantitative and qualitative analysis and specializes in process and outcome evaluations. One of her current assignments with UNICEF Communication for Development (C4D) involves bringing together a national report covering the work done by C4D across its thematic areas as part of the 2013-2017 Country Action Plan. In another of her assignments, she has been working to understand the impact of nutrition focused programmes aiming to improve the dietary diversity of estate workers and their families in Assam and Tamil Nadu. As a manager she is also responsible for client and project management for her portfolio.

Shubh Sharma is Senior Programme Officer (Results and Learning) with the Aga Khan Foundation's India office. Her role is to lead monitoring, evaluation and learning initiatives for the Foundation in India across its sectors of intervention, including agriculture and food security, economic inclusion, education, ECD, WASH and governance. She brings around ten years of experience in evaluation and policy research on women's education, work and wellbeing. She has worked on a programme for understanding and strengthening evaluation capacity based on gender and participatory approaches in India.

Ratna M. Sudarshan has been Director of the Institute of Social Studies Trust (ISST), where she is now a member of the Board of Trustees. She has worked at the National Council of Applied Economic Research and been a Fellow at the National University of Educational Planning and Administration. Her research has mainly focused on the linkages between women's work, the informal economy and education. She initiated ISST's work on feminist evaluation and continues to be associated with this project.

Enakshi Ganguly Thukral is founder Co-Director of HAQ: Centre for Child Rights Delhi. She is a Sociologist by training and a human rights activist in her heart. She has researched, lobbied, advocated and fought on a range of issues since she started working over three decades ago. These include the rights of displaced persons, women's rights, housing rights and child rights. She has a number of publications, which includes edited books, contributions to books, newspapers and journals on diverse subjects including issues concerning children, women, and displacement of people due to development projects.

Sonal Zaveri is a founder member and Vice President of Community of Evaluators South Asia; coordinator of GENSA, the Gender and Equity Network South Asia, member of the EvalGender+ global management group, co-chair of the Tools and Approaches task group for gender sensitive and equity responsive evaluation, member of the working group on the South2South Evaluation initiative and international advisor to the Child-to-Child Trust, University of London. She is an independent consultant with experience in strategic planning, capacity building and evaluation. She has worked in more than 25 countries in Asia, East and West Africa, Asia-Pacific, Central Asia, Middle East and Eastern Europe. Sonal's interests relate to how rights, participation and gender intersect with various evaluation approaches such as outcome mapping, utilization-focused and developmental evaluation, as well as feminist evaluation. She has various publications and webinars to her credit.